The Merchant U-Boat

The Merchant U-Boat

Adventures of the *Deutschland* 1916–1918

Dwight R. Messimer

Naval Institute Press
Annapolis, Maryland

Library of Congress Cataloging-in-Publication Data
Messimer, Dwight R., 1937–
  The merchant U-boat : adventures of the Deutschland, 1916–1918 /
  Dwight R. Messimer.
    p.   cm.
  Bibliography: p.
  Includes index.
  ISBN 0-87021-771-2 :
  1. Deutschland (Submarine) 2. World War, 1914–1918—Naval
operations—Submarine. 3. World War, 1914–1918—Naval operations,
German. 4. Merchant marine—Germany—History—20th century.
I. Title.
D592.D4M47   1988   88-22786
940.4'512—dc19   CIP

Designed by Moira Megargee

Printed in the United States of America

To my daughter-in-law
Dina

CONTENTS

Chapter 16.   Shutting Down the Program, 1 February–6 April   156
              1917

Chapter 17.   War Boat, 6 April–21 August 1917   165

Chapter 18.   The Final Year   185

              Epilogue   195

              Notes   207

              Bibliography   223

              Appendix   227

              Index   229

PREFACE

Sometime before World War II, I think around 1940, my parents gave me a toy submarine. It was typical of the toys at that time—solidly built of metal, painted blue, and had a key sticking out of the conning tower. I remember that it had a saw-tooth net cutter on the bow, and was equipped with only bow planes. It was a rather basic design. But it was a great bathtub toy, running on the surface until it rammed the end of the tub, and diving until it bounced off the bottom and popped back to the surface, where it stayed until it rammed the end of the tub again. The effect was most satisfying.

There was no name on the submarine, not even a number. It was just a blue submarine. Thirty years later there was a song about a yellow submarine, but in 1940 real submarines were definitely not blue. But it did not matter.

The point is that the toy given to me in 1940 may have been just a representation of submarines in general. It probably was. But recalling that wonderful toy, I remember its tremendous beam relative to its length, and the peculiar shape of its conning tower. I also remember that the key rusted into an inoperative mass after about a dozen trips down the bathtub.

Forty years later I saw a photograph of a submarine that looked remarkably like the toy that had been given to me in 1940. The photograph was of the *Deutschland*. The conning tower was the same shape, and her beam was enough to make her look obese. Was it the same boat? Probably not, though the toy maker may have been influenced by the submarine whose name became a household word during World War I.

The end result of that parental indulgence is this book. It is intended to be informative and entertaining, because the story of the *Deutschland* is just that. In 1916 the Germans tried an unorthodox scheme to break the British blockade. They failed. This, then, is the account of what they tried to do and why it did not work.

ACKNOWLEDGMENTS

During the twenty-two years that I have been a cop, I have learned that no investigation will be successful without help. Usually, the help comes from one or two people, a good partner or a good informant. I have also learned that if you want the answer to a question, just ask enough people and someone will give you the answer. Researching a historical event works the same way.

On this project I got all my help from a long-time and good friend, Charles Burdick. The man is a living warehouse of information about German military history. He knows where the records are, who is alive and can talk about it, and what written material might be even remotely related to the topic. On top of that, he kept sending me copies of documents and articles from his own enormous files. Charles is that rare person who is both a good partner and a good informant. As a matter of fact, I never have met the combination being a cop. But if I ever do, my case-clearance rate will skyrocket.

I asked a lot of people a lot of questions and got the answers I needed. The people I asked were archivists in the United States, Germany, and Great Britain. They are too many to name individually here, but their organizations are listed in the bibliography. In some cases I wrote letters and in others I went there. In every case, the archivists did exactly what I hoped they would do—well, in nearly every case.

The Merchant U-Boat

CHAPTER ONE

MAY 1915

Smoke and flame erupted from the muzzle of the 6-inch gun, accompanied by a flat, listless boom that had no sharp definition or punch. There was no subsequent splash, no column of water rising from the sea to mark the projectile's impact. There was just a sprinkle of wadding and debris on the sea's surface. The round was a blank. Nevertheless, it had the desired effect.

Five thousand yards away, the SS *Atlantic Empire* started to slow, her captain standing on the starboard bridge wing, peering at HMS *Alsatian* through binoculars. He had seen her before. She had been an Allan liner before the war, touted as the largest and fastest steamer running to Canada. Now she was an auxiliary cruiser, the flagship of Admiral Sir Dudley de Chair's Tenth Cruiser Squadron. The *Atlantic Empire*'s skipper was not at all happy about being stopped.

The American freighter was loaded with cotton, wheat, and corn consigned to a firm in Oslo. The captain knew the company was a front that would transship the cargo to Germany, but that made no difference to him. His ship was an American flag carrier, he was an American citizen, and so were his crewmen. So far as he was concerned, his was a neutral vessel doing business with a neutral country, and the British had no right to stop him. But the cold, lonely waters east of the Faeroes were no place for a merchantman to argue with an armed auxiliary.

The *Alsatian* turned at right angles to the wind and sea, slowed to two knots, and lowered a boat. Signal flags ran up the mast ordering the *Atlantic Empire* to fall astern and come up on the boat. The freighter complied, and soon the boarding party went up her side. She was now dead in the water, the *Alsatian* standing off her starboard side, her 6-inch guns trained on the freighter.

Lieutenant Commander J. W. Williams, RNR, and Sub-Lieutenant John Barton, RNR, led the boarding party. Together with a signalman, the two officers inspected the ship's papers, questioned the crew, and made a quick examination of the cargo. Coxswain John Leslie and four oarsmen remained in the boat. One of the oarsmen, Michael Lynch, was kept busy fending the small boat away from the freighter's side as the big ship rolled in the moderate sea. The whole affair took about an hour.

Aboard the *Alsatian,* Captain George Trewby, RN, kept an eye on the freighter, waiting for a signal. If Williams was satisfied, the boarding party would return and the *Atlantic Empire* would go on her way. But if Williams found something suspicious, the freighter would be sent to Kirkwall in the Orkneys with an armed guard aboard. The signal was short, CONTRABAND.

Quickly a second boat was lowered, an officer and six armed men aboard. According to the Reprisals Order issued on 11 March 1916, all Atlantic freight of German origin or destination was subject to seizure. That included cargo sent to dummy firms for transshipment. British intelligence was precise about those firms, and every boarding officer had a list of their names. Though it was no comfort to the *Atlantic Empire*'s skipper, he and his ship were just one of many being stopped and seized. The Tenth Cruiser Squadron was very effective.[1]

By 1915, the Royal Navy had effectively sealed off Germany from the rest of the world. The English Channel was heavily mined and patrolled, and the North Sea was closely guarded by the Tenth Cruiser Squadron. Through a series of ever-restrictive Orders in Council, the British government was tightening the blockade around Germany. Critically needed imports had slowed to a trickle and in some cases were nonexistent.

By the first week in July 1915 the Tenth Cruiser Squadron had stopped over sixteen hundred neutral ships and had sent nearly four hundred into British ports. By the end of the year the figures had more than doubled. The effect on Germany was devastating.[2]

The Germans had planned for, and expected, a short war. In August 1914 they fully expected their victorious armies to be home by that Christmas. As a result they had almost no strategic reserves of raw materials and no food reserves. It was a short-sighted view for a country that imported one-third of its food and most of its industrial supplies. The first indication that disaster was brewing came in October 1914 when an ammunition crisis developed. All existing stocks had been used up, and the army was entirely dependent on new production. But the amount of ammunition coming out of German factories was so inadequate that by 14 November German artillery on the Western Front was down to a four-day supply.[3]

To head off disaster and bring order to developing chaos, the Germans established the War Raw Materials Section (*Kriegsrohstoffabteilung*). The organization's purpose was to distribute scarce materials to firms directly engaged in the war effort. Their task was formidable.

Copper stocks assembled before the war were nearly exhausted by the summer of 1915. Before the war Germany had imported 200,000 tons of copper each year, mostly from the United States. For all of 1915, copper imports amounted to a meager 13,000 tons, to which Germany could add only a pitiful 40,000 tons through domestic production. In May 1915 the government ordered manufacturers to declare their copper stocks. In July the stocks were confiscated. By December copper articles were being stripped from households to feed the war effort.[4]

The British declared cotton a contraband on 22 August 1915 and virtually stopped importation into Germany, permitting just 40,000 tons to be delivered by the end of the year. Before the war Germany had used over 400,000 tons each year just to produce fabrics. But by 1915 the German munitions makers alone were using 1,000 tons per day, and another 500 tons per day were being used to make military clothing and equipment. At that rate of consumption Germany's cotton supplies would soon be exhausted. In fact, by December textile production for the civilian market had been reduced 70 percent.[5]

In mid-July 1915 the German government assumed control of the entire coal supply.[6]

The growing crisis resulted in an energetic program to find substitutes for the things that were unattainable. Aluminum replaced copper in much of Germany's electrical equipment. Cellulose for explosives was developed from wood, reducing some of Germany's dependency on cotton. Paper was used to manufacture civilian clothing.[7] But inventiveness was not the sole answer to the problem, and some things could not be replaced with substitutes. One of those things was food.

By early 1915 the food crisis at home was as serious as the ammunition crisis on the front. Individual meat allowances were reduced to five hundred grams (17.7 ounces) per week, and two days

Before World War I, Admiral Alfred von Tirpitz put his faith in newly constructed battleships to wrest control of the sea from the British. But experience during the war showed the inadequacy of his prewar efforts. (Author's collection)

each week were designated as meatless. Milk supplies were cut in half, and bread rationing was started in June. German harvests declined for lack of fertilizers, reducing wheat and rye supplies by 30 to 50 percent. The production of beer fell 40 percent.[8]

Shortages were accompanied by soaring prices. By May 1915 all food prices in Berlin were up 50 percent, meat prices had doubled, and the price of corn was over four times its prewar figure.[9]

German soldiers, no better off than the civilians, were the most poorly fed of all the troops fighting on the Western Front. In June 1915 the individual meat ration was cut to 280 grams per day, one year later it was cut to 168 grams, and the staple diet became a thin pea soup with a few lumps of fat and some gristle.[10]

In an attempt to get food and raw materials past the British blockade, the Germans rerouted imports through the neutral countries—Holland, Norway, Denmark, and Sweden. Consigned to friendly companies in those countries, the cargoes were then transshipped to Germany along more secure routes across the Baltic. The British quickly responded to the ploy by blacklisting companies that traded with the Germans through that scheme. The British also put enormous diplomatic and economic pressure on the four neutrals. As a result, the trick was only marginally successful, and the shipments

SMS *Blücher* joined the fleet in 1909, and was sunk six years later at Dogger Bank, on 24 January 1915. Only 61 men from a crew of 853 survived. Dogger Bank was the last major engagement before the Battle of Jutland sixteen months later. (Author's collection)

received through the four neutrals came nowhere near making up Germany's shortages.

By the end of 1915, the home-front situation was so grim that General Erich von Falkenhayn, chief of the General Staff, was convinced that the people would not support the war beyond 1916.[11] Alfred Hugenberg, chief director of the armaments giant, Krupp, would have agreed, but for a different reason. Krupp desperately needed nickel for war production. But their stocks were rapidly dwindling, and there was no replenishment in sight. Once the existing stores were gone, estimated to occur by the end of 1916, Germany would be unable to continue the war.[12]

It was during this period that the argument over how the war at sea should be fought became heated. On one side the German navy wanted to increase submarine production and wage unrestricted submarine warfare. The German naval command insisted that the quickest way to force Britain to accept a negotiated peace was to paralyze her with a crippling U-boat campaign. On the other side the civilian government wanted to stick to existing law and find a way through the blockade.

In February 1915, one month after Dogger Bank, Admiral Reinhold von Scheer told the kaiser that an unrestricted U-boat campaign was the only thing that would defeat the British. U-boats like these were to torpedo enemy and neutral merchant ships without warning. (Author's collection)

Before the war, Grand Admiral Alfred von Tirpitz had overseen the construction of a balanced fleet. It was the battle line, not submarines, that would wrest control of the sea from the British. But events early in World War I proved the inadequacy of Admiral von Tirpitz's prewar efforts.

The first blow to German confidence came in August 1914 when the Royal Navy raided the Helgoland Bight, sinking the cruisers SMS *Ariadne, Mainz,* and *Köln,* along with the destroyer SMS *V-187.* Two other light cruisers were damaged. Four and a half months later both sides tangled on the Dogger Bank, and the Germans lost the SMS *Blücher.* The German fleet stayed in port until May 1916 when it ventured out to fight the Battle of Jutland, the last major role played by the German fleet.

The developing stalemate on the Western Front and the naval setbacks prompted General Erich von Falkenhayn, soon to be chief of the General Staff, to see the kaiser. In November 1914 he told the kaiser that unless France or Russia could be defeated, Germany would lose the war.[13]

There was more bad news in February 1915 when Admiral Reinhard Scheer told the kaiser that the German battle fleet could not

This staged photo was used by the Germans to drum up support for an unrestricted U-boat campaign. Armed British ships regularly flew neutral flags—in this case American. Any U-boat that surfaced and approached such a freighter, in compliance with the prize rules, was running a serious risk of being sunk. (Author's collection)

defeat Britain at sea. The only alternative, Admiral Scheer said, lay in an unrestricted U-boat campaign against commercial shipping.[14]

Lacking the ships needed to stop, search, and seize merchant ships bound for Britain, the Admiral proposed to sink them without warning. The U-boats would end the war quickly by doing to Britain what Britain was doing to Germany—they would starve her out. Britain and Germany would be like two men trying to strangle each other—the one who squeezed the hardest and held out the longest would win.

Opposing Admiral Scheer's view was the civilian government led by Reich Chancellor Theobald von Bethmann-Hollweg. The chancellor warned the kaiser that unrestricted U-boat warfare would turn world opinion against Germany and bring the United States into the war on the Allied side. Bethmann-Hollweg's fears were based on the nature of international law in 1916.

Briefly stated, the law, incorporated in a set of regulations called the prize rules, said that merchant ships could not be attacked without warning. According to the prize rules, the warship had to stop the merchantman, board the vessel, and inspect her cargo. If contraband was found on board, the ship could be seized as a prize and sent into port. If for some good reason the ship could not be taken to port, the crew had to be put in a place of safety and the ship sunk. Usually the crew was taken aboard the warship. Putting the crewmen into lifeboats was only permitted if the sea was calm and they were close enough to land to row ashore.

To Americans who witnessed the savage Battle of the North Atlantic, and applauded the wholesale destruction of the Japanese merchant fleet during the Second World War, the idea that there was something wrong with unrestricted submarine warfare seems out of place. But during World War I, people still expected commanders of warships to behave like gentlemen.

Initially the Germans tried to play by the rules, but the realities of war soon made that impractical. The British started arming their merchant ships early in the war, and many flew neutral flags. U-boat captains increasingly found themselves being shot at when they surfaced to inspect an apparently unarmed neutral ship. As the war progressed, more and more British merchant ships were armed, making the visit-and-search aspect of the prize rules very hazardous.

Worried by the reports made by General von Falkenhayn and Admiral Scheer, the kaiser gave his approval for unrestricted U-boat warfare against merchant shipping. In February 1915 a war zone was established around the British Isles, and neutrals were warned that their ships were subject to being torpedoed without warning. Most of the German skippers continued to operate by the prize rules, but within a short time many were torpedoing ships without showing more than a periscope. The neutrals were aghast at such a horrible practice.

Their outrage took a quantum leap on 7 May 1915 when the RMS *Lusitania* was sunk by Kapitänleutnant Walter Schwieger in the *U-20*. The Cunard liner was within sight of land when she was torpedoed and sunk in less than twenty minutes. Nearly twelve hundred people went down with her.

The howl of protest from the United States threatened to bring her into the war on the side of the British. And that was something the Germans wanted to avoid at all costs—at least in 1915.

Chancellor Bethmann-Hollweg used the opportunity to get to the kaiser. Worried by the chancellor's report on America's reaction to the sinking, a reaction that was underscored by a strong warning from President Wilson, the kaiser backed off. On 31 May he ordered his U-boat captains not to attack large enemy or neutral passenger ships, a decision that sparked an angry reaction from the admirals. Despite the admirals' outrage, the kaiser continued to back his chancellor—at least for the moment.

But the diplomatic crisis deepened in August when the *U-24* sank the SS *Arabic,* a White Star liner about half the size of the *Lusitania.* But she was still a passenger ship, and there were Americans aboard. The *Arabic,* outward bound to the United States, was just fifty miles south of Kinsale when the torpedo hit, sinking her in less than ten minutes.

The neutrals were outraged, and America was on the brink of going to war. Chancellor Bethmann-Hollweg urged the kaiser to stop placing limited restrictions on the unrestricted U-boat campaign and return to the prize rules. The kaiser, shaken by the neutrals' reaction, again listened to his chancellor. In September 1915 the unrestricted U-boat campaign was stopped.

But the Germans were still faced with the fact that the British blockade was very effective and that Germany was being starved for food and war materials while Britain was being regularly supplied. Either something had to be done to cut Britain's supply lines, or a way through the British blockade had to be found.

CHAPTER TWO

THE *ETAPPENDIENST*

The words were painted in large black letters across the front of the building, above the big sliding doors: NEW YORK DOCK CO. WAREHOUSE 104. A heavy chain and a massive lock secured the door, the windows were covered with tar paper, and a watchman patrolled the dock. The precautions were not unusual. Warehouse contents are often very valuable, and burglars know that. And the contents of warehouse 104 were valuable, but they would have been very difficult for burglars to carry away. Inside warehouse 104 were 560 tons of refined nickel, packed in casks weighing 1,000 pounds each.[1]

There was a similar warehouse in Pittsburgh.

Dr. Heinrich Albert had purchased the ore from the International Nickel Company in New Jersey. The purchase was only half legal. Heinrich Albert, the German commercial attaché in Washington, was apparently acting on Krupp's behalf when he made the purchases in November 1914. The war was just three months old, and already the blockade was starting to hurt. The world's supply of nickel came from Canada, and an agreement had been reached between the Canadians and the big American nickel houses not to sell the ore to any of the Central Powers or their agents.

But Albert had been able to convince the International Nickel Company that the ore he wanted to buy had been obtained from Canada *before* the war, and was, therefore, exempt from the agreement. He may have been right; at least he convinced the Americans he was.

But neither Albert nor the Americans were convinced the British would agree, so the sale was done secretly.

Albert shipped the ore to the Nassau Smelting and Refining Company in New York City, where it was refined, cast in buckshot form, and packed in casks. It was then shipped to the warehouses in Brooklyn and Pittsburgh where the ore was joined by another batch purchased early in 1915 by Kuhn, Loeb, and Company. Having purchased and collected the ore, Albert's next problem was getting the nickel to Germany. And there he was stuck. Because of the blockade, the nickel sat in the warehouses, out of Krupp's reach.

The purchases had been done under the direction of the *Etappendienst,* an organization whose name gives some clue to its purpose. *Etappe* has several meanings, one of them being the military expression for rear area communications or logistics. *Dienst* simply means service. But the organization was really much more than just a logistics service.

Funded and directed by the navy, the very secret *Etappendienst* was established about 1896 and charged with ensuring that Germany receive the raw materials needed to fight a war. But its mission was also to ensure that, regardless of the war's outcome, Germany's industrial complex and international business network would remain intact.

To accomplish those goals the *Etappendienst* drew on the combined skills of the navy, the diplomatic corps, the business community, and the industrialists. The result was a complex, international network of agents, dummy companies, and bank accounts in virtually every country in the world. The extent of the organization is demonstrated by the fact that as late as 1948 the *Etappendienst* cell in Japan was still functioning.[2]

Today, historians still do not have a clear picture of what this organization was all about, because many of its files were destroyed at the end of World War II. What follows is, to some degree, conjecture based on circumstantial evidence supported by bits and pieces of documented facts. But there is no conjecture about the situation in the autumn of 1915.

The war was at a standstill on the Western Front, and there was no sign of a breakthrough. Germany's merchant fleet had been driven from the seas, she was totally cut off from her prewar markets, and her economy was on the verge of collapse. The civilian government was locked in a life-and-death struggle with the military over how the war should be conducted. In order to win that struggle, the civilian government had to find a way to break the blockade without angering the neutrals—especially the United States. That requirement went hand-in-glove with the goals of the *Etappendienst*.

Starting in early 1915, a scheme was hatched wherein large cargo U-boats would be built and sent on regular runs to the United States. They would carry dyestuffs and pharmaceuticals to the United States and return with rubber, copper, and nickel. They would also provide a means for sending secret information between Germany and the German ambassador to the United States, Count Johann von Bernstorff. The cargo U-boats would also be a secure way to send agents to the United States.

The idea of building cargo U-boats was not new. A Krupp engineer and designer, Rudolf Erbach, had submitted a design for a cargo U-boat as early as 1914, but it was pigeonholed and ignored until 1915. The oversight was due, in part, to German overoptimism and shortsightedness.

Until well into 1915 many Germans clung to the belief that the war would be over quickly. They believed the brutal stalemate on the Western Front would soon be broken by a combination of German élan and superior weapons. Even after the start of the first major U-boat construction program in February 1916, the head of the Bureau of Yards and Docks was openly asking what was to be done with all those extra submarines if peace were suddenly made.[3]

But by spring of 1915, there were many Germans who believed the war was going to drag on for a long time. They were the people most affected by the British blockade, and the armaments giant, Krupp, was one of the first to feel the pinch. Closely linked to the *Etappendienst*, Krupp's priority goal was to recover the nickel stored in warehouse 104.

Krupp needed the nickel for several projects, but the most urgent was U-boat construction—U-boat pressure hulls were built of nickel-steel—and Krupp suggested building a cargo U-boat to get it. An order was sent to the design department, and the navy was asked for authorization to build the boat. The request was sweetened by an offer to make a gift of the boat to the nation—provided it was used to transport Krupp's nickel.

In the meantime, the German state secretary was making a similar suggestion, though his idea was still rather general and vague. He wanted cargo U-boats to bring in "essential supplies," which would have included nickel, but without the paramount emphasis on Krupp's specific need.[4]

Alfred Lohmann, a prominent businessman from Bremen, now entered the picture. Officially he was a businessman who was also interested in building a freight U-boat. The truth was probably something else.

He was the son of a former chairman of the board of the powerful Norddeutsche Lloyd (North German Lloyd). Lohmann was not in the shipping business, but he was the chairman of the board of at least three major corporations. One of those companies was his own Lohmann and Company with offices in Bremen, Sydney, and Melbourne. In addition he was the president of the Bremen Chamber of Commerce. As a businessman with connections in shipping, importing, and exporting, he was ideally suited to play the role of public coordinator for the *Deutschland* project.[5]

Lohmann also had another interesting, and probably significant, connection. His brother, Walter, was a captain in the German navy. At the time, Walter Lohmann was serving inconspicuously in a noncombatant, logistics slot. In fact, he remained in that slot throughout the war. But it may have been more a place to hide him than to use him.

After the war Walter was given complete charge of the navy's "black funds" that were used for clandestine operations. He used the money in a number of commercial ventures that included submarine design and construction in Holland and Spain. There is little doubt that in 1915, Captain Walter Lohmann was an *Etappendienst* agent.[6]

During the spring and summer of 1915, Alfred Lohmann made several trips to Berlin to discuss the cargo U-boat idea with government officials. The discussions took place in the elegant Hotel Adlon, and resulted in a holding company being formed that included representatives of Norddeutsche Lloyd and the Deutsche Bank. Called the Deutsche Ozean Reederei GmbH (German Ocean Navigation Company), the company would be the public owners and operators of the cargo submarines.

Alfred Lohmann was named chairman of the board. The general director was Philipp Heineken, president of Norddeutsche Lloyd, the treasurer was Paul Millington-Herrmann, director of the Deutsche Bank, and another Lloyd director, Karl Stapelfeld, was named director in charge of freight. All had ties with the *Etappendienst*. Though not openly represented, the navy and Krupp were also involved.[7]

Around mid-September a Krupp competitor, Vulcan, got wind of the cargo U-boat idea and wanted in. At the time Vulcan was building two mine-laying U-boats, *U-79* and *U-80*, and Vulcan suggested those two boats be modified to carry freight.[8]

It would have been a quick way to get the project started, but the navy rejected the offer. The minelayers were needed for their designed purpose, and in any event they were too small to do the job planned for the cargo U-boats. As things worked out, the *U-79* and *U-80* also lacked the speed and range for the job.

In October, Vulcan countered with a bid to build four cargo U-boats. At the same time, Lohmann, representing the Deutsche Ozean Reederei, was negotiating with another Krupp competitor, A. G. Weser. The Bremen-based shipbuilders responded to Lohmann's request for a 600- to 800-ton design by submitting plans for a 600-ton boat. The design was too small, probably because of A. G. Weser's relative inexperience with building large boats. But an even bigger problem was that A. G. Weser had no engines readily available.[9]

At that point the government stepped in, demonstrating the degree of their involvement in the project. Both Vulcan's and A. G. Weser's bids were rejected, and Krupp was awarded a contract for two cargo U-boats.[10]

Ostensibly the boats were to be controlled by civilians and were known publicly as the *Deutschland* and the *Bremen*. In fact, the navy carried the two boats in their files as the *U-200* and the *U-201*, and throughout their relatively short careers, the navy exercised enormous control over the two boats—even to the point of abruptly ordering the *Deutschland* converted to a war boat.

But insofar as the German public and the rest of the world were concerned, the two boats were being privately built for the newly created Deutsche Ozean Reederei. And it was important to make people believe that.[11]

The key to the entire episode was the alleged civilian status of the two boats. The United States was still neutral in 1915, and Germany wanted her to stay that way. Because the United States was neutral, any belligerent warship that remained in a United States port longer than twenty-four hours would be interned for the duration of the war. Legitimate commercial vessels had a much longer grace period to dock and take on cargo.

If the two cargo U-boats were accepted as civilian vessels, they could regularly carry freight between the United States and Germany without being interned by the United States government. Two boats might become four and four might become eight. The possibilities were limitless. If the plan worked, the blockade would be broken.

On 8 November 1915 the Deutsche Ozean Reederei was officially founded, shielded by a complex network of company charters, inter-

The after section of the *Deutschland*'s pressure hull under construction at Flensburger Schiffbau AG. The fact that the frames were inside the hull was noted by the American officers who inspected her in Baltimore and New London. One wrote, ". . . it is noteworthy as the inner hull of most double hull submarines is framed on the outside." (Bibliothek für Zeitgeschichte, Stuttgart)

locking directorships, and joint company operations. The whole operation was a joint government-business venture, with the government making the decisions and the businessmen managing the operations.[12] The relationship was best described as a sweetheart deal for the businessmen.

Lohmann and his associates put up 2 million Marks of their own money, and each man's investment was substantial. Lohmann invested a half million Marks only to have that figure surpassed by Philipp Heineken and Paul Millington-Herrmann, who each invested three quarters of a million Marks. But those were safe investments, protected by the government, with a guaranteed 5-percent return. The investors could not lose.[13]

The money was held in a special account in the Deutsche Bank in Berlin, supposedly to pay the building costs of the two cargo U-

The outer hull's raised walkway has been attached to the pressure hull, as have the fuel and ballast tanks. Cargo that could withstand immersion in sea water was stored atop the tanks and beneath the walkway. There was also space beneath the walkway to store two small boats. (Bibliothek für Zeitgeschichte, Stuttgart)

boats. In fact, the construction materials and skilled shipyard labor were supplied by Krupp and paid for by the navy. Even the diesel engines, designed as diesel-generators for the battleship SMS *Sachsen* and the heavy cruiser SMS *Ersatz Gneisenau*, were Krupp products. They were diverted to the cargo U-boat program.

Not surprisingly, the crews for the *Deutschland* and the *Bremen* were selected from among experienced U-boat crews.[14] After all, the boats were submarines, complex vessels that required special training and skill to operate. And that kind of skill was not found in the merchant marine.

What is surprising is that during the diplomatic flap that attended the *Deutschland*'s arrival later in Baltimore no one questioned the crew's status. And the German navy was very careful to keep the crew's real status a secret. In an unsigned, secret document dated 27 July 1916 a German Naval Staff member wrote:

The navy supported the operation by providing construction labor, material and the diesel engines, and later the crew who had been trained in U-boats and was released from active service. The crew was, whenever possible, selected from former Lloyd personnel. The Captain of the *Deutschland* had commanded a Lloyd steamer between America and the Mediterranean before the war.[15]

The man referred to in the secret document, Paul Lebrecht König, had literally been plucked from obscurity to command the *Deutschland*. An officer with Norddeutsche Lloyd since 1896, he had been promoted to captain in 1911 when he took command of the SS *Schleswig*. Until the war started in August 1914, Captain König spent most of his time in the Mediterranean commanding the SS *Schleswig* or the SS *Prinzess Irene*. Both were passenger ships that catered to wealthy tourists.[16]

Dressed in civilian clothes, Paul König would have been lost in a crowd. He was forty-eight years old when he was selected, though he looked at least ten years older. He was a small man about five feet eight inches tall and weighed 155 pounds. His iron-grey hair was combed straight back and closely cropped, military style, above his slightly oversized ears. His face was small, weather-beaten, and somewhat homely. One reporter described him as "elf-like." But in uniform, on board his ship, he was a charming, elegant man whom the passengers adored.

A casual glance at Paul König's record revealed no outstanding feature beyond his being a competent officer. But under closer inspection several facts came to light. For one thing, he spoke English fluently, though with a heavy German accent.

As a youth König had studied Latin at the Frankeschen Stiftungen zu Halle where his mother had him enrolled to prepare for the priesthood. Though his father had been a pastor, a career in religion was not something Paul wanted. But he did have an ear for languages. The several trips he later made to the United States as a junior officer with Norddeutsche Lloyd gave him the opportunity to learn English. His already well-developed ability to speak English took a huge leap forward in 1900 when he met an English woman, Kathleen Marie Pennington. Like his own father, hers had been a clergyman, and was deceased.

She had been a passenger and he was the second officer when they met, and a romance developed quickly. They were married in Winchester, England, on 5 September 1901. On the marriage certificate his occupation is listed as first lieutenant, Imperial Naval Reserve. Why did he not use his real full-time occupation: merchant marine officer?

The Königs established a residence in Winchester, although it is not clear how much time Paul really spent there. He sailed out of Bremerhaven, and the commute between home and work would have been a long one. But whatever arrangements they worked out in regard to his career and family, he was around long enough to father three sons between 1901 and 1914. And at the same time he perfected his English.

The runs to the United States had provided him with firsthand knowledge of American harbors and a clearer understanding of the workings of the American mind. Those were important considerations when selecting the man to command a cargo U-boat intended to visit American ports. But resourcefulness, the ability to function well under pressure, and the disposition to follow orders without question were equally important. Paul König's record showed that he had those three traits.

When the war started in August 1914 he was in command of the SS *Schleswig* off the coast of Norway. Under orders to either duck into a neutral port or run for home, he chose to run for home. It was not an easy decision. He was responsible for the safety of his passengers, and an encounter with the Royal Navy could have ended in terrible humiliation or disaster. The decision was the right one, however, and the *Schleswig* reached Bremerhaven safely. The press loved it, Norddeutsche Lloyd was relieved, and the Imperial German Navy immediately ordered Captain König to active service.

For the next fifteen months he served aboard the old battleship SMS *Brandenburg* as a Kapitänleutnant. During that time he moved up from watch officer to first officer, and took part in the naval campaign against the Russians. For his part in those actions he received the Iron Cross, Second Class.

His service in the Imperial Navy and his participation in combat operations against the Russians are important points for two reasons. They counted heavily in the decision to give him command of the *Deutschland*, and they were carefully hidden from the public after that decision was made.

In December 1915 Kapitänleutnant König was relieved of his duties aboard the *Brandenburg* and assigned to the special personnel division of the Navy Department (*Matrosendivision zur Verfügung*). There

Taken in March 1916, this photo shows the *Deutschland* nearly ready to launch. The after part of the conning tower is solid and a ladder is built into the tower to allow access to and from the deck. As a war boat the conning tower was open in the rear to allow more speedy access. The slots in the hull allow seawater to flow freely between the hulls. This is also a good view of the vertical and horizontal rudders. The *Deutschland*'s diving planes in the bow, and her horizontal rudders in the stern were always rigged out. (Bibliothek für Zeitgeschichte, Stuttgart)

he assisted in the selection of the men who would be assigned to the *Deutschland*. Among the men he helped select was Lieutenant Franz Krapohl.

Lieutenant Krapohl was thirty-seven years old, over six feet tall, and ruggedly handsome. Unlike the elf-like König, Krapohl was the image of what a U-boat officer should look like. He had entered the Imperial Navy officer corps in 1909, but his service record to 1917 is missing. One source suggests that he may have been a member of naval intelligence. More likely, he was probably a member of the *Etappendienst*.[17]

The only other officer selected with König's help was Ensign Paul

Bow view of the *Deutschland* taken in March 1916, just before she was launched. Her straight stem is typical of surface-ship design during the early twentieth century. (Bibliothek für Zeitgeschichte, Stuttgart)

Eyring. Ensign Eyring, a twenty-nine-year-old reservist, had already seen action aboard the light cruiser SMS *Karlsruhe* during her raiding cruise in the West Indies and off Brazil in 1914.[18]

On 4 November 1914 the *Karlsruhe* was steaming north, in company with the SS *Rio Negro* and the SS *Indrani*. Without warning a huge explosion blew away the entire forward part of the cruiser, sending her to the bottom like a rock, and taking 263 crewmen with her. There were only 110 survivors, and Ensign Eyring was among them.

Rescued by the *Rio Negro*, Eyring and the other survivors were aboard her when she slipped through the British blockade and returned to Germany. He stayed aboard the *Rio Negro* as a watch officer after she was designated a blockade runner, and he was aboard her when she broke through the blockade, carrying supplies to German

The *Deutschland* had only one anchor, and the fact that it was completely
flush with the hull impressed the American officers who inspected her. Note
the bow planes permanently rigged out. (Bibliothek für Zeitgeschichte,
Stuttgart)

On 28 March 1916, without fanfare and in strict secrecy, the *Deutschland* was launched in Flensburg. She was then towed to Kiel for fitting out. Despite the tight security, information, rumors, and gossip about the boat were heard in bars from Flensburg to Kiel. (Bibliothek für Zeitgeschichte, Stuttgart)

troops in Africa. From September 1915 to January 1916 he commanded a small patrol boat operating out of Ems.

As was done with König, both officers' service records were sealed. Officially they were ex-merchant officers who after a period of forced leave were being returned to work in the merchant fleet. Oddly, no one questioned that assertion.

From January to April the three officers received training in U-boats while the *Deutschland* and the *Bremen* were being built. The *Deutschland* was completed first. She was launched on 28 March 1916, completed her sea trials in May, and was placed in service in June.

By 1916 standards, the *Deutschland* was a big submarine. Her length, 213 feet (65 meters), was not really exceptional, but her beam, 29.2 feet (8.9 meters), was. She had double-hull construction, common among U-boats, but the space between the hulls—thirteen feet at one point—was enormous. So large, in fact, that it was used to stow several tons of so-called "wet cargo." Loaded she drew seventeen feet, and the measurement from the top of her conning tower to the bottom of her keel was 30.3 feet (9.25 meters). Her builders estimated that she could carry 1,000 tons of cargo, about half the amount carried by many freighters.[19]

The *Deutschland* conducted her sea trials in April and May 1916. Her crew, selected from among experienced U-boat crews, is seen here dressed in German navy uniforms. The ship in dry dock is a *Kaiser*-class battleship. The *Deutschland* was 213 feet long, and had a 29.20-foot beam. She drew 17 feet. (Bibliothek für Zeitgeschichte, Stuttgart)

While the crew was being selected and trained and the two boats were being built, the *Etappendienst* was busy setting up the organization to handle the U-boats at the American end of the line. Early in 1916 Henry G. Hilken and Paul H. L. Hilken were contacted. They were a father-and-son team that owned A. Schumacher and Company, the United States agents for the Norddeutsche Lloyd. The Hilkens were told to establish a new company to handle the U-boat cargo business, and to buy waterfront property for landing and loading cargo. But the Hilkens were really just front men for Captain Frederich Hinsch, from whom they took their orders.[20]

Captain Hinsch was the skipper of the Lloyd liner SS *Neckar,* at that time interned in Baltimore. At the start of the war, the *Neckar* had been in Havana, where she was taken over by the German navy as a supply ship for the light cruiser SMS *Karlsruhe*. On 9 September 1914, the *Neckar* was with three other ships waiting for the *Karls-*

April 1916. The *Deutschland* is nearly ready to be commissioned. There is a formation forward of the conning tower, and an officer is saluting. Only the helmsman is atop the conning tower. All very military and hardly in keeping with a "civilian" boat. Her hull and conning tower were painted sea green, the tank tops black, and the periscopes were a mottled sea green and white. Note the ladder built into the conning tower, port side aft. (Bibliothek für Zeitgeschichte, Stuttgart)

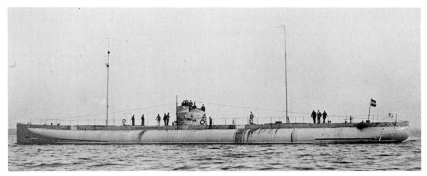

The *Deutschland* returning from sea trials in April 1916. Her crew is now dressed in civilian attire, and the boat shows signs of hard use. Both radio antenna masts are raised and her jumper antenna is rigged from the stern, across the conning tower, and down to the bow. In practice, she used her jumper antenna since raising and lowering the masts were terribly time consuming. Note the crow's nest on the forward mast. (National Archives)

Kapitän Paul Lebrecht König, the *Deutschland*'s skipper. A former skipper with Norddeutsche Lloyd, König was a competent seaman with a natural gift for public relations. He spoke English fluently, though with a heavy German accent. The hat badge represents the Deutsche Ozean Reederei, but he was an officer in the Imperial German Navy. (National Archives)

ruhe just east of Trinidad when the British cruiser HMS *Berwick* showed up.

The ships scattered in four directions like hares before the hound. By evening of the following day, three of the German supply ships had been captured, and the *Neckar* was running toward Baltimore where, as a naval auxiliary vessel, she was interned.[21]

Working closely with Captain Hinsch, the Hilkens established the Eastern Forwarding Company, bought waterfront property in Baltimore, and also leased the newly constructed State Pier in New London, Connecticut. Despite the name, the pier was owned by the T. A. Scott Dredging Company.[22]

Early in May they bought a coal-fired tug, the *Timmins*, in New York and brought her to Baltimore where:

> An army of workmen were busied upon her day and night. In the utmost secrecy they tuned up her engines, crammed her bunkers full of coal, installed efficient wireless apparatus, Morse electric code signals not ordinarily used on boats of her character.[23]

With the exception of security measures at the two dock sites, everything was ready by 14 June. On that day the *Deutschland* left the Germania Shipyard outfitting pier.

CHAPTER THREE

DEPARTURE,

14–23 JUNE 1916

The *Deutschland* lay port-side-to along the Germania outfitting pier in Kiel, her bow and stern lines slack, her fat, grey-green hull pushed against the dock by the flooding tide. Captain Paul König looked down from the conning tower, mentally noting the current that was setting his boat against the pier. Then he looked aft.

The tug *Charlotte* lay a short distance off the *Deutschland*'s starboard quarter, a tow line from her stern to the stern of the U-boat. König glanced at his watch. 1100. Then he turned his attention to the men standing by the bow and stern lines. They were ready. He gripped the steel rim of the conning tower and listened to the steady rumble of the U-boat's idling diesels. The noise of the unmuffled engines drowned out the soft hum of her electric motors.[1] Under his hands the boat felt alive, powerful.

"All stations report manned and ready." The speaker was Lieutenant Franz Krapohl, the *Deutschland*'s first officer.[2]

Captain König acknowledged the report and bent over the speaking tube. "Achtung, achtung, achtung," he spoke into the tube and then straightened up, raising his hand.

"Cast off aft," he shouted, dropping his hand. The stern line splashed into the oily water as dockhands hastily hauled it in. König turned to face the tug, cupping his hands around his mouth. "Pull away, *Charlotte*."

The tug's engine telegraph jingled and the line went taut. As the

Deutschland's stern swung away from the dock, the captain turned forward.

"Cast off forward." The last line fell away. He leaned forward to the speaking tube. "Port back one-half. Starboard ahead slow." Again he straightened up, this time speaking to the helmsman on the platform forward of the conning tower. "Starboard rudder, twenty degrees."

"Aye, aye sir. Starboard rudder, twenty degrees," the seaman answered, ensuring that he had understood the order as given.

Captain König was performing a maneuver called twisting. It is used in tight spaces and causes the bow to swing in one direction while the stern swings in the other. In this case, the captain wanted to turn the *Deutschland* a full 180 degrees, and was twisting her to the left as she backed slowly away from the pier. The bow swung left slowly, the tidal current trying to push it back against the pier. The boat was at right angles to the pier, moving slowly back, gripped by the current. The *Deutschland* needed help from the tug.

Captain König again faced the tug, cupping his hands around his mouth. "Pull away, *Charlotte*," he shouted. The tug took up the slack, the U-boat's stern swung toward the tug and her bow pointed down channel.

"All stop," he said quickly into the speaking tube. The twin screws stopped turning. "Cast off aft." The tow line was hastily cast off and taken aboard the tug. König waited a fraction of a minute to make sure that the line was clear of his propellers before giving the next command.

"All ahead half. Port standard rudder."

The *Deutschland* moved forward, turning to the left to avoid a U-boat that was being fitted out just aft of the spot the *Deutschland* had left. The *Deutschland* slid past the war boat and Captain König gave the next command.

"All ahead full. Rudder amidships."

The *Deutschland* slowly gathered speed, her bow pointed toward the Kaiser Wilhelm Canal, the North Sea, and Baltimore. Between her and her goal were the auxiliary cruisers of Admiral Sir Dudley De Chair's Tenth Cruiser Squadron. To any normal U-boat, that may not have posed a serious problem, since the cruisers had as much to fear from a U-boat as the U-boat did from the cruisers. But the *Deutschland* was no normal U-boat. She was an unarmed merchant vessel.

There had been no fanfare when the cargo U-boat left on her maiden voyage. There was no band, no cheering crowd, and no weeping loved ones. There was not even a notice in the paper. Everything about the *Deutschland* up to this point was shrouded in secrecy. The fact that the German Ocean Navigation Company had been founded was public knowledge, but only if you read shipping trade journals. And its purpose was vaguely stated.

The American consul in Bremen, William Thomas Fee, had issued a bill of health and certified invoices to the boat on 13 June 1916. But at the request of company representatives, and in direct violation of State Department rules, he did not report the *Deutschland*'s departure to the American Embassy in Berlin. The Germans told him that making the boat's departure public would place it in extreme danger. Fee agreed.[3]

The British would certainly do all they could to stop the boat if they could locate it. In fact they would certainly sink it. The British saw no difference between a U-boat built for war and one built to break the blockade. A U-boat was a U-boat. But how would the Americans react? That was the main issue at hand.

If the Americans accepted the *Deutschland* as a commercial vessel, the route through the blockade was open. And the cargo U-boat would enjoy the same protection under international law as any surface commercial vessel. That would mean that the British could not *legally* sink her on sight, without warning. That would probably have been a hollow victory since no one was really convinced that the British would observe the law in regard to the *Deutschland* anyway.

But if the Americans agreed with the British view that U-boats were all alike, she would be treated as a war boat. And that would be disastrous to the German plan. As a war boat, the *Deutschland* would not only be subject to attack without warning, but she would be denied entry into American ports. And a cargo U-boat that could not go where the cargo was would be totally useless. But the point was that the Germans wanted to ensure that the boat reached the United States so that the question could be resolved one way or the other. Therefore, secrecy was vital.

To further hide the boat's movements, the Germans decided to hold it at Helgoland until 23 June.[4] Their big worry was spies, and they believed that the British had plenty in and around Kiel. In fact, there were rarely any British spies in the area, and none reported any information about the *Deutschland*. But the Royal Navy did know about the big U-boat.

Part of their information came from loose-lipped yard workers, shop managers, and executives. The bits and pieces they let slip in bars, restaurants, and clubs were picked up by the press. As early as April 1916 a Dutch newspaper had published a story about a whole fleet of cargo U-boats being built by the Germans. The newspaper report was passed on to London by the British consulate in Stockholm. Other bits and pieces made their way to cocktail parties hosted by neutral consulates and embassies, where they were overheard by British sympathizers and agents. From there the information took the shortest route to British Naval Intelligence.[5]

So far all the British had were rumors that the Germans were building some kind of a super U-boat with cargo capability. In a broad sense the rumors were correct, but they lacked specific details. The British did not know, for example, if the U-boat freighter would be armed or not. They assumed it would be. In addition to rumors the British got some information directly from the German navy.

Unknown to the Germans the British had broken all the German navy codes by the end of 1914. Virtually every message sent by the Germans was intercepted and decoded by the British. And the Germans did use the radio. U-boats routinely radioed their departures, arrivals on station, their successes, failures, and positions. The British copied most of the messages.[6]

The *Deutschland* had reported her departure to Wilhelmshaven when she left Kiel. She also told headquarters when she cleared the Kaiser Wilhelm Canal and when she reached Helgoland. And when she headed north on the 23rd she broadcast that too.[7] The British knew she was at sea, but they did not know when she was scheduled to arrive off the United States. Could they catch her anyway?

CHAPTER FOUR

THE FIRST CROSSING,

23 JUNE–8 JULY 1916

A heavy sea broke over the *Deutschland*'s bow, burying the deck and crashing against the conning tower.[1] Ensign Eyring and the lookout ducked behind the windscreen as the wave exploded. A wall of water rose up in front of the conning tower, folded over, and cascaded down on the two men. Water swirled around their feet before pouring out through the scuppers. Eyring and the seaman stood up again and peered across the tossing sea.

The night was clear, but a strong wind out of the northwest heaped the sea into a succession of white-topped waves that curled and rolled. Loaded with seven hundred and fifty tons of cargo, ballasted with two hundred and fifty tons of scrap iron, and trimmed down nearly to the main deck, the *Deutschland* plowed through each oncoming wave.

Standing watch was wet work, but it was a piece of cake compared to what was happening below. The *Deutschland* had developed a vicious snap roll. Men were hurled from one side to another as the boat plunged through the heavy seas. In the days of sail men aloft said, "one hand for the sail and one hand for yourself." The adage applied to the men aboard the *Deutschland*.

The roll was so quick that if a bottle were standing on the table and it started to fall to starboard, on the roll to starboard, it would be caught by the return roll to port before it could finish the fall.[2]

The *Deutschland*'s crew was made up of experienced seamen. But even the most experienced old salt could not handle that kind of move-ment. The entire crew was seasick.

Ensign Eyring gripped the edge of the conning tower as he scanned the sea ahead. Then he saw it. Zigzagging toward the U-boat was a large ship with two funnels.

"Captain to the bridge," he shouted down the speaking tube.

In the control central Lieutenant Krapohl heard the call and passed the word forward by the speaking tube. The steward, Adolf Stucke, woke the captain. Grabbing his oil skins, Captain König hur-ried aft, scrambled up the ladder, and climbed through the hatch atop the conning tower.

"What is it?" he asked his second officer.

"There's a steamer almost dead ahead and zigzagging toward us." Ensign Eyring pointed forward.

Captain König lifted his binoculars and braced himself against the side of the lurching conning tower. "Probably an auxiliary cruiser. Stand by to dive."[3]

Ensign Eyring leaned over the speaking tube. "Stand by to dive."

König studied the strange ship for a few moments longer. The sea was too rough, the distance too great, and the light too poor to be sure. But the ship looked like one of the Tenth Cruiser Squadron auxiliary cruisers. Sure or not, this was no time to hesitate. "Dive," he shouted.

"Dive, dive, dive." Despite the distortion caused by the speaking tube, Eyring's voice rang with urgency.

Gong alarms rang throughout the boat as the bridge crew tum-bled through the hatch and slammed it shut. Orders were given to flood tanks. Bells clanged and red lights flicked on next to the flood-ing valves.

The pounding of the diesel engines was replaced by the hum of electric motors. The bow dropped down eight degrees as the bow diving planes bit in and the stern planes pushed the stern up. Water poured into the tanks.

> Compressed air escaped hissing from the tanks. At the same time a gigantic, intermittent snorting ensued, like the blowing and belching of some prehistoric monster. There was an uncomfortable pressure in our ears, then the noise became more regular, followed by a buzzing and a shrill hum.[4]

"Dive to twenty meters." Captain König watched the depth gauge needle swing slowly down. At that depth the *Deutschland* would be twenty-four feet below her periscope depth. He would then bring her up slowly until his periscope cleared the surface.

Lieutenant Krapohl was watching his stopwatch. It could take up to two minutes for the *Deutschland* to get under in a calm sea. With this sea running it might take longer.

"Twelve meters." A seaman stood facing the depth gauge calling out the depth as the boat descended.

"Two minutes," Lieutenant Krapohl said, punching the button on his stopwatch. The *Deutschland* was under.

Reports now came from all parts of the U-boat—the central, the engine room, the bow, the stern, the cargo spaces, the battery room— all tight.

"Fourteen tons negative."

"Start main pump."

The low-pressure pump whirred and hummed, driving air into the ballast tanks and driving water out. The descent slowed and then stopped.

"Six tons negative."

"Secure pumps. Hold her at twenty meters."

The boat leveled off, a scant one degree down at the bow. Captain König, Lieutenant Krapohl, and Ensign Eyring listened for the sound of propellers overhead. There was nothing.

"Take her up to periscope depth." The captain was already standing at the brass tube that rose from the deck. The boat rose easily.

After I had made sure that there were no vibrations from propellers to be heard in the vicinity and no steamer with which one might collide, we mastered the so-called blind moment. This is the interval during which the boat has already risen so high as to be rammed, but is still too far under the water to permit the use of the periscope.[5]

The *Deutschland* passed through the blind moment, the periscope rose above the surface, and Captain König made a three hundred and sixty degree sweep. He could not see much. Thick hills of water swept over the glass. In the interval between waves he saw only a witch's cauldron of black water and white spray.

"Down periscope." The brass tube slid past him into the deck. "Take her down to forty meters. We'll wait till dawn and then surface."

Was the ship they had seen really an auxiliary cruiser? Maybe. At the time they were between the Orkney Islands and the Shetland Islands and well within the Tenth Cruiser Squadron's patrol area. During the day, while on the surface, they had been spotted by a British trawler patrolling off Pentland Firth. The trawler had not attacked the U-boat because of heavy seas, but it did transmit "MAX LUCY." No one aboard the *Deutschland* knew for sure what MAX LUCY meant, but they assumed it was a coded alarm sent to British warships in the area. And the appearance of the large, fast steamer appeared to confirm that.[6]

At 0400 they surfaced. The sky was overcast and a big sea was running, but the seasick crewmen, desperate for relief from the terrible conditions below, huddled in shifts at the base of the conning tower. Throughout the day lookouts spotted several fishing boats and a few steamers, and Captain König noted that many of the fishing boats had the same paint scheme, a black hull with large white letters and numbers along the side. All appeared to be harmless fishing boats—one was even drying a net in its upperworks—except for the radio antennas they carried.

In fact, the northern route taken by the *Deutschland* was heavily patrolled by a vast fleet of fishing boats, yachts, auxiliary cruisers, and Q-ships. The latter were floating traps set to catch U-boats.

Typically, a nondescript, rather battered old freighter would be heavily armed. With its guns well hidden behind phony deck cargo and canvas superstructure, the Q-ship steamed slowly through areas where the U-boats operated. If things worked out, a U-boat would surface, stop the Q-ship, and move in close to send over a boarding party. With the U-boat dead in the water, the Q-ship would unmask its 6-inch guns, and open fire. The ensuing battle was usually short, and fatal to the U-boat.

North of the Hebrides the *Deutschland* was spotted by a steamer flying a Swedish flag. The U-boat's lookouts had been watching the steamer for some time and were suspicious about it because of its apparently aimless wanderings. It did not seem to be going anywhere in particular, except that it was working itself closer to the *Deutschland*. When the ship turned toward them in an attempt to ram, the *Deutschland* dove.[7]

The strange ship was probably a Q-ship. Flying a neutral flag was a common practice intended to put the U-boat's skipper off guard. In this case the *Deutschland*, not being a war boat, made no move to close on the willing victim. The Q-ship's captain may have thought that the submarine's lookouts had not seen him, and decided to launch his attack. Why he did not fire on the *Deutschland* is not clear. He certainly sent out a sighting report and that may have led to the *Deutschland*'s third narrow escape.

That night Captain König ordered the *Deutschland* to submerge and remain under "during the darkest hours of the night, 2300 to 0100." When the boat surfaced, the sky was clear but a heavy swell was still running.[8] It was, he said, "a pretty bit o' weather."[9] And a pretty bit it was.

In the pale light of early dawn the already monstrous mountains of water looked even more formidable. Each wave curled at the top, the white crest streaming downwind in a horizontal sheet of water. The boat labored head on, sometimes falling away violently. The deck was completely under water, and the conning tower shuddered every time a wall of water slammed into it. The boat rolled heavily.

Clutching the rim of the conning tower, Captain König and a seaman searched the horizon. The electric motors were still running and Captain König was just about to order the diesels cut in when his lookout shouted. Looking in the direction the man was pointing König saw what looked like a wisp of smoke on the horizon.

At first it was just a faint, dark line. Was it really there? Captain König braced himself against the steel side of the conning tower and peered through his binoculars. Water poured over him as the boat plunged into another wave. Spotted with water, his binoculars provided a hazy view of the horizon, but it was a magnified hazy view. König saw smoke.

Another sea lurched against the conning tower, bursting into a dense shower of spray. Captain König lost sight of the smoke. A few moments later he spotted it again and below it a thin needle—a masthead. As he strained to get a better look, a larger shape heaved up on the jagged horizon. The dark shape was visible for only a moment, briefly suspended below the smoke. In that brief moment Captain König counted four smoke stacks.

"Donnerwetter," he exclaimed. "A destroyer." And then turning to the seaman he shouted, "Clear the bridge."[10]

The lookout instantly disappeared down the hatch, followed closely by König who stopped just long enough to slam the hatch shut and dog it down. As he spun the wheel he shouted to the men in the command central, "Alarm! Dive quickly!"

No on asked what was going on. The captain's abrupt entrance through the hatch and the urgency in his voice told them something serious was up. Red lights flicked on as tons of water poured into the tanks and the bow angled down. Under the best circumstances the *Deutschland* was slow to dive. In a heavy sea she was very slow.

The normal procedure for diving in a heavy sea was to lay the boat in the trough, put her two degrees down by the head, and go forward on the electric motors at about two knots. In this case Captain König wanted to get under as quickly as possible, and procedure went out the window.[11]

The diving planes were angled down sharply as the electric motors drove the boat ahead at full power. The hull quivered under the strain. The *Deutschland*, still plowing head on into the waves, staggered, pitched violently, and made "several leaps." But she remained on the surface. Then with a sudden jerk her bow angled down steeply and she plunged beneath the surface.

The boat was out of control. The down angle soon reached thirty-six degrees, the depth gauge rapidly indicating greater and greater depth. Men grabbed whatever they could to keep from being thrown forward. Captain König slipped, tumbled forward, and grabbed the periscope ocular. He ordered the diving planes up-angled and the tanks to be blown in a desperate attempt to halt the wild dive. The *Deutschland* would soon be below her maximum rated depth of one hundred and sixty feet. And then she hit bottom.

A tremendous crash echoed through the boat. Men were hurled to the floor and anything not fastened down flew forward. The *Deutschland* was still angled down thirty-six degrees, and her electric motors were "raving away at intervals that made the whole boat shake from stem to stern."[12]

The shocked, stunned men were slow to react to the new danger. The boat's bow was rammed into the ocean floor and her stern was protruding above the surface. The "raving" of the electric motors was caused by the propellers being alternately submerged as a wave rolled over and then spinning wildly as the wave passed.

In the interval between stunned inactivity and reaction they found themselves "in the queerest attitudes" and simply stared at one another. There was a grim moment of silence among them that was finally broken by Lieutenant Krapohl.

"Well, we seem to have arrived," he said.

The dry comment broke the ghastly tension. Chief Engineer Heinrich Klees jumped up from his crouched position and swept the engine signal dial to STOP. Almost immediately the howling din ceased and the men untangled themselves.

Thinking clearly again, Captain König quickly considered what he should do to stabilize the situation and bring the *Deutschland* back under control. His first concern was the nearly twenty feet of stern that protruded above the surface, an attractive target if the destroyer was actually on their trail. He was sure that the whirling propellers had thrown up a cloud of spray each time they emerged from the water. If that were true, he believed that the destroyer must have spotted it. Therefore, the immediate goal was to get the stern under before the destroyer started firing at it. He ordered the after tanks flooded.

The stern dropped slowly beneath the surface, forced down by tons of water flooding the tanks. The crew held its breath. As the minutes ticked away Captain König decided that the destroyer had not seen them. It was not yet full daylight and the poor visibility may have combined with the heavy sea to conceal the low-lying submarine. Her grey-green hull color undoubtedly helped.

Reports from all compartments were good—the hull was tight, there were no leaks. The stern sank deeper, the down angle decreased, and the men gave a sigh of relief.

She still by no means lay horizontal as yet—she had stuck her nose too deeply in the mud for that. Nevertheless we were now completely under water and could proceed with our work. The forward tanks were partially emptied. By balancing and trimming with the tanks we were able to get the bow clear of the bottom. We began to rise, but were at once obliged to offset the inclination to oscillate caused by the full after tanks. After a time the center of gravity was again restored and I once more had the *Deutschland* under control.[13]

Captain König, Lieutenant Krapohl, Ensign Eyring, and Chief Engineer Klees met to discuss what had gone wrong. They decided that the problem was a result of a chain of circumstances that started with the unusually high seas. Because of the sea state the *Deutschland* was already having difficulty diving. Owing to the presence of the destroyer the bow was given too much down angle before the after tanks were completely flooded. Added to that was the sudden dynamic force exerted by the diving planes which, combined with the full thrust of the engines and the crushing weight of a particularly heavy sea, had given the boat its dangerous down angle.

We were in a position similar to that of a dirigible that approaches its landing at too steep an angle, and then is crushed to the ground with double force owing to a sudden downward blast of air.[14]

Only the *Deutschland*'s solid construction had saved her from serious damage.

At 0400 she surfaced and proceeded on her way to America. There were no more alarms, and the lookouts reported only small fishing boats. But the weather remained sloppy. Log book entries became repetitive: "A heavy sea; Stiff wind from WNW, Force 8; Storm; Heavy seas sweep over the entire boat, even the conning tower; The boat is traveling under water almost the entire time."[15] The last entry was not a reference to being submerged. It simply describes a boat being constantly buried under mountainous waves. In fact, during the sixteen-day passage to America, the *Deutschland* covered only ninety nautical miles under water, and that may have been about all the crew could take.

Conditions inside the *Deutschland* were awful. The temperature reached 128° F (53° C), and the humidity was so high that the men found it almost impossible to breathe.[16] Every surface was slick with condensation, wooden drawers swelled and jammed shut, and mold grew on clothing and bulkheads. The air was permeated with the odor of diesel, carried through the boat by the crude ventilating system.

Clad only in shorts and undershirts, the sweating crewmen struggled through each four-hour watch. Crushing fatigue dulled their senses. Routine tasks became formidable undertakings, performed mechanically, and accomplished through sheer will power. And there was no respite in sleep.

Exhausted crewmen lay naked in their berths until they fell into a dull stupor. Moments later they were awakened by sweat running from their foreheads into their eyes. The process was repeated over and over, allowing the men only a fitful rest.[17]

The few who stood their watches atop the conning tower were the lucky ones. For four hours they were free of the oppressive heat and choking humidity below. But their relief was short-lived. Soaking wet, covered with salt, they returned to the sweat box. Their wet clothing added to the moisture in the air, and "helped spread a pestilence through the narrow spaces."[18]

By the time she reached the mid-Atlantic, the *Deutschland* was alone and the seas had calmed. Both deck hatches were opened, allowing fresh air into the boat, and the men gathered on deck to smoke and enjoy the sun. Conditions below changed little, but the ability to find relief on deck was a major improvement. There was even an opportunity to use the "surf bath."[19]

The so-called surf bath was the brain child of Second Engineer

O. Kisling. Captain König assumed that the man must have been struck by the idea during one of his frequent trips aft to check the diesel engine exhaust. Many of those trips were made across the flooded after deck during the height of a storm, and Kisling always came back soaked to the skin. Whether or not that was the source of the idea, Kisling's discovery was a good one.

The *Deutschland*'s outer hull was built over the cylinder-like pressure hull, and gave the submarine its distinctive shape. The lower portion of the space between the inner and outer hulls was taken up by the fuel and ballast tanks. The top of those tanks was called the tank deck. The upper portion of the space between the hulls was called the wet-cargo space because cargo that would not be damaged by immersion in seawater was stowed there. The entire upper area was open to the sea through many openings, holes and slits, and was, therefore, always flooded. Access to the wet-cargo space was through hatches in the deck. When standing on the tank deck there was enough room between the hulls for a man to stand upright in the wet-cargo space.

When the submarine was under way, seawater poured through the openings, surged across the pressure hull, and was carried out through openings farther aft. Depending upon how deeply the boat was trimmed down, the wet-cargo space would be anything from partially to totally flooded. To use the surf bath a man simply descended through a hatch into the wet-cargo space and hung on. According to Captain König, the practice was completely safe. There was, however, one drawback.

In case you stepped into the surf bath after we had surfaced, you would get not a bath but a regular oil bath. The oil bunkers are seldom hermetically tight, especially after a long and difficult passage. And it happens that a rising boat often breaks through a layer of its own oil as the boat surfaces. The oil then covers the hatches and decks and remains on top of the water in the outer tanks. That water does not change very rapidly. It usually took more than a day before the oily water had streamed away and was replaced by new. Whoever took a bath during that period would come out covered with oil.[20]

Leaking oil was a problem for many early U-boats, because one of the telltale signs that patrol boats watched for was an oil trace on the surface. In some cases the leak was bad enough that the oil formed an unbroken track across the surface that led directly to the U-boat.[21]

The *Deutschland*'s oil leaks were the result of the pounding she took during the several days she slugged her way through heavy seas. The leaks were not too bad, and as long as the water remained rough there was little chance that the oil would be spotted. But Captain König could not count on that. In any event, there was nothing he could do about the leaks until he got back to Germany, except hope for the best.[22]

To what degree was the *Deutschland* actually endangered during her passage to America? Assuming that her lookouts were alert and she was not caught napping, not much. The most common methods of sinking a U-boat were by gunfire or ramming.[23] To accomplish that, the U-boat had to be caught on the surface, though there were instances when a U-boat at periscope depth was run down by a warship. All other antisubmarine measures were largely ineffective.

Depth charges were just coming into use. In fact, on 6 July 1916 the mine-laying U-boat, *UC-7*, became the first victim of a depth-charge attack.[24] But that was a fluke, since at that time depth charges were unreliable, and in very short supply, a condition that existed until well into 1917.[25]

There was a form of underwater listening device called the hydrophone. But those early models were only partially effective, and hard to use. In order to locate a target with any accuracy, several vessels equipped with hydrophones were needed, and the listening ships had to stop their engines to keep from drowning out the U-boat's propeller noise.[26]

The British had strung nets across the Dover Strait and laid mines in great numbers. The nets were enormous steel affairs, supported on the surface by cork or glass floats, that hung down about sixty feet. The nets often stretched for several miles in individual segments, and some nets were fitted with explosive charges. Fishing boats armed with outdated guns, and in some cases explosive sweeps, patrolled the nets watching for signs that a U-boat was entangled.[27]

The first indication that a U-boat was caught in a net came when a whole row of floats was abruptly jerked below the surface or took off at high speed across the water. When that happened the patrol boats would fire the net charges, if the net had them, or trail their explosive sweeps across the U-boat's suspected location. More often they simply gathered around and waited for the trapped U-boat to surface, at which time they would take it under fire with their deck guns.

The reality was that not too many U-boats became entangled and most that did managed to tear through the nets. The nets themselves were almost unmanageable. They tore away from their moorings, became tangled, and sometimes simply sank. The patrol boats guarded them only during the day so that most U-boat skippers just waited until dark and crossed them on the surface. In fact, the net lines were easily recognized by the cork and glass floats bobbing on the surface. In some instances U-boat captains dove under the nets, but that was the least popular way to avoid them.[28]

British mines were little better. In fact, they were so unreliable that U-boat crews were told by the German Navy Department that "British mines don't explode." And it was not just morale-building propaganda. The British mine was so poor that the British discontinued mining activities during 1915, a decision that may have been prompted by reports that German warships were carrying souvenir British mines on their decks. There were even reports that U-boats could "carry these ineffective engines on their bows, shake them off, or bump against them with impunity."[29]

The reports were undoubtedly overstated, but the fact that British mines and nets were only marginally effective was clearly recognized. Despite that, the U-boat skippers who had tangled with the nets came back home with hair-raising stories. As a result of those reports the larger German U-boats were forbidden to attempt passage through the Dover Strait and were ordered to take the longer way, north around Scotland. Since the *Deutschland* was a very large U-boat, she too used the northern route.

And that was a sound decision. Though there was a strong probability that she could have successfully made her way through the Dover Strait, there was no need to add any risks to the undertaking. The distance to America was about the same whether she went north or south, and the risks were substantially less along the northern route.

Omitting mines and nets from the list of threats left only gun-armed surface ships. And she could avoid those by keeping a sharp lookout and diving. But her slow diving time was something to keep in mind.

Fast ships, especially destroyers and cruisers, could run down a U-boat before she got deep enough to pass under the attacker. Since it took the *Deutschland* up to two and a half minutes just to get under, an attacker might have as much as six minutes to find and ram her.

Leaking oil had not been a problem on the passage through the North Sea, but it might become one as she neared the coast of the United States. Particularly if the British had information about the boat and were expecting her. It would simply be a matter of forcing her under and then following the oil trail until she was forced to surface to charge her batteries and replenish her air. There were British and French warships off the American coast, so the question was: what did they know about the *Deutschland* and her schedule?

The British certainly knew she existed, though they did not know all the details about her. They also knew she was at sea, having intercepted and decoded the radio message she sent when she departed Helgoland. It appears that from that point forward, the *Deutschland* maintained radio silence so that the British had no precise information about her location, exact destination, or projected arrival date. But there were plenty of rumors.

Despite the best security precautions possible and rigid press censorship, the Germans could not prevent some information from leaking out. Workmen from Krupp, dockworkers in Kiel, and sailors who had watched the *Deutschland* come and go from her sea trials all had something to tell. And they did. The recipients of most of the loose talk were members of the press.[30]

An American reporter, Carl W. Ackerman, had gathered an amazing amount of information that was surprisingly accurate.[31] He suspected, for example, that the *Deutschland*'s officers were assigned to naval intelligence, and he knew that the crewmen had been selected from experienced U-boat crews. He also knew that the German Ocean Navigation Company was a front. But he was wrong in believing that Krupp controlled the operation on behalf of the navy. If anything, Norddeutsche Lloyd was in that position.

He sat on the story because he did not want to be arrested as a spy. And the only way he could publish his story was to leave Germany, something he was not ready to do. It was a dilemma that would not bother today's newsmen, but in 1916 the press had to be considerably more careful about what it printed.

There were German newspaper reporters who had almost as much information. Doctor Emil Leimdörfer, editor of the sensationalistic Berlin newspaper *BZ* (*Berliner Zeitung*), was one of them. He had sniffed out rumors about a plan to establish submarine service to America, operated by the Hamburg-America Steamship Company. He had submitted an article about it to the censors in March 1916. The censors spiked the story, and that made Leimdörfer really suspicious. By the first week in July he had just about put the whole thing together, and he was asking many more questions.

Among the things he wanted to know was the date set for the

Deutschland's arrival in America. He also wanted to know her destination. To get the answers, Leimdörfer arranged to meet with Alfred Lohmann in the *BZ* offices on 6 July 1916.[32] He did not know it, but in just four days the *Deutschland* would arrive in Baltimore.

In the meantime, Lohmann had already written an article for publication in the *Weserzeitung* and the *Bremer Tageblatt* and had cleared it through the censor's office.[33] The article, constructed to appear as though it had been written by the editorial staffs of the two newspapers, carefully avoided any reference to the boat's relationship to the navy. In fact, the claim that the venture was entirely a civilian undertaking was made several times. The article was to be the official and only word about the *Deutschland.*

Imagine his shocked surprise when Leimdörfer told him how much he knew and demanded to be let in on the rest of the story. Lohmann immediately exploded, telling Leimdörfer where to go. But the editor was not about to be put off. He had a story and Lohmann's reaction confirmed that most of it was true.

For his part, Lohmann was desperate to control any information that was put out. He could certainly get the censors to spike anything that Leimdörfer might submit—but suppose the man leaked the story to a foreign paper? Regard for the scruples of the press was about as low in 1916 as it is seventy years later.

In the end, Lohmann agreed to write an article for *BZ* on the condition that his name not appear. Like the material submitted to *Weserzeitung* and *Bremer Tageblatt,* the article must appear to have been written by the editorial staff. There was a final stipulation. News of the *Deutschland*'s arrival in Baltimore was not to be printed until at least two hours after Leimdörfer received notice of the arrival. Lohmann needed the delay in order to notify the kaiser first. "I don't want him to find out about it in the press," he said.[34] Leimdörfer accepted the deal, happy that *BZ* would be the first to break the news in the nation's capital.

But the leak to the foreign press that Lohmann feared so much had already happened. On 1 July the *New York Times* claimed that the *Deutschland* had already arrived in Baltimore. Citing a full page ad placed in a local Hungarian-language newspaper by the Trans-Atlantic Trust Company, the *Times* said that the submarine was hidden, "presumably under the waters of Chesapeake Bay." The claim was ridiculous, and several people interviewed by the *Times* were quick to point that out. Why did the Trans-Atlantic Trust Company run the ad?

The company was the unofficial financial agent for the Austrian and German governments. According to the ad, people who wanted to send gold, currency, or securities back to Germany aboard the *Deutschland* could do so through the company. But the Trans-Atlantic Trust Company was in no way associated with the German Ocean Navigation Company. And navy officials in Germany, upon learning about the ad, treated it as a joke.[35] What was not funny was the fact that the Trans-Atlantic Trust Company had named Baltimore as the *Deutschland*'s destination. The Germans wanted the British to think the *Deutschland* had two options.

The article also reported that German authorities in Washington had already contacted the United States government regarding the boat's status as a commercial vessel. It was reported that the German Embassy feared the submarine might be regarded as a warship by the United States authorities, and as such ordered out of American waters within twenty-four hours.

In a second article datelined Baltimore, even more information was disclosed that could help the British warships to lay a trap for the *Deutschland*.

> The mystery surrounding the reported arrival of the German supersubmarine has taken a new turn in connection with the movements of the tug *Thomas J. Timmins*. The tug in command of Captain Zack Cullison is now cruising off the Virginia Capes, waiting to convoy the submersible to Baltimore, according to rumor, and watching for a four-masted schooner to tow to port, according to Paul G. L. Hilken, Baltimore agent for the North German Lloyd Steamship Company and principal owner of the tug.[36]

Hilken was, of course, trying to scotch the surprisingly accurate rumors with his statement about the four-masted schooner. His efforts were undermined by the several "experts" to whom the press turned to for more information. According to an assortment of unnamed "naval officers and shipping men," it was possible for a submarine to cross the Atlantic Ocean and remain off the Virginia Capes in deep water. The cat was clearly out of the bag and the entire East Coast knew about it. The question was, would the Royal Navy act on the information? The British Embassy in Washington certainly did.

As early as 27 June, just four days after the *Deutschland* had sailed from Helgoland, the British Embassy in Washington had filed a protest with the United States Department of State. The British did not want the Americans to allow the *Deutschland* to dock in an American port. In the British view, all U-boats were alike.

On 3 July, two days after the *New York Times* report, the British submitted another protest. Citing "persistent rumors" that a German submarine was on its way to a United States port, the ambassador offered the British government's views on such a visit. The first point he made was that it was "unlikely that a German submarine would cross to an American port except for the purpose of conducting hostile operations on this side of the Atlantic." He then cited international law and precedence that governed whatever access a belligerent's warship might have to a neutral port. But if the *Deutschland* did enter a United States port, she should be interned "unless it has been driven into port by necessity."[37]

The British intelligence clearly knew she was a cargo vessel, and they suspected that the civilian status of the crew was a bogus claim. What they did not know was to what degree, if any, the *Deutschland* had been built as a war boat. Once she arrived in Baltimore, they wanted the Americans to fill in the missing pieces. As things worked out, they got only about half of what they were after.

On the afternoon of 8 July, when the *Deutschland* was about one hundred miles off the Virginia Capes, Captain König and his two officers discussed the best way to approach the coast. König, ever cautious, felt they should hold a position about ten miles out from the three-mile limit and wait for dawn on the 9th.

I was of the opinion that we should wait in deep water for the coming of the dawn ... and then assure ourselves as to whether any hostile measures had been taken against us. In case indefinite rumors of our voyage had leaked out, there was small doubt that we would have to reckon with such measures on the part of the enemy.[38]

Krapohl and Eyring suggested that they approach the coast as closely as possible under cover of darkness. A compromise was reached when Captain König decided to move in closer toward the coast at dusk and wait to see what happened. As things worked out, the plan forwarded by Krapohl and Eyring was the one they used.

As they stood in toward shore a stiff southwest breeze came up clearing away the thick haze that had reduced visibility to a few miles. The breeze brought unlimited visibility, but it also raised a short, choppy sea. Soon the *Deutschland* was rolling violently. Satisfied that he knew his position, the skipper laid out a course for Cape Henry that would get them out of the disagreeable chop.

Captain König's earlier intention to remain offshore had been well founded. He had recently received a coded message that eight enemy cruisers were waiting for him near the entrance to the Chesapeake Bay. The information came from German agents and was confirmed by "a well-placed member of the United States Navy."

The message also warned that American fishing boats previously employed by the Germans to report Allied ship movements, were now working for the British. According to the report, the British had purchased about two miles of fishing net to use as a U-boat indicator. The idea was to string the net across the U-boat's route, not to stop the *Deutschland*, but to reveal the U-boat's position. König was told that the net had already been strung across the south channel that the *Deutschland* would use on her approach to Hampton Roads.[39]

As they moved closer to the coast, the lookout reported a pale glow on the horizon that flared up and then vanished. Captain König watched the light flash again, recognized it as the Cape Henry Light, and relaxed a bit. Several minutes passed as the boat moved through the dark, the Cape Henry Light guiding them in. Suddenly another light flashed to starboard. It disappeared instantly and then flashed again several times. Almost at once another light flashed off the port bow and then remained on. The officers on the bridge felt an adrenalin surge as their stomachs knotted. Those lights looked like signals sent by warships.

Captain König ordered the boat trimmed down until just the conning tower protruded above the water, and reduced speed to half. With the crew at diving stations, the *Deutschland* crept forward through the dark.

The sources of the strange lights turned out to be a small schooner and the masthead light on a coastal steamer. The schooner was sailing without side lights, merely displaying a white light from time to time. The men were visibly relieved, but to be safe the *Deutschland* remained trimmed down, her decks awash.

At 2330 on 8 July the *Deutschland* reached the United States three-mile limit.[40] Both the Cape Henry Light and the Cape Charles Light were clearly visible, but there was one thing missing—the tug *Thomas J. Timmins* that was supposed to meet them. As had been correctly reported in the *New York Times,* the *Timmins* had been patrolling offshore since the first of July, waiting for the *Deutschland* to arrive. According to information sent from Germany several weeks earlier, the U-boat was to have arrived on 4 July. That date had come and gone and still no sign of the *Deutschland,* only rumors. On the afternoon of 8 July, the tug had moved back into Chesapeake Bay to give the crew a much-needed rest.[41]

Captain König now brought the boat fully to the surface and spent the next two hours looking for the *Timmins*. Unable to find her, he gave up looking and approached the pilot boat, *Relief*. At 0200 Captain König stopped and lit a blue flare, the signal that he wanted a pilot. From atop the *Relief*'s wheelhouse a searchlight stabbed through the night, illuminating the U-boat. Confused by the vessel's odd shape the *Relief* approached slowly, keeping its spotlight on the *Deutschland*. Finally a voice boomed out across the water.[42]

"What ship are you?"

"The *Deutschland*, sixteen days out of Bremerhaven." The answer was not entirely accurate, but it was in keeping with the claim that the vessel was completely civilian in nature. It would hardly have helped matters to have said they were twenty-five days out of Kiel via the U-boat base at Helgoland.

"Where are you bound?"

"Baltimore."

A boat was lowered and the pilot, Captain Fred Cocke, was soon standing on the *Deutschland*'s deck.[43] "I'll be damned," he said with feeling. "Here she is."

CHAPTER FIVE

A QUESTION OF STATUS,

9 JULY–14 JULY 1916

The *Deutschland* lay starboard side to along the five-hundred-foot pier, screened from the land by a large L-shaped warehouse. The short leg of the L was formed by a section of the warehouse that lay along the river bank. The long leg of the L extended down the pier, about one hundred and fifty feet. Attached to the end of the warehouse and running to the end of the pier was a twelve-foot high, solid wooden fence, topped with barbed wire.

As if that were not enough, the Lloyd liner SS *Neckar* lay along the other side of the pier, sandwiching the warehouse and fence between her and the *Deutschland*. She served to further shield the *Deutschland* from view, and provided quarters for the crewmen during their stay in Baltimore.[1]

Despite a pouring rain, hundreds of people were crowded around the Eastern Forwarding Company's offices at the foot of Andre Street, eager to get a look at the U-boat. Dozens pressed against the gate while others tried to climb the fence. Burly guards pushed them back and jerked them off the fence, roughing up anyone who objected. Not to be deterred, some of the crowd worked their way around the right-hand end of the warehouse where there was at least a partial view of the U-boat.

Fourteen feet of her bow protruded beyond the stern of the lighter *George May*, made fast along the U-boat's port side. And the upper portion of the conning tower could just be seen above the *George May*'s frame and canvas superstructure. It was not much of a

Baltimore, 9 July 1916. The *Deutschland* alongside the Eastern Forwarding Company's tug, *Efco*. (National Archives)

view, but at least it was something. But getting a view from the water was even more disappointing.

Several small steam yachts, sailboats, and rowboats were clustered around the end of the pier in the Patapsco River. The tug *Timmins* was positioned between the boats and a small barge that formed a barrier across the U-boat's stern. The Germans had also erected several wooden panels on the barge to further screen the *Deutschland*. Some of the small boats had slipped past the tug in an attempt to get close enough for a look, but it was a waste of time. A heavy log boom constructed of telephone poles stretched the length of the pier, forming a barrier one hundred feet outboard of the *George May*.

Armed guards supplied by a local private agency patrolled the property line, admitting only those who had company authorization. And there were very few who did.[2]

It had already been raining when the *Deutschland* tied up at the pier at 0700, and Captain König, dressed in his oil skins, went ashore to present his papers. Newsmen, straining to get a view of the boat and a statement from the captain, were largely disappointed.[3] A few noted that the *Deutschland*'s crew wore the "regulation uniform of the German Merchant Marine" and appeared to be 18 to 23 years old. Others spotted "only two grizzled old tars."[4] The observations might

Security was so tight in Baltimore that few people got a good look at the *Deutschland*. And fewer got aboard. There is a white man in the lower right corner of the picture, a rare sight on the Eastern Forwarding Company's pier. For security reasons, the Germans used only black stevedores to handle the cargo. (National Archives)

appear harmless, but in fact they were potentially disastrous to the Germans.

When the captain emerged from the customshouse, he made just one short statement. "My orders are from my home government," he said. "No one can go aboard without authority. I am sorry. I would like the whole world to see."[5] It was his second slip of the tongue in less than twelve hours.

Captain König had said that his orders came from the German government rather than from the German Ocean Navigation Company. Eleven hours earlier, as the U-boat passed Sandy Point, he had told a boatload of reporters that his departure had been made from Helgoland. Both statements were widely reported in the press. Surprisingly, only a few people picked up the meaning of those two slips.

The issue at hand was the boat's status. Was it a warship, as the Allies insisted, or was it a "harmless merchant vessel," as the Germans maintained? The determination had to be made by the United States government, and it had to be made with great care.

There were several elements to be examined. Those elements had been spelled out by the British on 3 July 1916 in a note sent by the British Embassy in Washington to the Department of State.

If a submarine should enter a neutral port flying the mercantile flag, His Majesty's Government are of the opinion that it is the duty of the neutral authorities concerned to enquire closely into its right to fly that flag, to inspect the vessel thoroughly and, in the event of torpedoes, torpedo tubes or guns being found on board to refuse to recognize it as a merchant ship.[6]

There were also questions about the crew's status as merchant seamen. Were they actually civilians? And who really owned the boat, the German Ocean Navigation Company or the German government? Captain König's apparently innocent statements had touched on both those questions.

If Captain König's slip went unnoticed by the State Department, it was brought to their attention by E. Mitchell Ferriday. Mr. Ferriday, a Waterbury, Connecticut, resident, fired off a telegram to Frank L. Polk acting Secretary of State.

IN NEW YORK TIMES OF TODAY CAPTAIN KOENIG OF THE GER-MAN SUBMARINE IS QUOTED AS SAYING MY ORDERS ARE FROM MY HOME GOVERNMENT STOP THE STATUS OF THE WARSHIP NOW HARBORED IN OUR NEUTRAL PORT IS THAT CLEARLY DEFINED STOP MAY OUR GOVERNMENT TAKE HEED.[7]

Apparently Mr. Ferriday's warning fell on deaf ears.

At 0800 on 10 July, William P. Ryan, the senior customs officer in Baltimore, boarded the *Deutschland* to determine her status. With him were two civilian marine surveyors, Guy W. Steele and his deputy, F. Sydney Hayward. The American officials were warmly greeted by the Germans who made an effort to show they had nothing to hide. Insofar as the U-boat was concerned, that was true, but the crew's background was another matter.

The German tactic worked. Ryan and his assistants, impressed by the Germans' sincerity, conducted as thorough an examination as

Even after the crowd worked its way around the end of the office building, the view was restricted. All that could be seen was the tip of the *Deutschland*'s bow protruding beyond the barge, *George May*. The log boom kept boaters back 100 feet, and the *Neckar*, in the background, formed a solid wall. (National Archives)

they could, and paid little attention to the crew. At the conclusion of their survey they wrote:

> There were no guns aboard nor were there port holes from which torpedoes could be discharged. The only firearms aboard were for the purpose of discharging rockets as signals and which were listed on the stores list of the vessel, as also 420 cartridges, 36 rockets and blue lights, and 12 gun shots.
> The master states, and the members of the crew verify the statement, that all officers and crew belonged to the German merchant marine.[8]

That last statement was, at best, only technically correct. William Ryan and his assistants did not know it, but every man in that crew had until recently served in the Imperial German Navy.

The Treasury Department, receiving William Ryan's report that evening, passed the information on to the State Department. What Ryan told them was what they had expected to hear. In fact, German credibility in regard to the *Deutschland* was good, and their claim that she was a merchant vessel had already been pretty much accepted by the State Department. Still, the United States had to be sure.

But Ryan's report was not enough. The British, French, and Italian governments were putting pressure on the United States to declare the *Deutschland* a war boat.[9] And they were supported in their views by a vocal American group of British sympathizers. On the other hand, there were large numbers of equally vocal German sympathizers and powerful business interests that were anxious to find a way to break the British blockade.

Added to the political and economic concerns was the fact that the *Deutschland* was unique. As one writer pointed out, the evolution of merchant ships to warships was well documented, and the difference between them was easily recognized by their shapes. The fact that conventional ships remained on the surface made identification relatively easy, even at a distance. But submarines represented the reverse evolution. Until the *Deutschland* came along submarines were only built for war and their status under international law was clear— they were warships.[10]

The submarine's ability to submerge and thus avoid detection became a key issue. According to international law at that time merchant ships had to be stopped and examined before they could be sunk. And then they could only be sunk if they were found to be carrying contraband to an enemy port and there was no way to take them into port as a prize. It was also required that the crew be put in a place of safety before their ship was sent to the bottom, since sinking without warning was simply not allowed at the time. That is why the Germans were in so much hot water over their use of unrestricted submarine warfare. The introduction of the merchant submarine literally added a new dimension to the problem.

For example, how was a warship to tell the difference between a merchant submarine and a war boat? They certainly looked alike, and to make a mistake would probably be fatal for the warship. More importantly, in regard to the law, was the danger that misidentification would result in the unlawful deaths of the merchant submarine's crew.

The situation threatened to put armed merchant vessels and all U-boats on the same footing in regard to the law. As things stood in

1916, anytime an armed merchantman spotted a U-boat on the surface the merchantman had the unlimited right to open fire. The U-
boat, on the other hand, was supposed to stop the merchantman
instead of simply firing a torpedo.

But the advent of unarmed cargo U-boats would take away the
merchantman's right to fire first and ask questions later. Unless, of
course the law were changed. A change in the relationship of merchantmen to U-boats, and any changes in the prize rules were things
the British wanted to avoid. And there was another problem.

The Germans argued that the British Q-ships, and the British
practice of arming merchantmen, already made the rules of stop and
search too risky for a U-boat. How was a U-boat skipper to know if
the ship he was approaching on the surface was armed or not? He
sure could not tell at a distance, and when he got in close enough to
see, it was too late.

But if cargo U-boats became a reality and were accorded the same
status as surface vessels, the British merchant captains would find
themselves in the same situation as the U-boat skippers.

What it all boiled down to was that the British would have to
behave like the Germans. If that happened, they ran a real risk of
losing American support, something they wanted to avoid at almost
any cost.

The rising clamor on both sides made Ryan's report totally inadequate, though it was accurate insofar as the question of armaments was concerned. What it lacked was the credibility needed to
satisfy the boat's enemies—if such a thing were possible. On 11 July
three navy officers were sent to Baltimore to inspect the boat again.

Unknown to the State Department the *Deutschland* had already
been visited by a navy officer. While Ryan and his men were conducting their initial inspection on 10 July, Lieutenant J. H. Klein, USN,
showed up at the pier. His presence had been arranged through the
Justice Department and was independent of what the State Department was doing. Lieutenant Klein was a member of Naval
Intelligence.[11]

He made a thorough inspection aided greatly by the fact that he
spoke flawless German. When he first went aboard he had intended
to keep his language ability a secret, hoping to pick up information
from the casual talk of the unsuspecting crewmen. But he quickly
abandoned that plan when he found that the crewmen were surprisingly loose-lipped.

When he told them he had recently read several publications on

German submarines, they "became very talkative and explained much that I might not have heard otherwise," such as comparative specifications on some of Germany's newer U-boats.

The amount of information the men had regarding the U-boats should have alerted Klein to the crew's real status. Apparently it did not, or he chose to ignore it. When the mates "stated most emphatically that none of the officers and men belonged to the Imperial German Navy," Klein accepted that. He noted, however, that the "mates' caps were quite new."[12]

That afternoon Lieutenant Klein's report went to his boss, the director of Naval Intelligence. The following day, 11 July, Captain C. F. Hughes and two lieutenants went aboard to make their inspection, totally unaware of what Klein had found out.

Both Captain König and Lieutenant Krapohl were away when the three officers arrived at the gangplank, but their arrival came as no surprise to the officer of the deck, Emil Eyring. That three navy officers would inspect the boat had been front-page news in the nation's newspapers, news that had been roundly criticized by Paul and Henry Hilken, owners of the Eastern Forwarding Company.

In a public statement that appeared on 11 July, Paul said that the officers should not be allowed to board the boat. According to the younger Hilken, "in Germany only our navy officers are permitted to go aboard our submarines."[13] Again, no one seemed to pick up the meaning of his statement.

Captain König was more cooperative, adopting the attitude that if the United States government wanted three navy officers to inspect the boat, they were welcome aboard. "We have nothing to hide," he said.[14]

Captain Hughes was shown through the boat by Chief Engineer Klees. The tour included "all parts of the ship not occupied by cargo and fuel oil, except the central ballast tank...." Captain Hughes found no sign of any armaments.

Naval Constructor Lieutenant Herbert S. Howard, USN, also found no evidence of provisions for weapons. But, like Lieutenant Klein, he found the crew very willing to talk. While in the conning tower he was told how the *Deutschland* differed from conventional war boats. He learned that the conning towers in the war boats were larger and that the torpedoes were fired from that position. It apparently did not occur to him that the civilian crewmen were unusually well informed about the workings of Germany's U-boats.

Lieutenant J. O. Fisher, USN, representing the Bureau of Steam

Engineering, spent most of his time in the engine room. His guide was Senior Machinist O. Kisling who, like the other Germans, went out of his way to be helpful. There was nothing Kisling would not talk about. As a result, Lieutenant Fisher came away with a wealth of information and a solid respect for German construction and engineering. In a private letter to Admiral Grant he said, "I wish we were laying down one of this size in preference to one of our boats." Later he added that "practically the entire engine was cast steel. Steel casting of this description cannot at present be obtained in this country."[15]

Jointly, the three officers concluded that the *Deutschland* was a merchant vessel and could not "be converted to a war vessel without extensive alterations." The report was sent to the Treasury Department and forwarded to the State Department.

On 12 July, while the State Department was reading the inspection reports, Mr. Samuel H. Hobbin, an American citizen, wrote a letter to Frank L. Polk, Acting Secretary of State. Mr. Hobbin was questioning the status of the *Deutschland*'s crew. Reacting to what he had read in the newspapers, Mr. Hobbin wrote:

> Can the owners show affirmatively that the crew of twenty-nine men . . . are definitely discharged from all present and future duty to the German Empire during this war? Let them produce their discharges from the German navy. It is not enough to masquerade in uniforms of the North German Lloyd S. S. CO. It is inconceivable that there are twenty-nine able seamen of military age, expert in submarine operation, who are not attached to the colors.[16]

Mr. Hobbin had a very good point.

On 12 July, Frank Polk sent all copies of the reports to the Neutrality Board for their consideration. It was really a formality intended to strengthen the government's position when it issued a decision in favor of the *Deutschland*. The date set to announce the decision was 14 July.

On the appointed date the board gave its opinion to the acting Secretary of State. There were no surprises in the five-page document, but the board did offer some good advice. Every submarine that came to the United States claiming to be a merchantman should be inspected, the board said. And that should be done on every visit no matter how many times the boat came into an American port. But the best advice was in the last paragraph of the document:

In view of the novelty and importance of the question at issue, the Board suggests to the Department of State the advisability of accompanying any decision that it reaches with a statement to the effect that its decision is subject to revision at a later date, should experience suggest the propriety of such revision.[17]

The State Department recognized good advice when it saw it and acted accordingly. That day Frank Polk announced that the United States government recognized the *Deutschland* as a merchant vessel, and she would be treated accordingly. He hastened to add, however, that the decision was not a precedent, and that each and every future case would be considered on its own merits.

The Germans were thrilled. But at the same time they recognized the absolute necessity of preserving the boat's guise of civilian status. The Americans' decision was at best a frail victory for the Germans.

The British were understandably disappointed, but not overcome by the decision. They had expected it. Still, they protested loudly after Mr. Polk's public announcement. Their arguments were based on three points. The *Deutschland* could be armed outside the three-mile limit, probably by some sort of "mother ship." In view of the findings made by Captain Hughes and his staff, that argument just did not hold water. The second argument was that the nature of the *Deutschland*'s construction made it a warship. Since she was unarmed and carried only cargo, that argument did not have much impact either. But the last argument, that she could not be stopped and searched like a surface vessel, had merit.[18]

The last point became a major issue about three weeks later.

CHAPTER SIX

BALTIMORE,

9–19 JULY 1916,

THE REACTION

While the diplomats argued whether the *Deutschland* was a warship or a freighter, the press was going wild over the boat's arrival. The *New York Times* said it was " . . . an incident which compels admiration and stirs the imagination."[1] Even the *Manchester Guardian* praised the *Deutschland*'s success, spotlighting her skipper. "Captain König appears to be a sportsman and has earned his laurels cleanly," the editor wrote.[2] However, he raised the question of the crew's status when he added, "If the captain and the crew are members of the Imperial German Navy, the submarine may be dealt with as a naval auxiliary." But the most astute observation about the event was made by the *New York Tribune*.

> The use of such vessels is the most signal tribute yet paid to the effectiveness of the work done by the blockading fleets. There was probably never any reason since the war began why submarines should not have been used if it had been thought worthwhile to use them. If, therefore, after two years they have been turned to account, we may readily surmise how desperate the state of affairs in Germany must be. . . . The wild excitement of the populace over the exploit of a single blockade runner is a pathetic demonstration of their plight.[3]

The editorial was right on the mark.

Even in Germany, where the news of the *Deutschland*'s arrival in Baltimore was received with wild enthusiasm, there were detractors. Admiral Scheer and his supporters were unimpressed. They insisted on an immediate return to unrestricted U-boat warfare, and set their goal at 600,000 tons of enemy shipping monthly. Only by destroying the merchant fleets of the leading powers could Britain be paralyzed and the war brought to a speedy conclusion. At the supreme headquarters in Pless the kaiser promised to resume unrestricted U-boat warfare as soon as the Romanian campaign was successfully completed.

Had there been enough U-boats to do the job, that plan might have worked. But there were not, and construction of new boats was still too slow to provide the two hundred, plus, boats they needed. In 1916, the poor state of antisubmarine warfare permitted an advantageous situation for U-boats to carry out such a campaign. But by 1917 that advantage was fast disappearing, and by 1918 it was virtually nonexistent. For Admiral Scheer and his ardent supporters, 1916 was a now-or-never year.

But the rumblings from Berlin were largely drowned in the swirling controversy that attended the *Deutschland*'s visit. Both sides, her pro-German supporters on one and her pro-British detractors on the other, added fuel to the fire on a daily basis. And the press reported every new development with uncontained enthusiasm. The controversies raised were often related, and all were argued in the shadow of the much larger diplomatic controversy about her status. The first controversy to surface was started by Simon Lake.

The moment he learned that a German cargo submarine had passed through the Capes, he called a press conference. As founder of the Lake Torpedo Boat Company, and visionary of vast undersea commercial fleets, he threatened to sue the *Deutschland* and her owners for infringing on his patents.

It is entirely possible for a German submarine to cross the Atlantic. But if one does enter an American port it will be met by a process server. The crew will be surprised at the reception, no doubt, but in America the Lake Torpedo Boat Company controls the rights to make and use my devices.[4]

The British were overjoyed. If Lake could tie up the boat in the American courts, she might never get back to Germany. In anticipation of his court action, Lake telegraphed the State Department demanding to know who owned the *Deutschland*. After all, he wanted the right people named in his suit.[5]

Lake's charges were not entirely without foundation. Just sixteen years earlier he had been one of the world's leading figures in submarine development. Though his designs had been rejected by the

United States Navy in favor of boats built by John Holland, Lake had continued to act as a consultant to Russia, Germany, and England. And many of the ideas he had suggested were being used in German U-boats. In fact, the double-hulled design, characteristic of most U-boats, including the *Deutschland*, had been introduced by Simon Lake.[6]

While the telegram was being read at the State Department, Lake and his chief counsel, Fred B. Whitney, went to the Eastern Forwarding Company's pier in Baltimore. They intended to go aboard the *Deutschland*, conduct their own examination, and produce evidence of patent infringement. Instead, they ran into a stone wall—Captain König refused to allow them aboard.[7]

Retreating to the warehouse office, Lake and Whitney spent thirty minutes discussing the issue with Captain König. The captain was a charmer. In fact, he was so charming that when Lake left the meeting he praised the German's accomplishment, saying that it had vindicated his own ideas. The frosting on the cake came when Fred Whitney told reporters that Lake had been approached with a scheme to build a fleet of cargo submarines.

Confirmation came two days later when Simon Lake held a press conference in the offices of North German Lloyd.[8] Lake told the press that he, the Hilkens, and Krupp would form a company in the United States to build *Deutschland*-type boats here. The initial capital needed was $100,000,000.00, and that was apparently available.

The boats, much larger than the *Deutschland*, would cost about $1,250,000.00 each to build. The boats would sail under the American flag, linking Baltimore with Bremen and other German ports. William Prusse, a Krupp engineer who had come across in the *Deutschland* as "supercargo," would supervise construction, with Lake acting as technical consultant.

Lake, ever the visionary when it came to commercial applications for submarines, was serious about the plan. How serious the Germans were is unclear, since the idea may have been a ploy to divert Lake's attention from his civil action against the *Deutschland*. If that is true, the ploy worked. But regardless of who was serious and who was not, the British immediately recognized the threat.

If large, long-range submarines were built in the United States and sent to Germany as freighters, the German Navy would have ready access to a steady supply of new U-boats. The Hughes report had simply said that the *Deutschland* could not be converted to a warship without "extensive alterations." There would be nothing to prevent those alterations being made in Kiel.

Such a delivery system would be almost impossible to stop since the boats could easily dive to avoid the British patrols. And if the cargo U-boats were considered to be merchantmen under the law, the British would be legally restrained from attacking them without warning while they were still on the surface.

British concern was expressed in a lengthy Foreign Office memo addressed to Sir Cecil Spring-Rice.

The submersible cargo boat for all her peaceful appearance possesses and must always possess qualities which would enable her at very short notice to be converted into a fighting vessel of the most formidable kind; her case is therefore exceptional and calls for exceptional treatment. If this be denied it would seem to follow that unarmed submarines might be constructed in any number in neutral countries and then be armed by the belligerent purchaser with necessary torpedo tubes. . . . [9]

The Foreign Office pointed out that the ability to avoid being stopped and searched would also be a problem to the United States.

In the future there could be no coast protection for any country; that through submarines customs could be evaded, and that henceforth espionage was made very simple, in that a submarine could land on the coast and carry on espionage work.[10]

But the whole issue of the submarine's status on the high seas was a philosophical one that the State Department avoided. When confronted with the question of how would the United States react if the Allies sank the *Deutschland* without warning, the State Department declined to speculate.[11] For the moment the burning issue of the *Deutschland*'s status was laid to rest. But there were plenty of other issues to keep the pot boiling.

The debate over the *Deutschland*'s status and the flap about possible patent infringements were old news by 14 July. But the question about who was going to get the cargo of dyestuffs was still unanswered. Closely associated with that question was the matter of profit.

The *Deutschland*'s detractors loudly pointed out that the U-boat was a poor substitute for a surface freighter. The cargo was too small to bring a profit, and whatever cargo she took home to Germany was just a drop in the bucket compared to what the Germans needed to survive. They were only half right.

The war materials she was capable of taking back to Germany

were indeed a pathetic drop in the bucket. But the plan was to build at least seven cargo U-boats. Operating on a regular schedule, and bolstered by a growing fleet of Lake-built boats, the plan just might have worked. Certainly the British feared it would.[12] Alone, however, the *Deutschland*'s ability to deliver war supplies in any useful amount was nonexistent. But profits were another matter.

Before the First World War, Germany held the monopoly on the world's production of aniline dyes, and American fabric companies were among her best customers, buying about 15,000 tons per year. The war had crippled both the United States fabric makers and the German dye industry. Desperate for dyes, the Americans had already shifted over to synthetic substitutes. But the quality was low and the cost was high. The Germans were even harder hit. They virtually had no market they could reach to sell their dyes.[13]

The firms most interested in receiving dyes from Germany were Farbwerke-Hoechst Company, Badische and Company, Casella Color Company, and Bayer and Company. The arrival of the dyes was big news, and each company was anxious to obtain its share of the shipment. But the decision on how the cargo was to be divided was withheld by the Eastern Forwarding Company.[14]

One hundred and thirty stevedores worked around the clock to unload 3,042 cases of dyestuffs, each case weighing about five hundred pounds. Security around the dock was particularly tight, which added to speculation about the cargo's value.

The prewar price for German dyestuffs was about two cents per ounce, which made the *Deutschland*'s cargo worth about a half a million dollars. But the war had driven the price up to twice that, and the Germans publicly estimated the cargo's value at one million dollars. Actually it was worth a lot more.

Herman A. Metz, a New York importer, told the press that the normal dye consumption in the United States was three thousand tons per week. That made the *Deutschland*'s cargo, just 760.5 tons, a mere drop in the bucket. But wartime, synthetic substitutes cost at least three dollars per ounce and were not nearly as good as the genuine German product. Therefore, Metz estimated the value of the *Deutschland*'s cargo at around six million dollars.

On 17 July, the Hilkens told the anxious buyers that the entire cargo was consigned to their own company, A. Schumacher and Company. The American firms were stunned and then irate. The Hilkens were in a position to gouge out any price they wanted. Prodded by rumors that the dyes, in concentrated form, would be sold for $100,000,000.00, the Americans dug in their heels and refused to buy.

In the end, the selling price was close to Herman Metz's six million dollar estimate, and the four big firms were given preference for sales. But the Germans' high-handedness in shuffling title to the cargo between two companies owned by the Hilkens, in order to drive up the price, left a sour taste. But the behind-the-scenes flap over the cargo the *Deutschland* was to take home made the British look equally bad.

The *Deutschland* was scheduled to take back up to 400 tons of bagged nickel, about 90 tons of tin in pigs, about 400 tons of crude rubber, and a half-ton of jute.[15] The cargo's value was in excess of a million and a half dollars. The controversy over the return cargo had to do with the nickel and rubber.

Canada was virtually the world's sole supplier of nickel, a resource that the British guarded jealously. That was the reason for the agreement forced on American buyers not to resell it to any of the Central Powers. But there was nickel being delivered to the Eastern Forwarding Company's warehouse in Baltimore that had obviously come from Canada. But who had sold it to the Germans?

British Intelligence got on it right away and soon learned that at least part of it had passed through Kuhn, Loeb, and Company in 1915.[16] But the British were not yet able to follow the paper trail left by Dr. Heinrich Albert. Still, the Kuhn, Loeb, and Company connection was a start, so, working backwards, the British now hoped to answer the question: who sold it to Kuhn, Loeb, and Company? In the meantime, the British threatened to blacklist any American firm that was found to have been involved in the transaction. That did not sit well with the American public.

The British were also threatening to cut off America's source of South American rubber. There was no prohibition on the re-export of rubber from the United States because the British had no control over the source. But the possibility that a fleet of cargo U-boats might be able to supply South American rubber to Germany via the United States demanded action, and the British let it be known that they might exercise the "distant blockade to block transshipment of rubber through the United States." The veiled threat angered the Americans and provided fuel to Germany's propaganda effect.

The loading of cargo went on around the clock until 19 July. During that time rumors from "reliable sources" said that the *Deutsch-*

land was making haste to get under way, her departure widely said to be scheduled for any moment. And that claim was bolstered by rumors that the *Bremen* was already on her way to the United States.

Since the day that the *Deutschland* had arrived, there had been talk of another U-boat arriving hard on her heels. Rumor had it that the *Bremen* had sailed immediately after the *Deutschland,* which explained the apparent haste to unload the *Deutschland*'s cargo, because the *Deutschland* had to make room for her sister ship. But another rumor said that the *Bremen* was en route to Rio De Janeiro.

Fuel was added to the fire when the tug *Timmins* suddenly left the Charles Rhode and Sons dry dock on 11 July and headed down the Chesapeake. The *New York Times* speculated that the tug was headed toward the Virginia Capes to meet the *Bremen.* But in the same article citing "usually reliable sources," the *Times* acknowledged that at midnight the *Timmins* had not been seen anywhere near the Capes. The conspicuous absence did not deter the *Times* reporter. He felt the *Timmins* was probably hiding in Lynnhaven Bay.[17]

Several days passed and the *Bremen* failed to appear. She was delayed, the press reported, having been forced to evade Allied patrols off the American coast. Rumor had it for certain that she would arrive by 22 July in either Boston or New York. If that were the case why was the *Deutschland* hurrying so to take aboard her cargo? Because the *Amerika* was also on the way.[18]

By 19 July, the day that the *Deutschland* completed her loading, the *New York Times* had a "confirmed report" that the *Bremen* was in Long Island Sound. She had left Bremen nine or ten days earlier. The fact was, the *Bremen* was still in Kiel.

After nearly a week and a half of wild speculation and reporting rumor-based "facts," the press abandoned the *Bremen* stories. But the rumor about a third cargo U-boat, the *Amerika,* provided a whole new series of articles. Supported by Captain König's statements about regular U-boat service between the United States and Germany, and Simon Lake's announced intention to build a fleet of cargo U-boats, the press was off and running.

As early as 12 July, they were reporting that eight new cargo U-boats were under construction in Kiel. They were very close to being right, and how they got the information is still a mystery. Actually, there were six new boats building. The pressure hulls were being built in different places, four in Hamburg, and one each in Flensburg and Bremen.[19] The completed pressure hulls were to be sent to the Germania yard in Kiel for fitting out. Those six added to the existing

Deutschland and *Bremen* would make eight. There was no *Amerika;* the first of the six new boats was named the *Oldenburg*. Presumably, the other five would also have been named for German cities.

The press reported another rumor that also had some basis in fact. Since the day the *Deutschland* had arrived in Baltimore, there had been talk about an American making the trip to Germany aboard the U-boat. The idea started among Americans who for one reason or another wanted to make the trip.

One such American was Sophie Viola Sherling.[20] Born in Berlin, Miss Sherling had come to the United States in 1910 to further her studies in medicine while working as a nurse. She had become an American citizen and was living in Washington, D. C. Her earnest wish to return to Germany was not based on patriotic reasons; her loyalties were firmly with her adopted country. But she did have a very personal reason for wanting to go home. Her brother and her mother, both doctors, had been killed on the Western Front in February 1916, and she wanted to visit their graves.

Captain König, a friend of the family, gave her request his personal attention. Though he had to turn her down, he drove to Washington to explain why.

Other applicants were pro-Germans who wanted to join the crew, and wealthy adventurers who wanted to enjoy the novelty and thrill of being a passenger aboard the U-boat. The latter were the people who got the publicity.

By 13 July, the North German Lloyd offices in New York were flooded with requests from people who wanted to book passage to Germany. Most of the applicants offered to pay one thousand to five thousand dollars for a ticket, several offered ten thousand, and there was one who was willing to pay fifty thousand. All the requests were refused.

Henry G. Hilken, pointing out that the boat had only accommodations for the crew, told reporters that "under no circumstances will a passenger be carried."[21] But the matter did not end there. Amidst the debate over the boat's status, the kaiser suggested to the navy that taking an American crewman or passenger aboard might be a good idea. If that were done, he said, the United States would be put in the position of having to extend protection to the *Deutschland*.[22]

Despite the apparent soundness of the idea it was anything but. In a lengthy and very diplomatic reply, the navy squashed the plan. In the first place, the United States did not extend protection to Americans who crewed aboard foreign ships. And as Henry Hilken had said, there was not room in the U-boat for a passenger. But somehow, the British obtained a copy of the kaiser's idea.

Based on the information they had, the press reports about people clamoring for a place in the *Deutschland* took on a different meaning. In fact, the British hoped the Germans would take a passenger. If they did, the British planned to block the U-boat's departure under the La Follette-Seams Act. The act required that all ships carrying passengers had to be equipped with lifeboats and davits. Passenger-carrying ships that lacked those safety features would not be allowed to leave an American port.[23]

It was a clever ploy by the British, but even if the Germans had been serious about taking a passenger, it might not have worked. Since the La Follette-Seams Act applied only to United States flag carriers, the *Deutschland* was not covered. Out of all that, the question remains: where did the press get all its information to start those rumors?

The press got some of it from the *Deutschland*'s talkative crew. They enjoyed talking about their boat, and they equally enjoyed spreading deliberate misinformation about their trip across the Atlantic. Along the way they embellished a few points and made up some outright lies. Lacking a better source, the press and the American public swallowed the tales hook, line, and sinker. And the crew had plenty of opportunity to talk.

From 13 to 19 July the *Deutschland*'s crew was constantly on the move from one social event to another. Captain König, in a double-breasted, blue serge suit and a straw hat, became a common sight in and around Baltimore. He frequently was seen hurrying to his social appointments, seated in the front seat of Captain Hinsch's "high-powered runabout."[24]

The Germans capitalized on every opportunity to have the captain seen and photographed with American and German dignitaries. Typical was a luncheon held on 13 July at the Germania Club. Present were Baltimore Mayor James P. Preston, German Ambassador Count Johann von Bernstorff, Dr. Heinrich Albert, the count's privy counselor, and Hugo Schmidt, New York agent for the German Bank. United States flags were conspicuously paired with German flags throughout the hall.[25]

Lunch dates often became spontaneous demonstrations of German-American friendship. The scenario was always the same. König and his party would be near a large crowd, and someone would recognize the captain. One wonders how it happened that the captain

The German sailors were easily recognized in Baltimore, and wherever they went they attracted a crowd. The uniform, leather jacket and boots, was distinctive but not actually navy regulation. Still, the men looked official, but few Americans questioned their claim that twenty-eight men of service age, trained to operate a U-boat, were civilians. In fact all were members of the Imperial German Navy. (National Archives)

was so frequently recognized by people who had never laid eyes on the man. Scheduling had a lot to do with it, and having the captain shoulder to shoulder with an easily recognized local personality helped. But having a plant in the crowd worked every time.

A typical example of that sort of thing occurred on 15 July when Captain König, the Hilkens, and four ladies went to lunch at the

Hotel Belvedere. There just happened to be an Elks convention there. As König and his party were crossing the lobby, someone shouted, "There's the captain. It's Captain König, captain of the *Deutschland.*" That got everyone's attention. The captain was immediately surrounded by a legion of handshakers, while inside the hall the band struck up *Die Wacht am Rhein,* followed by the national anthem. By coincidence, the press was there to cover the story.[26]

While the captain was being seen, photographed, and cheered, the crewmen were sent off in groups to attend events hosted by a dozen German societies. But even the social events provided opportunities for controversy.

Six of the crewmen got themselves in a jam when they took an unauthorized trip to Washington, D. C. How and where they obtained the car was not reported, but the fact that they were arrested for speeding was. Oddly, nothing was said about the driver being unlicensed. Today speeding is a small matter, but it was not in 1916—especially when the violator was an unlicensed foreign national.

The six seamen were taken to the police station, the press was called, and the embarrassed Germans forked over twenty dollars to be held in bond.[27] By mid-morning they were back on the street. The capital's police may not have seen any advantage in dealing with the celebrity visitors, but the capital's politicians sure did.

While officialdom squashed the speeding ticket, the sailors were whisked away to the White House for a tour. There they asked if they could speak to the man who "is like our Grand Admiral von Tirpitz." Certainly they could, and the group was taken to the Navy Department where they were introduced to the young Franklin D. Roosevelt, under secretary of the navy. If the Germans were disappointed about being shown a civilian instead of an admiral, they quickly got over it. Roosevelt was a charming host who spoke to them in German.[28]

Another tempest in a teapot occurred over a silver loving cup presented to König and his crew. The cup, sixteen inches high and mounted on an ebony base, ostensibly was the idea of Christine Langenhan. A former diva of the Royal Opera in Berlin, she was living in New York with her American husband, Hugo Boucok, when the *Deutschland* arrived. Overcome with patriotic fervor, Mrs. Langenhan had the cup inscribed:

> Presented to the conqueror of English prestige on the sea and to the commander of the first merchant submarine, the Deutschland, the Captain Paul König and his crew in commemoration and appreciation of their service by Christine Langenhan, Royal Opera singer, 15 July 1916.[29]

Christine Langenhan caused an uproar when she presented Paul König with an engraved loving cup. (National Archives)

The uproar over the cup had nothing to do with the words inscribed on the side. The problem was the United States flag that was inscribed above the words. Americans were very sensitive about how their flag was used, especially pro-British Americans. Frederick T. Blakeman, a landscape architect in New York, protested to Secretary of State, Robert Lansing. Quoting the inscription, Blakeman wrote:

Is not this an illegal use of this country's flag (the flag of a neutral country) and a direct slight to a friendly nation? Must this overt act be classed with the countless other unneutral acts by the German-Americans, violating the statutes of this country? ... the importance of this misuse of our flag certainly should not be overlooked.[30]

Mr. Blakeman and several dozen other writers received a noncommittal reply.

Equally patriotic, but much more practical and noncontroversial, was the ten-thousand-dollar gift presented to the crew by August Hecker of New York. He intended the money to be divided among the officers and men on a graduated scale based on rank. Hecker obviously believed the Germans' claim that the crewmen were not members of the German navy. In fact, all were members of the German navy and could not accept the money. An embarrassing situation was avoided when the crew turned over the entire amount to the German Red Cross, thus side-stepping the problem and creating a valuable piece of propaganda.[31]

The German University League jumped on the bandwagon by organizing a memorial to the *Deutschland,* to be exhibited in New York on 18 July. Anyone who wanted his or her name on the memorial had only to donate one dollar to the German Red Cross.[32]

But most of the recognition for the crew was in the form of lunches, banquets, and tours. They met with President Wilson, toured New York, and danced with the daughters of the German League. Everywhere they went there seemed to be a band or an orchestra that played the national anthem and *Die Wacht am Rhein.* It was a noisy, sometimes spontaneous but usually choreographed, experience that ended abruptly on 19 July.

CHAPTER SEVEN

WAITING TO GO,

17 JULY–1 AUGUST 1916

Four sweating, black stevedores hauled and pushed a heavy cart through the warehouse door and onto the dock. Outside the warehouse the heat seemed twenty degrees hotter, the humidity as thick as water. Straining against the weight, the four men wrestled the cart into a left turn, and moved it alongside the U-boat.

On deck, Fritz Humke swung the boom of one of the *Deutschland*'s four electric cranes over the cart, lowered the hook, and waited for the men to make it fast. One hundred and two feet aft, Wilhelm Mueller was operating another crane. One of the stevedores raised his arm, and Humke pulled a lever. The pallet rose. Humke pushed another lever and the boom swung the pallet over an open hatch. From inside the hold arms reached up to guide the pallet through the opening as it descended below the deck.

The work had started before dawn, but the stevedores were already sweating in the cool morning air as they loaded bulk rubber into the after wet-cargo spaces.[1] By the time the rubber was stowed aboard it was 0900 and the temperature had already climbed to over eighty degrees. It was now nearly noon, and the thermometer was touching ninety.

It seemed cooler in the warehouse, at least it felt cooler to those who were not doing the work. Those privileged few were the guards who stood near the doors and windows. To the stevedores, being inside just meant they were out of the direct sunlight. It was still hot.

The SS *Kronprinzessin Cecilie*, shown here passing the Rotesand Light, was interned in Boston. It is believed that $4,000,000.00 in gold was smuggled out of her hold and on board the *Deutschland*. (Author's collection)

The men inside the warehouse were breaking open nickel-filled casks, transferring the contents into shot bags, and stacking them on pallets. They were the same casks that had been stored in warehouse 104 in Brooklyn. To all but one of those black stevedores, that bit of information was both unknown and unimportant. The one who cared was pretending to be repositioning ingots on a pallet.

The man knelt next to the pallet, glancing at the guards to be sure they were not watching. They ignored him. He began shifting and restacking several bars on the pallet, quickly examining each bar as he did. As he handled the bars he saw the word TIN stamped on the side of each one. That was odd. There was tin being loaded aboard, but it was cast in oblong pigs. This stuff was cast in small bars. Why?

Taking a chance, he took a penknife from his pocket, opened the blade, and scraped the surface of one of the bars. The dull greyish surface came away revealing a white undercoat. More scraping exposed metal that "had a yellowish hue about the color of gold."[2] Turning the bar so that the scraped area was hidden by the bar next to it, he stood up, slipping his knife back into his pocket. He walked quickly to a loaded cart and joined the men pushing it toward to door.

What had he seen? It may have been $4,000,000.00 in gold taken from the vault of the interned SS *Kronprinzessin Cecilie*. According to journalist Damon Runyon, an unnamed source told him that the gold had come from Boston by train under heavy guard. "This on the authority of a man who knows," Runyon wrote. "Nameless he must be: but he knows."[3] All very mysterious, but possibly true.

In 1966 a German writer, Fritz Brustat-Naval, told nearly the same story. According to Brustat-Naval, the gold was declared as nickel and brought aboard in small sacks, under very tight security.[4]

It is true that on 19 July, two days after the British spy had examined the suspicious tin bars, the entire crew was kept aboard the *Deutschland*.[5] Reporters watching the boat thought the sudden end of shore leave meant the *Deutschland* was getting ready to sail.[6] In fact, the Germans were not even nearly ready to leave, and the crew was probably kept aboard to protect the gold. In fact, with one exception on 21 July, crew members were not allowed ashore after the 18th.[7] Their abrupt disappearance from the bars around Locust Point was loudly lamented by the bartenders, a lamentation that was echoed by the Germans' American girlfriends.[8]

There is no German document to support the claim that the *Deutschland* took a fortune in gold back to Germany. In fact, both Paul Hilken and Paul König denied the allegation when asked by American reporters. But the evidence is strong that it happened.

An hour and a half after the spy had examined the suspicious cargo, loading was stopped so that two tank cars could be rolled onto the pier.[9] Heaving and groaning, their efforts coordinated by their black leadmen, the stevedores pushed the tank cars into position. Hoses were attached to the valves and bolted to the *Deutschland*'s fuel intakes. A German chemist took samples of the oil, pronounced it clean, and pumping started. By 1900 the contents of the two tank cars rolled outside the gate.[10]

The following morning, 18 July, two more tank cars arrived, but were left outside the gate. "Why were they there?" people asked. Obviously to refuel the *Bremen* when she arrived, the experts explained. And they were probably right.

The *Deutschland* had topped off her fuel tanks and had taken aboard 550 gallons of additional fuel in barrels.[11] According to the captain, when the *Deutschland* arrived in Baltimore she had plenty of fuel remaining for the trip home. If that were true, why take on more, especially so much more? His answer was probably honest. American diesel oil was much superior to what was available in Germany, and he wanted the best on board.

Americans accepted that because it made sense and fit in with their ideas about the superiority of American products. But in the process they overlooked the fact that Germany was not going to let that high-grade fuel stand idle while the *Deutschland* was in Germany preparing for the next trip. It is safe to assume that the fuel was pumped into an outbound war boat. And when the *Bremen* went home, she would also be topped off and carrying extra fuel.

That same day, more rubber was stowed in compartments five and seven, and crammed into the wet-cargo space forward of the conning tower. No other cargo was worked on the 18th. In fact, the stevedores were released early in the evening and returned to their quarters aboard the *Neckar*. That night the only cargo moved was handled by the *Deutschland*'s crew. And it was probably gold.

The following day, 19 July, the remaining rubber went aboard bringing the total to 348 tons, followed by 600 bags of nickel. She was now fully loaded with fuel, approximately 800 tons of cargo, and provisions for sixty days.[12] Everyone expected her to leave, but she stayed. In fact, she remained in her berth until 1 August 1916.

The delay has never been fully explained, but it was due in part to repairs that were carried out. Some of the piping was replaced with American-made piping that was more corrosion resistant, and a Baltimore firm made several bronze gears to replace German-made steel gears.[13] It may also have been that Captain König was waiting for the right moment to evade the Allied cruisers waiting outside the three-mile limit.

Whatever the reasons for the delayed departure, the fact is the boat remained tied to the pier for nearly two more weeks. During that time the press kept a close eye on her, ready to report any change. Two press boats, the *Ruth* and the *Beverly*, prowled the Patapsco River every night, pressing close to the log boom to get a better view. They were rarely successful.

Defending the log boom were the *Thomas J. Timmins* and the tiny *Efco*. Whenever a press boat came too close, the crew on the *Timmins* would illuminate it with its powerful searchlight. Irritated and blinded, the reporters would back off. On the night of 22 July, the helmsman on the *Beverly*, his night vision destroyed by the glare of the search-light, ran aground leaving the reporters aboard the *Ruth* with a dilemma.[14] Should they applaud their competitor's plight or denounce German obstructionism?

On another occasion, the *Efco* conducted a counter-patrol of its own. Damon Runyon described the small launch as "a noisy little boat with a dinky searchlight that is always prying and poking into other people's business." The *Efco* and the *Ruth* got into a searchlight battle trying to blind one another. Both were ineffectual because "the two searchlights together were about as powerful as a two-candle-power kerosene lantern." The battle was decided for the *Efco* when the *Timmins* joined in.

Defeated, the reporters went ashore to try their luck there. Nearby was a large pile driver with a ladder to the top of the tower. Reporters had been climbing to the top during the day, and one tried it that night. When he shouted down his observations, the *Timmins* flooded the tower with light.[15] The next day the Germans paid off the pile driver's owner and no more reporters were allowed to use it as an observation platform.[16]

Unable to report any substantial change, the reporters rehashed old news, speculated, and passed on rumors. As time dragged on the rumors became wilder and more ridiculous. One said that the U-boat now tied up to the McLean Pier was not the *Deutschland*. It was the *Bremen* that had slipped in at night. The *Bremen*'s crew had taken the *Deutschland* home, leaving the *Deutschland*'s crew behind to hide the switch.[17]

That one was too much for Damon Runyon. He told his readers that actually the U-boat tied up at the pier was not the *Deutschland* or the *Bremen*. In fact, it was not a U-boat at all. What was tied up to the McLean Pier was an inflated rubber model, left behind to fool everyone.[18]

On 24 July the press finally had something new to report. Actually, there were two events to report, one that supported the belief that the *Deutschland* was about to leave, and another to contradict it.

Before the *Deutschland* arrived, a channel had been dredged from the Patapsco River to the McLean Pier. The depth was thirty-five feet, which was just enough for the boat to submerge, with her keel on the bottom and her conning tower just below the surface.[19] On the 24th, Captain König conducted a test dive alongside the pier, giving the press positive proof that she was about to leave.[20]

But that same day, William P. Ryan, collector of the port, and R. Y. Camdus, radio inspector, went aboard the U-boat to seal up her radio.[21] The *Deutschland* had been in port two weeks, and that was as long as she could stay and still have an operating radio. It was really a formality since the *Deutschland* had only used her radio twice since 10 July. On both occasions she had received the time from Arlington. In fact, her antenna was not even up except on those two occasions.[22]

The next day the excitement was heightened by a report that a British cruiser had entered the Chesapeake Bay and had come in as far as Fortress Monroe.[23] The public was outraged. Violating American neutrality was one thing, but to do it without warning and without a pilot aboard compounded the crime.

The report is probably true, though the British denied it. Watch officers aboard the battleship USS *Louisiana* reported seeing the ship. So did officers aboard the nearby collier, USS *Neptune*. The State Department said they were wrong, they had simply seen each other.[24] In fact, the diplomats suggested that the *Neptune* was playing a trick on the battlewagon.

Angered over the accusation that impugned their professional reputation, the American officers dropped the subject. That pleased the State Department, who now said that even if a British warship had entered the Chesapeake, no violation had occurred. But on 26 July, the armored cruiser USS *North Carolina* upped anchor and steamed out to the three-mile limit to make sure there were no more nocturnal visitors.[25]

The British had said publicly that they would sink the *Deutschland* on sight, and eight Allied warships were reported off the Virginia Capes. The number was undoubtedly exaggerated as were reports that five hundred armored subchasers were coming from Britain to "join in a cordon of Allied warships across the Capes."[26] Despite the exaggeration, the Germans knew the British were out to stop the U-boat from reaching Bremen, and Count von Bernstorff asked the United States for protection.

In a letter to Frank Polk, the ambassador expressed the Germans' concern:

> I beg you to be good enough to request the Navy Department to give the *Deutschland* protection within the three-mile limit for some time as it is to be expected that our enemies will attack her within this limit unless protection is given by the American Navy.[27]

The request was denied because the destroyer *Sterrett* and the armored cruiser *North Carolina* were already maintaining a neutrality patrol off the Virginia Capes.

On 29 July, Captain König, fearing that British sympathizers would attempt to damage his boat as she moved down the Chesapeake, asked the collector of customs in Baltimore to provide escort for the *Deutschland.* That request was also denied.[28] The federal government saw no reason to treat the departure of a merchantman— even if she were a U-boat—any differently from any other departure.

However, after reconsideration a compromise was reached. The government agreed to provide an escort to keep boats away from the U-boat as she headed toward the sea, on the same basis as they provided escorts to large yacht-racing events.[29]

After two more days of delay, false starts, and rampant rumors, the *Deutschland* showed the first positive signs of getting under way. At 1800 the small workboat *Efco* cleared away the log boom while the *Timmins* towed the barge, *George May,* clear. Then the two boats dragged the channel for mines.

By noon word of the preparations was out and a large crowd gathered outside the Eastern Forwarding Company offices, and along the river bank. The press had chartered two large boats, the steam yacht *Valiant* owned by Edward Toulson, and a powerful speed boat, the *Esperanza,* owned by Dr. R. T. Somers. There were twenty reporters, photographers, and movie cameramen aboard the *Valiant,* and six or seven reporters aboard the *Esperanza.* Their insistence on getting in close to the *Deutschland* irked the customs officials who were handling the last-minute details.

Shortly after noon a customs official went aboard the *Valiant* and told the owner that he could not carry passengers for hire. Citing a law that required charter boats to register at the customshouse, he ordered Toulson to put his passengers ashore. Edward Toulson was outraged, the reporters were irate, and the customs official was adamant.

What about the reporters aboard the *Esperanza?* They were not covered by the law because the owner, Doctor Somers, had them aboard as nonpaying guests, the customs agent replied. That decision pleased the reporters in the *Esperanza,* who knew it was too late for their competitors to charter another boat.

Toulson exploded. Years earlier he had tried to register the *Valiant,* but was told that registration was unnecessary. Since then he had been carrying passengers on a regular basis. He even advertised. The customs official was unimpressed.

Exasperated, Toulson hurried ashore to call his attorney, while twenty reporters "burned up the wires to have the yacht released." Within an hour they were reassembled on the *Valiant* where Toulson said loudly enough for all to hear, "All I ask is that you sign a paper making affidavit that I did not accept money from you. And please don't give me any. I'll even buy the gasoline."

Loaded with guests, the *Valiant* rejoined the growing mob of boats that surrounded the *Deutschland*.[30]

At 1600 the Coast Guard cutter *Wissahickon* and the Baltimore police boat *Lannan* arrived. For an hour the two government boats and the *Timmins* lay alongside one another discussing plans for the escort down the bay. At 1730 the government boats took their positions, and the *Timmins* passed a line to the *Deutschland*. At 1738 the U-boat started her voyage home.[31]

Amidst the din of saluting horns, whistles, and bells, the *Deutschland* was turned around and proceeded into the Patapsco River. Hundreds of people lined the river banks, shouting, cheering, and waving handkerchiefs. American and German flags dotted the crowd. As the U-boat pushed forward, she was surrounded by a huge fleet of small boats that formed an "unwanted escort."

As the procession moved down the bay a stiff breeze came up, accompanied by a short, steep chop that quickly forced the smaller boats to fall away and run for shelter. When the convoy passed Annapolis at 2045 most of the unwanted escort had disappeared. By 2355 when the *Deutschland* and her two escorts passed Cove Point, only the two press boats were following them. By the time they reached Solomon's Island at 0230 on 2 August, the *Valiant* had also given up. A short time later the *Esperanza* developed engine trouble and disappeared astern.[32]

The *Deutschland* spent all afternoon on 2 August holed up in a small bay near New Point Comfort. Just twenty minutes from the channel, hidden by the hills, and protected by the *Timmins* and the *Wissahickon*, she waited for nightfall.[33]

Outside, several Allied warships were spread out along a five-mile line, waiting. The water at that point was too shallow to dive under them, so that Captain König was faced with the necessity of breaking through on the surface. The weather forecast for that night was for cool, cloudy weather with no moon. A stiff breeze was expected that would cover the sea with white caps, hiding the *Deutschland*'s wake. A dark night and a rough sea were what Captain König wanted. He would, however, have preferred deep water.

CHAPTER EIGHT

THE FIRST TRIP HOME,

2–24 AUGUST 1916

Trimmed down, her decks awash, the *Deutschland* pushed through the night. Captain König looked at his watch—2200. The *Deutschland* was an hour outside the Capes, well within the three-mile limit, and moving south along the coast. As long as she stayed inside the three-mile limit the *Deutschland* remained under American protection, a factor as important to König's plan as was the night departure. And his plan was simple. He was going to hug the coast, working his way south, until he could hook around the end of the Allied patrol line. Once he was around the line, he would turn north.

According to information supplied by the German Embassy, Captain Hinsch, and the Hilkens, British sympathizers in fishing boats had strung nets to snag the *Deutschland*.[1] The same warning had been given when the U-boat arrived off the United States coast on 8 July. Nothing had come of it on that occasion, but Captain König was nonetheless alert. With just the conning tower above the surface, hidden by darkness, Captain König was becoming increasingly confident that his plan would work.

Captain König and his first officer, Franz Krapohl, were peering into the night when suddenly two searchlight beams stabbed through the night from starboard. The conning tower was bathed in light. Startled, the two officers were momentarily frozen in place, their night vision destroyed. The lights abruptly rotated upward, their twin beams pointing directly overhead. The upward sweep was repeated twice and then the lights went out. Moments later a single shaft of light, pointing straight up, appeared on the headlands.

Recovering from their shock and surprise, the Germans strained to see into the dark. A short distance away they saw the dim forms of two fishing boats.

"They're signaling the British," Krapohl said. "They are giving away our position."

"Yes," König answered, pointing ahead. "Look."

Another beam of light rose into the sky. More lights dotted the sea ahead, their beams sweeping the surface. Captain König looked aft at the Cape Henry Light, mentally noting his position, and recalled the soundings on the chart. Not much water here, but enough. Still inside the three-mile limit the *Deutschland* dove.[2]

For thirty minutes the *Deutschland* remained under, holding her southerly course. At 2240 she surfaced. Concerned about the depth, and piloting by dead reckoning, Captain König wanted to establish his exact position.

Water was still streaming from the conning tower when the captain opened the hatch. A quick look around revealed a dozen searchlights probing the night ahead of them. It also revealed the lights of a large ship moving quickly toward the U-boat.

"Dive, dive, dive," König shouted, sliding down the ladder, slamming the hatch shut. Bells clanged and horns blared as the *Deutschland*'s bow angled sharply downward. Above the roar of water surging into the tanks the crew could hear the noise of screws churning the water.

"It's the *North Carolina*," König told the men around him. "She must have been attracted by the lights."

"She's very close," Krapohl said, listening to the noise.

"Yes." Captain König looked at the depth gauge—twelve meters, about thirty-nine feet. At that depth the *Deutschland* conning tower was only about nine feet beneath the surface, and could be rammed by any large surface vessel. But König could not take his boat any deeper, there was not enough water.

"Steady at twelve meters," he said stepping to the periscope. "Up periscope."

The tube rose quickly. Pressing his eye to the lens, the captain rotated the tube and peered aft. The *North Carolina*'s white stern light was drawing away. Looking forward he saw just a few searchlights in the distance. There was nothing on either side.

"Surface."

Shortly after 2300 the *Deutschland* rose to the surface and Captain König fixed his position. He then came about, dove, and headed north toward Cape Charles. Through the periscope he watched the searchlights "continuing to indicate our southward advance." That is exactly what he wanted. Instead of going end-around, he would move north. Hopefully, the British would continue to believe he was headed south and leave the north end of their line uncovered.

At midnight he was forced to surface because of shallow water. Continuing north he reached Cape Charles, turned east, and dove in fifteen meters of water. It was a tight fit between the surface and the bottom, but it "was enough to keep us out of sight." At 0120 on 3 August the *Deutschland* surfaced outside the Allied patrol line. She had broken through.

In Germany the news about the *Deutschland* was received through the Reuters news service, but the reports were not always entirely accurate. According to Reuters, the U-boat had left on 30 July. Alfred Lohmann immediately notified the navy and the kaiser that the *Deutschland* was expected to be off the English coast on 16 August and should arrive in Helgoland on the 19th.[3] The news set a number of wheels in motion.

The *Deutschland*'s visit to Baltimore had been a huge propaganda success, and her return to Germany was to further capitalize on that success. Dr. Ernst Bischof, a journalist, was employed to ghostwrite a book about the feat, naming Paul König as the author. Arrangements were now made to put Doctor Bischof aboard the *Deutschland* at Helgoland so that he could interview Captain König as the U-boat made her way to Bremen.[4]

But most of the book had been written even before he stepped aboard the *Deutschland*. Using material provided by Alfred Lohmann and the newspaper accounts from America, Bischof prepared the text that has become the standard account of the trip. Sticking to the official line, the text described the private nature of the venture, the civilian status of the crew, and routed the *Deutschland* through the English Channel. Nevertheless, König's contribution was substantial, since he gave accounts of the boat under way, described conditions aboard, and even recounted two near disasters.

While Doctor Bischof was organizing material for the book, the *Bremen* was being readied. By 5 August the second cargo-carrying U-boat was ready in all respects, and arrangements were being made for the directors of Krupp-Essen to have a special look at her. But authorization for them to go aboard had to first be obtained from the navy; a curious requirement for a "civilian" boat.[5] At the same time, Alfred Lohmann was making arrangements for the *Deutschland* and the *Bremen* to meet in Helgoland.

He wanted the *Bremen*'s captain to have the benefit of Paul König's experience, and Lohmann wanted to be present when the information was exchanged.[6] Getting the boats together was no problem, but having Lohmann present required cutting through red tape. Helgoland was a U-boat base, and getting permission for a civilian— any civilian—to go onto the base was a bureaucratic nightmare. Permission was finally granted, but Berlin warned everyone involved to be careful not to reveal the connection between the two U-boats and the navy.[7]

In the meantime plans were being made for a huge reception when the *Deutschland* arrived in Bremen. The kaiser would not be present, but every member of the crew would receive a decoration in his name. The decorations were carefully selected to represent the magnitude of the accomplishment, but at the same time were not military awards.[8] Parades, banquets, and speaking tours were scheduled, and press releases went out to the nation's newspapers, hyping Paul König.

One lengthy release described his life in colorful terms. His was the story of the poor boy who made good.[9] Orphaned at an early age, rejected by a heartless uncle, Paul shoveled coal for a few pennies a day. Somehow he found his way into a maritime academy, passed his tests, and went to sea. The tale was only half true, and the truth was a much better story.[10]

His father, a Lutheran pastor, died in 1876 when Paul was nine, leaving a widow, three daughters, and a son. Two years later his mother died, and Paul was sent to live with an uncle. The uncle was anything but cruel and heartless. Honoring his late brother's wishes, the uncle kept Paul in the Frankeschen Stiftungen zu Halle where he was studying to be a Lutheran pastor. But by the time Paul was sixteen it was obvious that the plan was not going to work. And in 1883 the uncle used his influence to find Paul a berth as a cabin boy aboard a freighter.

For the next eleven years, Paul alternately went to school and went to sea. In 1894 he successfully completed the course of study at the Maritime School in Bremen and passed his examinations for his master's license. Two years later he became an officer for Norddeutsche Lloyd.

Much more accurate was an account of his career up to the time he took command of the *Deutschland.* How it got past the censors is a mystery, but how it was overlooked by British Intelligence is an even greater mystery.

According to the article, Paul König had served as an active navy officer since the start of the war. The article even told about his participation in the Baltic operations against the Russians, for which he was awarded the Iron Cross Second Class. The information was correct in every detail, and provided the British with all they needed to convince the Americans to prohibit the *Deutschland* from entering port.

Another article reported his marriage to a British woman. According to the colorful account, she came to Germany in June 1914 so that their oldest son could receive special medical treatment. Paul had just returned from a Mediterranean cruise, and they met in Bremerhaven. Their reunion was short. The war broke out, and Kathleen, being loyal to her king and country, could not remain in Germany. Neither could the boy. Professing opposite nationalist sympathies, they parted full of high regard for each other's sense of loyalty and duty.

The lengthy article then shifted the scene to London in 1916. Kathleen was waiting at a train station when she saw a newspaper with Paul's picture on the front page. She was flabbergasted to read that her husband was the *Deutschland*'s skipper, "because he has never even been near a submarine." The account was attributed to the *London Mail.* In fact, the entire article was fabricated propaganda, and the *London Mail* never ran such an account.[11]

While the excitement at home was building, the *Deutschland* was plowing through heavy seas and battling stormy weather as she headed north. On the night of 13 August she maneuvered to avoid the RMS *Olympic* as the liner raced toward the United States. The U-boat was not spotted.[12]

The former White Star liner was one of few ships seen by König and his crew on the homeward trip. They did spot ships of the Tenth Cruiser Squadron off Muckle Fugga, as well as patrol boats off the Butt of Lewis and near Fair Island. But apparently the U-boat went unnoticed, and the trip home was uneventful. They were lucky.

The British intercepted a message sent on 15 August from Berlin to Kiel. Berlin wanted to know if *U-200* would pass through the Kattegat, between Denmark and Sweden.[13] Berlin must have thought that the *Deutschland* was returning to Kiel instead of Bremen, since there was no other reason to assume she would take that route. Berlin also wanted to know when the U-boat would enter German waters. Though confusing, the intercepted message gave the British a valuable clue to the *Deutschland*'s whereabouts.

Captain König was unaware that the British had broken the German codes, but he was nonetheless concerned that they might locate him. He was never sure that the patrol boats and auxiliaries he had seen had not also seen him. If the British were plotting his track according to sightings, and having a pretty good idea of his destination, they could easily set up an ambush. At 0600 on 22 August he thought that was what had happened.

The *Deutschland* was running on the surface, both deck hatches open, when the lookout next to König pointed dead ahead. There was something on the horizon. Even using binoculars the object was too far away to see clearly, but Captain König thought it was a sail. As the object drew nearer the captain became less certain and more concerned. The sail had a very odd shape.[14]

He ordered the deck hatches closed and trimmed the boat down until the decks were under and the sea broke against the conning tower. The wind was from the northwest at five knots, gusting to seven. The sky was overcast, visibility fifteen miles. The dark green conning tower, protruding barely five feet above the water, was almost invisible at that distance. The giveaway was the white foam trailing behind the conning tower. But that was an insignificant threat at this point.

Prepared to drop below the surface in a moment, the *Deutschland* moved cautiously forward. At three miles' distance the captain recognized the odd shape. It was a conning tower. But was it German or British? The fact that the boat was on the surface inclined König to think it was German. But a British submarine waiting for the unarmed *Deutschland* might also be on the surface.

A sharp-eyed lookout in *UB-35*'s conning tower spotted a strange object low in the water. Two years of war had sharpened his eye for just such a situation. He knew what the object was.

"U-Boat!" he shouted, pointing toward the object. "Two points off the port bow."

The officer next to him sighted down the extended arm and quickly raised his binoculars.

"Come left two zero degrees," he shouted down the speaking tube. "Stand by to dive." His hand slammed down the general-quarters alarm button, sending the crew scrambling to battle stations. There

24 August 1916, the *Deutschland* enters the Helgoland harbor for a meeting with her sister ship, the *Bremen*. (Bibliothek für Zeitgeschichte, Stuttgart)

was movement next to him as the captain leaned over the conning tower rim, squinting through his Zeiss binoculars.

"Is she German or British?" he asked no one in particular.

"Could be one of ours coming home," the younger officer answered, looking through his binoculars trying to recognize the stranger.

The *UB-35* was heading directly toward the strange object.

"Stand by to fire torpedoes," the captain spoke into the speaking tube. "Signal challenge of the day," he said, straightening up and raising his glasses to his eyes. Behind him three signal flags rose quickly up the halyard.

The *Deutschland*'s lookout was already diving through the hatch when Captain König read the signals. "She's German," he shouted down the hatch. "Blow ballast. Surface, surface."

The *Deutschland* came to the surface, her own signal flags fluttering, the crew pouring out on deck. In moments the two U-boats were alongside one another. The officers exchanged salutes, congratulations, and information. Then the boats parted, "we to our homecoming, and they to their work."[15]

At 1935 the *Deutschland* reported she was in 036Y, a grid west of the North Frisian Island, Sylt. During the three-minute transmission she asked for minefield information and an escort.[16] The British copied the message, but it was too late for them to react. Ten hours later the patrol boat SMS *Senator Sachse* radioed that she was leading the U-boat southward, toward Helgoland.[17] Eight hours later, the *Deutschland* was alongside the *Bremen* in Helgoland. It was 23 August 1916.[18]

Her stay in Helgoland was brief, just long enough for Paul König to brief the *Bremen*'s skipper, Captain Karl Schwartzkopf. At 0800 the following morning, the *Deutschland* left Helgoland under escort, headed for the mouth of the Weser.[19] At 1300 she passed the Rotesand lighthouse in light rain and headed upriver.[20] Despite the increasingly heavy rain, thousands of people were already lining the river banks to watch the U-boat come home.

CHAPTER NINE

HOMECOMING,

25 AUGUST 1916

Beneath low, grey clouds, a torrent of rain reduced visibility to less than three miles. Everything was dark and grey, even the masses of drenched onlookers that lined the banks of the Weser waiting for the *Deutschland* to pass. Ten-year-old Franz Eichberger squeezed through the crowd to the river's edge and peered downriver into the gloom. There were a few boats on the water, lucky people who would be close enough to get a really good look at the *Deutschland,* but still no sign of the U-boat.

Franz wiped the water from his face with a sodden sleeve and turned to push back into the crowd. Suddenly he stopped. A dull boom rolled upriver, followed by another and then another. Cannon were firing. Excited, the boy ran along the bank toward the sound. The crowd heard it too. The people pressed toward the noise but were packed too tightly to accomplish any movement that might afford a better view.

Voices from the crowd shouted, "It's coming. It's coming." A few followed Franz's example, scrambling along the bank, others stood on their toes, squinting their eyes against the rain. A band began to play *Deutschland, Deutschland Über Alles.*

From the crowd downriver came a roaring cheer. The upriver crowd heard it and saw the ripple of waving flags and fluttering handkerchiefs. Hats rose into the air. The mood was infectious. Soon everyone on both banks was cheering wildly. Several bands, playing several different marches, joined in. A boat on the river let loose with its steam siren. Horns blared, bells rang, and a fireboat pumped a

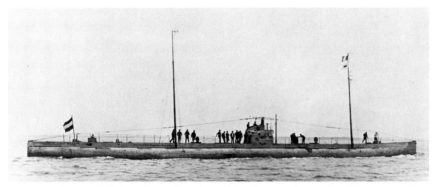

It was raining lightly when the *Deutschland* started up the Weser on the afternoon of 25 August 1916. (Bibliothek für Zeitgeschichte, Stuttgart)

stream of water from its single nozzle. The noise was indescribable and the crowd was delirious with patriotic fervor, but the river remained empty.

Franz Eichberger, exceptionally tall for his age, clambered up the side of a low, stone tower near the water's edge. Fifteen feet above the crowd, he had a clear view of the river in both directions. He had only enough time for one quick look downriver before the commanding voice of a policeman ordered him down. But Franz had seen what the others could not. Moving slowly toward him, convoyed by an assortment of private yachts, workboats, and navy patrol boats was the *Deutschland*.

"It's coming," he shouted and pointed. "I can see it."

The crowd went mad. A small cannon, positioned on the jetty, started firing a salute, the several bands tried to coordinate their efforts on a joint rendition of *Die Wacht am Rhein,* failed, and went their separate musical ways. In a preview of the type of mass demonstration that would characterize Germany in the 1930s, the crowd took up the chant, "*Deutschland, Deutschland, Deutschland.*"

Amidst the delirium, only the policeman was unaffected. Maintaining his official composure and never losing sight of his duty, he again ordered the boy down.[1]

At noon on 25 August 1916, the *Deutschland* entered the free harbor of Bremen, and made fast to her pier. Along the way from Bremerhaven she had passed an unbroken crowd of wildly cheering Germans. Salutes had been fired in every town and village, church bells rang, and military bands trumpeted her passage. Recalling the scene, Captain König said:

Fully dressed and her periscopes extended, she proceeds toward Bremen 25 August 1916. (Bibliothek für Zeitgeschichte, Stuttgart)

The spectacle was simply indescribable, this apparently endless multitude, these thousands upon thousands, like a black and living sea across which there passed a tidal motion of waving umbrellas, glimmering white muslin, and hands.[2]

The official reception in Bremen, followed by a state dinner that night, was a tumultuous and lavish affair. But the Germans were careful to ensure that the celebration had a decidedly civilian flavor. The army and the navy were represented, and the kaiser sent his congratulations, but the main players were civilians. The Grand Duke of Oldenburg led the civilian authorities and other dignitaries in greeting Captain König and his crew. Among the representatives of German industry, business, and banking, the most prominent was Count Ferdinand von Zeppelin.

The events of 25 August were carefully orchestrated to accomplish two propaganda goals. The first was to capitalize on the positive effect that the *Deutschland*'s visit had on the Americans. Alfred Lohmann, speaking at the dinner, said:

It was particularly agreeable to me to be assured of the warm interest and satisfaction with which the *Deutschland*'s arrival in America was greeted by all true Americans—that is to say, by all Americans possessed of the free spirit of Washington and Franklin, all whose judgement had not been warped by subversive Mammon. Our company takes pride in

Despite the rain the crowds that jammed the river banks numbered in the thousands. To the average German, the *Deutschland* represented an end to the British blockade, and her crewmen were national heroes. (Bibliothek für Zeitgeschichte, Stuttgart)

the thought it has succeeded in the very midst of war in sending dyestuffs to America under the German flag. America, herself, on the contrary, is not even able to secure the immunity of her post from Europe. I shall not mention the many other breaches of international and naval law committed against the Neutrals, and especially the smaller nations, by our enemies.[3]

The second goal was closer to home.

The German people needed a victory, one they could see, and one that offered salvation from the horrors of war. They needed to believe that the *Deutschland*'s success meant an end to the hardships caused by the British blockade, hardships that manifested themselves in a nearly starvation diet. They had to see an end to the carnage in which an entire generation was being slaughtered. The *Deutschland* did that.

And they needed heroes. Not heroes who had died for the Father-

The *Deutschland* tied up in Bremen in front of a temporary viewing stand. This was the only time the public—that is selected members—got to see the boat up close. If anything, security in Germany was much tighter than it had been in Baltimore. And it had been very tight in Baltimore. (Bibliothek für Zeitgeschichte, Stuttgart)

land—there were more than enough of those—but heroes who had succeeded for the Fatherland. They wanted to cheer men who had tweaked the lion's nose and then kicked him where it hurt. Captain König and his crew had done that.

Everyone was decorated—but with civilian medals. Captain König received the highest award, the Knight's Cross of the Hohenzollern House Order. Krapohl, Eyring, and Klees received the Royal Order of the Crown, 4th class, as did Prusse and two Krupp employees. Alfred Lohmann did much better with the same award in 2nd class. The Hilkens and Captain Hinsch shared the Order of the Red Eagle, 4th class, with a Krupp engineer. Based on rank, the rest of the crew received either the General Decoration in Silver, the General Decoration in Bronze, or the Medal of the Order of the Crown.[4]

There was a humorous situation that never reached the public. In November 1914 the kaiser had complained to a dinner guest that, "the General Staff tells me nothing and never asks my advice." His complaint was still valid two years later. When the *Deutschland* arrived at Helgoland on the 23rd, a telegram was sent to the kaiser at Pless, but was misrouted. Somewhere along the line German order and efficiency had broken down, and it was not until the evening of the 24th that he heard the news. Plans for the dazzling reception were already made, the stage was set, and the kaiser was totally in the dark about all of it. When he found out, he hit the roof. He demanded to know why he was not informed, and got a watered down excuse that really was not an answer at all. At the same time he was given a petty problem to solve.

His advisors were concerned that Alfred Lohmann was getting entirely too much personal publicity from the *Deutschland* operation and was grandstanding for his own gain. The royal advisors claimed "that was the view from all sides." Their solution lay in the telegram the kaiser would send to the *Deutschland*. The message, they said, should be addressed to everyone involved and not to Lohmann personally. It was the sort of problem the kaiser was eager to solve and he did it with admirable skill. He addressed the telegram to Captain König.[5]

CHAPTER TEN

BREMEN

Nearly one hundred sailors stood atop the Helgoland sea-wall watching the *Bremen* slowly cross the harbor toward the narrow entrance. For some of them it was like seeing something that had happened before—the U-boat looked exactly like the *Deutschland*. A small rowboat with two curious occupants drifted near the opening, and just outside a torpedo boat waited to escort the *Bremen* north. Off the U-boat's port beam a small tug maneuvered to give the photographer on her stern a better shot of the departing *Bremen*. As the *Bremen*'s bow neared the opening in the seawall, the photographer pressed the shutter release. The shutter opening whipped across the lens, a spurt of light burned an image on the gelatin surface of the film sheet, and the *Bremen* slid through the opening. The photographer lowered his heavy camera and waved to the men standing in the U-boat's conning tower. He had just taken the last photograph ever made of the *Bremen*.

At 1500 on 26 August, the *Deutschland*'s identical sister ship departed Helgoland and turned north. The sailors standing atop the seawall watched the U-boat until she disappeared over the horizon. She was never seen again, and no trace was ever found.

Her captain was forty-one-year-old Karl Schwartzkopf, a former first officer aboard the Lloyd liner SS *Prinz Friedrich Wilhelm*. Captain Schwartzkopf was born in Lübeck, the son of a goldsmith, and like Captain König he held a reserve commission. Since the war started he had been serving aboard the old SMS *Siegfried* as a watch officer, being relieved of that assignment in January 1916 when he was sent

The last photo taken of the *Bremen* was on 26 August 1916 as she headed north from Helgoland. She was never heard from again, and no trace of her or her crew was ever found. This may be the only photo of the *Bremen* in existence. (Bibliothek für Zeitgeschichte, Stuttgart)

to the U-boat training school in Kiel. He completed the course in June. That same month he was released from active service, given the reserve rank of Kapitänleutnant, and assigned command of the *Bremen.*[1]

Rumors about her arrival had been circulating along the U.S. East Coast since the day after the *Deutschland* had docked in Baltimore. But now there was tangible evidence that the second cargo U-boat was on the way. On 24 August an interned Lloyd liner, the SS *Willehad,* left East Boston Harbor headed for New London, Connecticut. Captain Hinsch, acting as the agent for the Eastern Forwarding Company, was in command.[2]

Early in 1916, Paul Hilken had leased the newly constructed State Pier in New London from the T. A. Scott Company. The lease said that the pier would be used as a terminal for a cargo U-boat, but did not name the U-boat. In July an ad appeared in the *New London Day:*

> Wanted—House carpenters. State Pier, New London, fifty cents an hour; overtime at time and a half; work all daylight hours, the T. A. Scott Company.[3]

Cryptic messages from the German Ocean Navigation Company to A. Schumacher and Company directing the American agents to gather the cargo were read by the press. The true meaning of the messages was a mystery to the reporters, but they could tell by the volume of traffic that things were happening. Raw materials started arriving at the State Pier, causing reporters to speculate about the

Bremen's destination. But cargo was also being gathered in Baltimore, and there were rumors that a pier had been purchased in Boston.

The *Bremen*'s arrival date was not made public, but Captain Hinsch knew that she was scheduled to arrive on 15 September. He did not worry too much when she was two or three days late, but after a week had passed he did worry. So did Alfred Lohmann, his associates, and German navy headquarters in Berlin.

Their fears were fueled by a flood of rumors that the U-boat had been sunk or captured. The frustrating part was that they were unable to dispel or confirm any of them. But one thing was certain, the *Bremen* was missing.

As early as 31 July there had been reports in American newspapers that the *Bremen* had been captured.[4] Sources were quoted as saying that the U-boat was seen being towed into a British port. The name of the port changed, and sometimes the source said she came in under her own power, but the rumors were consistent. Those rumors were easily discounted because the Germans knew that on 31 July, and until 26 August, the *Bremen* was safe at home. But after she disappeared it was another matter.

Information received by German naval intelligence came from agents in neutral countries and diplomatic staff, and some of their sources were considered to be very reliable. One such source reported on 20 September that according to talk among British sailors, the *Bremen* had been captured and taken to Liverpool.[5] The time element was about right, the source was considered reliable, and the scenario made sense. The report worried the Germans. Then there was a flash of hope.

Acting on a report filed in Rhode Island by Reuters, Dr. Emil Leimdörfer published an article in the *Vossische Zeitung* that the *Bremen,* after being long overdue, had arrived in New York.[6] The story was picked up by nearly every other German newspaper, and editors wrote front-page editorials praising Captain Schwartzkopf, his crew, Germania, and Alfred Lohmann. The German people had been totally unaware that the boat was overdue and missing, a fact the German censors had kept well under wraps. The word was out now, but the problem was past and the nation rejoiced.

Doctor Leimdörfer had used the same technique to put together the report of the *Bremen*'s arrival in New York that he had used to put together the story about the formation of a cargo U-boat company. The earlier story had been surprisingly accurate considering that he was working with unlinked bits of information. But in the earlier story he at least had several bits to work with. In the story about the *Bremen* he had no information other than a Reuters report that a tug had been dispatched to meet a cargo U-boat at Montauk Point.

What Reuters had neglected to say was that since 12 September, Captain Hinsch had been sending the tug, *T. A. Scott Jr.*, out to sea to wait for the *Bremen*. Later, when it became clear that something had probably happened to the *Bremen*, Hinsch recalled the tug but continued to send a small powerboat, the *Efco*, to wait at night in the "lower New London harbor." The movements of both boats were closely watched the the State Department.[7]

When the *Bremen* did not show up in New York, or anywhere else, the German government had to construct an explanation. Doing the only thing they could do under the circumstances, they said the *Bremen* was undoubtedly safe, her delay caused by extraordinary measures taken to evade the British fleet. And then they waited.

Ten-year-old Frederick Lakeman walked along the beach, head down, eyes searching the sand. Little Frederick probably was not looking for anything in particular. Anything would do. Suddenly he stopped, his attention fixed on a round life ring half buried in the sand. Overcome with excitement and pleasure at having stumbled upon such a wonderful find, the small boy struggled across the beach toward his parents, dragging his treasure.

His parents were even more excited. The life ring bore the name *Bremen* on both sides, and was marked with the Imperial crown. Above the crown was the word *Schutzmarke* (registered trade mark), and in small letters to one side were the words, V. Epping-Hoven, Wilhelmshaven. They were believed to be the name of the manufacturer. Certain that their son had found the remains of the *Bremen*, the parents rushed the life ring to the local police station.

Quartermaster A. J. Martinson, of the Coast Guard Cutter *Ossipee*, inspected the ring. The ring was well made and was the type used on German merchant vessels. But his sharp eyes had spotted the penciled outlines of the letters that had been painted, not stenciled, on the life ring. He also pointed out that the vessel's name should appear on only one side, not both. The ring was a fake.[8]

American newspapers reported the find on 2 October under banner headlines claiming that a ring with the name *Bremen* stenciled on it was found on "an Atlantic beach" near Cape Elizabeth, Maine.

Quartermaster Martinson's observations were not immediately reported. The story was picked up by Reuters and read in Germany, and the following day German naval intelligence sent a telegram to an agent in New Jersey. Sent through the German Ocean Navigation Company, signed by Spötter, the message said:

RING REPORTED DOES NOT BELONG TO STAPEL HIS PROPERTY BEARING NO INITIALS WHATSOEVER STOP HAVE YOU ANY NEWS ABOUT LUGGAGE[9]

The reference to the ring and initials said that the Germans knew the discovery was a fake. But they were hoping that the agent might have some word about wreckage—the luggage referred to in the message. There was none.

Three days later a German agent in Holland picked up a rumor that the *Bremen* had been captured in nets off the British coast and was now in an unnamed harbor. According to the agent's source, the life ring found near Cape Elizabeth had been planted there by British agents to hide the *Bremen*'s true fate. The report reached Berlin on 20 October.[10]

On 25 October a German agent in Amsterdam reported that the British naval attaché in the Hague was telling everyone that the *Bremen* was carrying provisions for U-boats. When those provisions had been distributed, she was to enter a United States port as a merchant ship to pick up cargo. But the Royal Navy had interfered with that plan, and the *Bremen* was forced to put about and return to Germany.[11] As with most of the reports the Germans were getting, there was a circumstance that appeared to give some credibility to the report.

On 21 September, six days after the *Bremen* was scheduled to arrive in New London, the *U-53* left Wilhelmshaven. She had been ordered to proceed to the area off New London, as a demonstration that German war boats could, if necessary, operate off the East Coast of the United States. It was a none too subtle warning and was recognized as such. But the *U-53* was also there to cover the *Bremen*'s exit when she crossed the three-mile limit on her trip home by attacking any enemy warship waiting outside.[12]

By the time the *U-53* left on her mission, the *Bremen* was already overdue, but there was no way to recall the war boat. At 1400 on 7 October 1916, the United States submarine *D-2* spotted the *U-53* three miles east of Point Judith, standing toward Newport, Rhode Island.

The *D-2* flashed a sighting report, and took up a position paralleling the German.

At the Brenton Reef Lightship, the *U-53*'s skipper, Kapitänleutnant Hans Rose, hailed the *D-2*, requesting permission to enter port. Permission was granted, and the U-boat was assigned Berth No. 1.[13]

Rose told the surprised Americans that he had just stopped by to pay his respects. He needed no supplies or assistance, and would be gone by 1800 that day. In the meantime, Captain Rose invited any American officer who wanted to see the *U-53* to come aboard. Several did.[14]

During the three hours the U-boat was in Newport, her captain managed to give an American journalist a letter addressed to Count von Bernstorff. The newspaperman mailed it, and in a similar way Rose was informed by the German Embassy that the *Bremen* was now considered missing. The *U-53* was ordered to return home.[15]

On the way home she sank five steamers off the American coast—three British, one Norwegian, and one Dutch. The Americans were outraged, but the lesson was clear. The fact that a German U-boat could reach the United States coast was not surprising. But many experts questioned if the *U-53* type could carry out operations there and still make it back to Germany. Those who doubted it believed that a supply ship would be necessary to make such operations possible. And the ideal supply ship was the *Bremen*.

That was not the case and the Germans knew it. But the suggestion was logical and the timing was right. Maybe the *Bremen* had run into a British squadron sent out to thwart an imagined resupply attempt. If that were true, she might have turned back and be on her way home. The Germans knew that was a very long shot, but they hoped. They decided to wait until the end of October. If the *Bremen* did not return by then, they would assume she was lost with all hands.

The German attaché in Stockholm heard that the British had sunk the *Bremen* in mid-October. According to the story, the British were keeping it secret because of the boat's popularity, and the adverse affect the news would have on American opinion.[16] But the most persistent rumors said that the boat had been captured and was in a British port. Those rumors continued until June 1917, and many were attributed to statements made by well-known people.

In December 1916 Lord Robert Cecil told Norwegian friends that the boat had been trapped in nets and was at Leith.[17] In January 1917 a German agent in Stockholm sent the same report, attributing it to an English engineer.[18] That same month the *Bremen* was reported in Chatham, having been towed there from Liverpool. She was also somewhere on the Avon and at Newcastle.[19]

The Germans discounted most of the reports. But from March to June 1917 they received a series of reports that they took more seriously. The first came from a German navy officer and was addressed to Alfred Lohmann.

The officer was working for naval intelligence in Norway. One of his contacts, a seaman on a freighter that made regular trips to Britain, said that the *Bremen* had been captured. So what else was new? The British had found twenty thousand cans of Salvarsan among the *Bremen*'s cargo.[20] That was new.

The *Bremen*'s cargo manifest was a closely guarded secret, though it was possible that it had been leaked. In addition to dyestuffs, the U-boat had been carrying pharmaceuticals, including Salvarsan. A form of arsenic used in the treatment of syphilis, Salvarsan was in demand throughout the world. The fact that the British had obtained an enormous supply would be news in any port, which explained how a common seaman would hear about it.

The report seemed credible to the Germans. How else would the British know that the *Bremen* carried Salvarsan unless they had captured the boat? The only thing about the report that did not fit was the amount reported seized. The *Bremen* had carried 32,500 cans of Salvarsan.[21] What had happened to the rest? That question opened up a whole new area of speculation.

Three weeks later a Swiss businessman had lunch with the British military attaché in Kopenhagen. The officer confided to his host that the *Bremen* was in Falmouth and that there were two survivors from the crew. They were being closely guarded and were not allowed any communication with the outside world. The businessman passed the information on to the Germans.[22]

Four weeks later, on 27 April, a German agent in England passed word back to Germany that the *Bremen* had been in Shirehampton Bay. Agent W.29c, considered very reliable, had gotten his information from a British sailor who had seen the boat supported between two wooden floats. The boat had been moved to another location sometime in March.[23]

Then on 23 May 1917, Marquis Cortina told a German agent in Madrid that he had just returned from England where he had gone aboard the captured *Bremen*. In June two more foreigners said they had seen the boat. An American claimed to have seen it in a Bristol dry dock, and a Swiss businessman said that he had seen it on display in London.[24]

According to the Swiss businessman, forty captured U-boats were on display, but were surrounded by a mesh fence that kept the crowd back a considerable distance. Each boat was identified by a large sign, and one of the signs bore the name *Bremen.*

The businessman's story was full of holes, the largest one being that by 1917 the British had not captured forty German U-boats. The Germans knew that they had lost sixty-three boats by the end of May 1917, but there was no way the British could have forty of them on display.[25] The display, if in fact one existed, was obviously a fake. There were too many contradictions and improbables in the story to make it acceptable to the Germans, but they could not be sure.

What happened to the *Bremen?* Was she captured, was she sunk, or did she suffer an accident? She probably was not captured. Keeping something like that a secret for more than seventy years would be nearly impossible, and there has never been any documentary evidence to support the claim. She may have been sunk by the Royal Navy, but probably not. There is a report that one of the Tenth Cruiser Squadron's ships struck a large underwater object off Iceland.[26] Time and location are about right, but again no documentary evidence has been found to support the claim. In fact, there is nothing in the available Admiralty records to suggest that the *Bremen* was lost as a result of action—intentional or accidental—by the Royal Navy.

Paul König said after the war that he doubted she had struck a mine. Had that happened, he said, there would have been at least some debris washed ashore. So what happened?

The most likely answer is a diving accident, and that is the official German explanation. The *Deutschland* had experienced a near disaster on her first trip to the United States when she made an uncontrolled dive and struck the bottom. The fact that she hit bottom probably saved her, since she would otherwise have gone deeper than the depth for which her hull was rated.

A similar thing happened to the *U-22* on 19 April 1915. She was taking the northern route, the same route used by the *Deutschland* and the *Bremen,* when suddenly her lookout spotted an auxiliary cruiser bearing down on them. The sky was heavily overcast and a big sea was running when the dive alarm sounded, and the crew ran to diving stations. If the term had been coined in 1915, the skipper would have yelled "crash dive!" Instead he shouted, "Auxiliary cruiser very close, as quickly as possible and with all power dive." A rather bulky command, but one that got everyone's attention.[27]

Tons of water flooding her ballast tanks, her bow planes angled down, and her twin AEG electric motors driving her forward, the *U-22* struggled to get under. Time after time, she was pitched up, causing her skipper to order more down angle on the bow planes. The men in the command central held their breath and prayed as they willed the needle on the depth gauge to move. Finally the boat started to sink slowly, the needle moving to 8, then 10, then 15 meters. Suddenly she pitched forward and shot toward the bottom.

In the control central it was reported that the bow planes were jammed in the hard-down position and could not be moved. The depth gauge showed seventy meters, and the bow was angling down more steeply. The boat was already 20 meters past its depth limit.

"Blow ballast!" the skipper ordered, desperate to halt the descent. Already rivets were starting to explode from the hull, whipping across the interior like bullets, splattering on the other side. Water spurted through the tiny openings. Slowly the boat slowed, the down angle eased, and she started up.

But now her ascent was uncontrolled. As she rose, she gained speed, until she literally erupted through the surface like a giant whale. The situation was critical. On the surface she was easy meat for the cruiser that she had just tried to escape. Again the ballast tanks were flooded and the U-boat plunged beneath the surface.

The bow planes were still jammed, and the bow was angled down sharply. But the rate of descent was much slower. Still, they could not get her to level off, and now the chief engineer reported a new problem. The batteries were spilling because of the sharp down angle, and chlorine gas was forming inside the boat. They had to surface.

Once more the *U-22* shot to the surface, this time to stay. As her conning tower broke surface, the hatch was thrown open, and the gun crew spilled out to man the deck gun. To their immense relief they found themselves wrapped in dense fog.

Discussing the problem later, the officers concluded that in their haste to dive, the forward tanks were flooded more quickly than the after tanks. Combined with the thrust of the propellers at full power, and the violent motion of the boat in the heavy seas, the difference in weight forced the bow down too sharply. That imparted an excessive dynamic load on the bow planes that jammed them hard down.

The circumstances that confronted the *U-22* were remarkably similar to those that confronted the *Deutschland* fourteen months later. The sea was rough, the boat was a poor diver even under good conditions, and they were threatened by an enemy warship. Even the location off Scotland's west coast was the same. Not surprisingly, their reaction to the threat, a crash dive, and the results were almost the same in both cases.

It is probable that the *Bremen* ran into the same set of circumstances, in about the same area, and reacted the same way. In her case she probably did not hit bottom before she had passed her depth limit like the *Deutschland*, and she was not able to recover in time like the *U-22*.

Or was she running on the surface with her hatches open when she was suddenly hit by a freak wave? Partially swamped, without power, and tons of water pouring through the open hatches, she might have gone down quickly. Whatever happened to the *Bremen*, her loss materially dampened the world's enthusiasm for commercial submarines.

CHAPTER ELEVEN

THE LAYOVER,

26 AUGUST–8 OCTOBER 1916

August Götze sat at the kitchen table fingering the letter for the twentieth time, finally putting it down and picking up a small photograph that had been enclosed with the letter. The photograph showed a soldier standing in front of a ruined building, apparently a farmhouse of some kind, the ground around his feet rough and littered with chunks of torn metal. A pole, maybe a telephone pole, lay at an angle across one corner of the demolished building.

"What's for dinner?" he asked in a low voice. He seemed disinterested in the answer that he knew was coming. It had been the same for the last several weeks.

"*Eintopf*," his wife answered, stirring a large, steaming pot.

August Götze just snorted. *Eintopf.* Cabbage, potatoes, turnips, and anything else they could get to throw in the pot. Largely tasteless except for the lone chunk of fatty bacon used to flavor the mess. He put the picture down and picked up an unopened envelope. He was a fiercely patriotic man, a good German who believed in the kaiser and the righteousness of the cause. But he was having his doubts. He turned the envelope over.

His shirt sleeves were rolled up exposing thick, muscular forearms, his collar was open, and his vest was unbuttoned. He stared at the letter while reaching for the beer bottle to his right, pulled the beer to him, and took a drink. Even the beer was weak and watery.

August was tired, physically tired. He had lost track of how long the Spandau plant had been working ten-hour shifts, six days a week.

It seemed forever. They were turning out machine guns by the hundreds, but it was never enough. It seemed that the longer they worked, the more guns they built, the smaller the food ration got. He was always hungry.

The army had said that the war would be over by Christmas. That had been two Christmases ago and there was still no end in sight. Victory was always just over the hill, around the corner, or hidden somewhere else. And now this.

The address on the letter had been written by August himself. He recognized it, he remembered doing it. It was addressed to his brother Alfred on the Western Front. But the letter had come back, arriving the same day as one written by Alfred to him. August looked at the envelope again, feeling the eternity expressed in the rubber-stamped message across the front. FÜR KAISER UND VATERLAND GEFALLEN. A gloriously noble way of saying killed in action. When will it all end? August asked himself.[1]

Since January 1916, many Germans had been asking the same questions, feeling the same doubts as August Götze. They were starting to show signs of war weariness brought on by a deteriorating economy, painful food shortages, and astronomically high casualty lists. The winter of 1916–17 would be known forever as the "Turnip Winter," named for the one staple that became the backbone of the German diet. And the rubber stamp FÜR KAISER UND VATERLAND GEFALLEN became as common as the postage stamp.

Throughout 1916 conditions in Germany were grim. The British blockade was proving to be very effective, its effect slow, but the inevitable outcome already apparent. The bread ration had been cut 35 percent from the 1915 allowance.[2] There was a terrible shortage of meat, dairy products, and grains. Long lines, exorbitant prices, and a flourishing black market had to be accepted as a part of one's everyday life.

There was a popular, bitter, joke about a butcher who had a surprisingly plentiful supply of *Wurst,* a cheap German sausage. Instead of scarce pork and beef, the butcher made his *Wurst* from rabbit—an unusual, but under the circumstances an acceptable, substitute. The question was: where did he get all those rabbits?

He was asked that question by his competitors, whose shelves were empty.

"Actually," he said, "the *Wurst* isn't just rabbit. I cut it one to one with horse meat."

"One to one!" exclaimed his competitors.

"Sure," explained the butcher. "One horse to one rabbit."

The bitterness of the joke stemmed, in part, from the inequity of food distribution. While workers went hungry and made do with barely acceptable substitutes, the wealthy continued to dine in prewar style. To be sure, the wealthy also were affected by shortages, but the shortages were relatively few. Butter, eggs, and meat were being brought in from Norway, Denmark, and Sweden. The amounts were not large, the prices were high, and almost none of those items reached the workers' tables.

Fearing a collapse of public support, General Erich von Falkenhayn sought a quick resolution to the war. But it was a resolution predicated on a total German victory, with no room for negotiation. How did he hope to achieve in 1916 what had eluded them in 1914 and 1915? The answer was at Verdun.

Unable to get at the British fleet and unable to cut Britain's transatlantic supply lines, the Germans decided to "break Britain's continental sword, France." The plan was to beat the French at Verdun so badly that they would withdraw from the war. Britain would then be forced to negotiate a peace on German terms.

On 21 February 1916, while the *Deutschland* was being built and her officers trained, the Germans opened their offensive at Verdun. Their attempt to roll over the French failed. By 21 July the Germans had gone over to the defensive and the French were counterattacking. The carnage finally ended on 18 December at a cost of nearly a million and a quarter casualties. Absolutely nothing had been accomplished.

Just nine days before the Germans went to the defensive at Verdun, and while the *Deutschland* was approaching Baltimore, the British opened their offensive at the Somme. Like the battle being fought at Verdun, the Somme offensive was also a bloodbath, costing the British sixty thousand men in one day. By the time the battle collapsed in the rain and mud on 18 November, another million casualties had been added to the lists. The result was a nine-mile gain of no strategic importance.

While the butchery at Verdun and the Somme ate up German youth without any prospect of ending the war, and while the *Deutschland* was in Baltimore, the uneasy relationship between Chancellor Bethmann-Hollweg and General von Falkenhayn was reaching the breaking point. By the time the *Deutschland* returned from her first trip to the United States, the relationship was over and Bethmann-Hollweg decided that Falkenhayn had to go. The chancellor needed a reliable chief of the General Staff who would support him in his campaign for a negotiated peace. But as he was working to undo General von Falkenhayn, the chancellor's adversaries were working to undo him.

In the middle was the kaiser, a weak, ineffective monarch who was unable to grasp the true meaning of the situation. The one thing he could do was protect his chancellor. And he did. But even that relationship was wearing thin, though in August 1916 the relationship was still strong enough for Bethmann-Hollweg to replace General von Falkenhayn with General, soon to be Field Marshall, Paul von Beneck-endorff und Hindenburg. The change in command took place on 29 August 1916, and Bethmann-Hollweg came away from the cere-mony in a state of ecstasy.[3] In just a few days he realized that he had made a terrible mistake.

General von Hindenburg, who had been enormously successful on the Eastern Front, enjoyed the peoples' trust and had not made any public statements about his position on peace with or without concessions. He seemed to be the man the country needed to pull itself together and end the war on an honorable basis.

But General von Hindenburg brought with him General Erich von Ludendorff, a man who has been described as "irritable and brutal and in the subtleties of life as inexperienced as a child."[4] He was nonetheless a brilliant tactician, both in war and politics, and a man for whom victory was an all-or-nothing matter. Like the chanting crowd on the banks of the Weser, General von Ludendorff was a precursor of the events of 1933–45. And he, not Hindenburg, was the real power in Germany.

The day following the appointment of the von Hindenburg-von Ludendorff team, a meeting was held at the Supreme Imperial Head-quarters at Pless to discuss the future conduct of the war. At the top of the agenda was what to do about Romania's entry into the war. The Romanians' declaration of war on Austria-Hungary on 27 August had introduced a military situation that had to be cleaned up as quickly as possible.

Chief of the Naval Staff Admiral von Holtzendorff immediately recommended the resumption of unrestricted U-boat warfare. Citing many of the same figures presented in 1915, the admiral said that the war could be ended in six months. The foreign minister and the secretary of state argued that the navy's figures were misleading, and the consequences of following the navy's recommendation would be catastrophic. Bethmann-Hollweg supported his fellow diplomats.

No decision was reached. Instead, the matter was tabled until the Romanian situation was cleared up, after which the decision for or against an unrestricted U-boat campaign would be made by von Hindenburg. The diplomats were still in control, but by a very slim margin.

What was the *Deutschland*'s role in those events? Her biggest role, not evident at the time, was as an indicator of who was in control: the civilians or the military. For so long as Bethmann-Hollweg could stave off the navy's intention to launch a new unrestricted U-boat campaign, the *Deutschland* would continue in her merchantman role. But once the navy got the upper hand, the *Deutschland* would change her appearance to that of a war boat.

While those events were taking place, the *Deutschland* was being prepared for a second trip to America. The fact that she continued to make preparations for a second trip reflected the outcome of the 30 August meeting at Pless. But first she had to go from Bremen to Kiel for unexplained repairs.

Alfred Lohmann told the navy that the fact that she had to make the trip in a nondiving condition posed no threat. Still, he requested extra navy escort, and asked to meet with a navy representative in Berlin to discuss the matter. What was said was not recorded.[5]

But the purpose of a passenger aboard the *Deutschland* during her trip to Kiel was recorded. Dr. Ernst Bischof, a member of the signals section of the Foreign Office, was to take advantage of the opportunity to further interview Captain König for the book he was ghostwriting under König's name.[6]

The *Deutschland* departed Bremen on Monday, 4 September, under close escort, and proceeded to Kiel via the North Sea Canal. Combined with the material provided by the navy, newspaper accounts, and two lengthy interviews with Paul König, Doctor Bischof had the book ready by the end of September. Two editions were published, one in English and one in German.

The English, or more accurately the American, edition was heavily slanted toward American readers. Even the photographs were different from what appeared in the German edition. Like Doctor Lohmann's speech in Bremen, the American edition played heavily on American sympathies and British perfidy. The German edition, however, played up the nationalist theme and offered the *Deutschland* as the answer to the British blockade. The German edition was available in Germany in September, and the American edition, in manuscript form, was shipped to the Hearst Syndicate aboard the *Deutschland* on her second trip to the United States.

The statements made at the *Deutschland*'s reception in Bremen, and the publication of the book, opened another propaganda front. In a widely publicized note, the American fishing boats that had signaled the U-boat's movement to the Allied warships off the Capes became the subject of an official protest to the United States.

On 7 September 1916, the State Department launched a "quiet investigation" into the charges that American fishing boats had aided the British in August.[7] Several government agencies, private firms, and fishing interests were contacted. The Association of Maryland Pilots reported that their people had seen "no unusual activity in reference to small craft and fishing boats ... but at the same time fishing steamers were about."[8] The German Ocean Navigation Company told the State Department investigators, "we have not succeeded in finding out anything definite."[9]

Special Deputy Collector N. A. Ryan (William P. Ryan's assistant) told the State Department that:

> The Menhaden Fisheries are famous in Virginia and have headquarters at Reedville where there is centered a large fishing fleet. The fishermen use very large nets to gather schools of fish. ... Fishing boats in the waters of the three-mile limit would, therefore, be the usual condition at the time of the *Deutschland*'s departure.[10]

It remained for the local fishermen—the prime suspects—to be more specific.[11] And they were. The fishermen told the State Department investigators that the boats in question were from Halifax, Nova Scotia. That made sense. Essentially British vessels, the Nova Scotia fishermen had both the motive for helping the British and a legitimate reason for being off the Virginia Capes. The State Department was satisfied with that explanation, but they had one more base to cover, just in case.

They asked the Neutrality Board for an opinion about whether or not America's neutrality would have been violated *if* American fishing vessels had aided the British. The Neutrality Board issued a long-winded statement that said "no."[12] Happy to be off the hook, the State Department passed its findings on to the Germans, who accepted them without comment.

But the Germans were not reassured. Everywhere they looked

they saw a threat. And some of the threats were real, though most were just rumor. One rumor that really worried them originated in the United States.

The rumor was started by W. A. Edwards, vice president of the Edwards Company, a wholesale fish company in Reedville, Virginia. In a telephone call to the Baltimore office of A. Schumacher and Company, Edwards told Captain Hinsch that a Baltimore firm had sold unusually large fishing nets to a group of Baltimore fishermen. Edwards said that he had confirmed the order by calling the Baltimore company that supplied the nets. It was his opinion that the nets were to be used to trap the *Deutschland*.[13]

Hard on the heels of the warning about nets came a rumor that the Americans were planning to seize the next cargo U-boat that arrived in the United States. That would be the *Bremen,* not yet reported overdue at the time the rumor was started. According to the rumor, the Americans were going to impound the vessel for lacking sufficient lifeboats and having inadequate ventilation.[14]

The rumor was unsupported by any documentation, but it was a possibility. Count von Bernstorff, the German ambassador to the United States, was asked about it. In a lengthy report, he described the tremendous feeling of goodwill that the *Deutschland*'s visit had created. He was particularly impressed with the cooperation the Germans had gotten from the American government and the navy, and on that basis he discounted the rumor.[15]

German suspicions about American intentions were matched by many Americans' suspicions about the *Deutschland*'s real mission. The big submarine's reported ability to make a round trip without refueling had been widely publicized in the United States. In fact, it was even claimed that the boat could make the round trip and still have fuel to spare. That and her large cargo capacity were recognized by many people as the ideal combination for a U-boat supply ship. And they were right.

While the *Deutschland* was in Baltimore, Captain König had often said that he had plenty of fuel for the return trip. But before the U-boat sailed, she was refueled from two railroad tank cars that had been rolled out onto the pier. If she had enough fuel to get home, why buy more? It was a question that lots of people asked.

In answer to the question, Captain König said that the diesel fuel available in the United States was much superior to what was available in Germany. And he wanted a load of the best for the trip home. It was a good answer, and probably true. But people did notice that despite the high praise for the quality of American diesel fuel, the *Deutschland*'s engineers carefully tested the fuel for signs of sabotage before running it through fine strainers and into the bunkers.

Most people believed the captain's explanation, but many wondered what the Germans were going to do with all that extra fuel when the *Deutschland* reached Germany. Probably pump it into an outbound war boat was the most common assumption. And they were probably right. From that low-grade suspicion it was an easy step to the idea that the *Deutschland* was actually a seagoing gas station.

C. W. Taintor, a Boston resident, put the question to the Department of State on 13 October:[16]

> I would respectfully ask if you think there is any possibility of the U-boat *Deutschland* being a mother ship for the *U-53* and the *U-61,* and the notice that she has returned to Germany and is to make a second trip is a masquerade to fool the American people?

He was closer to the truth than he knew.

Six weeks earlier a Professor Doctor Falk had suggested to the German navy that the *Deutschland* be used as bait on her next trip to the United States. The idea was to cover the exit from the American port with a wolf pack that would torpedo any Allied cruisers waiting off the coast. The professor suggested that after the cruisers were sunk, the *Deutschland* could refuel the wolf-pack boats with fuel obtained while she was in port. The plan was surprisingly similar to one already in effect for cooperation between the *Bremen* and the *U-53.*[17]

Suspicious of everyone, the Germans were very security conscious, and from the beginning everything about the *Deutschland* was kept under wraps. Most of the security precautions were necessary under wartime conditions, but some were overdone. For some reason, never explained, information about the cargo and the people to whom it was cosigned was classified GANZ GEHEIM; top secret. In fact, when the *Deutschland* departed from Bremen on her first trip, the Germans had convinced the American consul, Thomas Fee, not to tell his government.

That may have been cooperation on a personal level. But what happened in Baltimore was the type of cooperation at the government level that Count von Bernstorff had described in his report. In a letter to William P. Ryan, a State Department officer wrote:

In accordance with the advice of the Secretary of State and the Secretary of Commerce, the details of the cargo of the German merchant submarine *Deutschland* should not be furnished to the public until a reasonable period after clearance has elapsed. The Department regards thirty days as a reasonable period, but if the consignors should desire a longer period fixed, the Department will give due consideration to their request.[18]

What was there about legitimate cargo that warranted that degree of security? The answer is, nothing except unbounded paranoia. The Americans knew that, but were being careful not to appear unneutral.

The situation became more ridiculous as the departure date for the second trip approached. On 29 September, the American consul general in Dresden informed Washington that he had certified an invoice for chemicals to be carried aboard the *Deutschland*. American representatives throughout Germany were doing the same thing, especially Thomas Fee who had been righteously crushed for his earlier lapse.[19]

At the same time, Alfred Lohmann was sending a flood of telegrams to A. Schumacher and Company describing cargo that would be delivered and cargo to be picked up. The messages were sometimes coded, but often not. The point is that the British read them all.

But whatever damage might be caused by the British knowing the telegrams' contents was small compared to the delays caused by the overdone German security. Lohmann had to first submit the text of each telegram to the German censors, who deleted much of the information that the recipients needed to know. That and the normal bureaucratic delays finally drove the man to despair. In a strongly worded letter to the navy, he said:

I cannot understand the secrecy in regard to the cargo. The Swedish company that provides our insurance will not insure the cargo if they do not know what it is. We have to tell them. We have to tell the various American Consuls whose districts provide the cargo, and, in turn, they report to their government. Once the boat reaches the United States the manifest is made public. So why the secrecy?[20]

Documents related to the cargo continued to be stamped, GANZ GEHEIM.

There was, however, one item to be carried aboard the *Deutschland* about which secrecy was absolutely necessary. It was the new diplomatic code book to be delivered to Ambassador von Bernstorff in Washington. In order to protect it from discovery by United States customs officials, the book was placed in the sealed diplomatic pouch. Lieutenant Krapohl was the only man aboard the *Deutschland* who was authorized to deliver the pouch to the German ambassador.[21]

The new code, designated 0075, was intended to replace the old diplomatic code 13040. Unknown to the Germans, the British had broken 13040 sometime in 1915, and many messages sent by post with neutral carriers had been intercepted and read by the British. The new code would temporarily prevent the British from reading some of the Germans' diplomatic mail. But only some.

For some reason only one copy of 0075 was sent to von Bernstorff. He could use the new code to communicate with Berlin, but communications with the Mexican, Central American, and South American stations had to be done in 13040.[22] The groundwork for America's entry into World War I had been laid.

By 1 October, the insurance problems had been resolved, the *Deutschland* was fully loaded, and the Eastern Forwarding Company had been notified to expect her. Aided by a tug, the U-boat had just backed away from her pier and was starting to turn downriver, when the tug rammed her just forward of the conning tower on the port side. The damage was not serious, but some hull plates were started, and the *Deutschland* had to return to her berth.[23]

Alfred Lohmann sent a telegram to Berlin saying that there would be a forty-eight hour delay "due to trivial damage." But the damage was too serious to be repaired in Bremen, and the boat was sent to Wilhelmshaven. Lohmann's optimistic estimate proved to be too optimistic. It was a week before she was again ready.

In the meantime, Alfred Lohmann asked the navy for stronger escort to accompany the *Deutschland* as she headed north. He was increasingly concerned about the boat's safety since the loss of the *Bremen*, which he attributed to the Tenth Cruiser Squadron. He was sure they had sunk her near Iceland. He was not expecting the navy to escort the *Deutschland* that far, but he wanted her protected as far north as possible.[24] The navy added two torpedo boats to the escort, but authorized escort only so far as the regular outpost line.

Because the *Deutschland* had gone to Wilhelmshaven fully loaded with cargo, there was no need for her to return to Bremen in order to depart for America. On 8 October Wilhelmshaven notified Berlin by radio: COMMERCIAL U-BOAT DEUTSCHLAND DEPARTED JADE NORTH AT 11:00 A.M.[25] In London a naval intelligence officer flipped open a copy of the *Signalbuch der Kaiserlichen Marine* (SKM), and decoded the message.[26]

CHAPTER TWELVE

THE SECOND CROSSING,

8 OCTOBER–1 NOVEMBER 1916

Franz Krapohl ducked behind the steel rim of the conning tower to avoid the wall of water that bore down on the *Deutschland*. The huge wave exploded against the conning tower, the vertical column curling and collapsing in a deluge over Krapohl and the seaman next to him. The U-boat heaved up onto the next wave, hesitated, and plunged down into the trough. Krapohl and the seaman hung on. Water swirled around their knees, pouring through the scuppers that ringed the conning tower deck. Krapohl peered into the gloomy space between the heaving sea and the lead gray sky. He saw nothing.

Another wave swept across the main deck, smaller than its predecessor, and streamed past both sides of the conning tower. Krapohl counted the waves. Right on schedule the seventh wave rose up ahead of them, a towering wall of water, white-crested at the top, gray beards streaming toward them in the strong gale. The *Deutschland* tried to lift to meet the wave, failed, and slammed into it. The bow disappeared under tons of black-green water, and Krapohl noted that the top of the wave was still higher than the rim of the conning tower. He held his breath, hung on, and ducked.[1]

It had been blowing a gale since the U-boat left Bremerhaven, and the escort provided by the navy, four torpedo boats, had been too busy surviving to guard against the British fleet. Krapohl had watched them rolling heavily as they plowed through the mountainous seas, certain that the *Deutschland* would soon have to come about and pick up survivors. But they did not, and when they reached the outpost line and the torpedo boats turned back, Krapohl was glad to see them go.

Battling the southwesterly gales, the *Deutschland* had slugged her way across the North Sea, reaching the Orkneys in three and a half days. But the storm had at least one good point—British patrol boats and auxiliary cruisers were too busy just staying afloat to bother with the *Deutschland*. Nevertheless, she had been forced to dive twice. She went under off Fair Island after nearly running into a trawler, and again when she passed under the patrol line off the Butt of Lewis.[2]

Krapohl looked at his watch. It was nearly time for Eyring to relieve him, but Krapohl was not sure he wanted to be relieved. The *Deutschland* was buttoned up tighter than a drum, and the temperature below was up around 100° F. The moist air, filled with the disgusting odors of human sweat, excrement, and vomit, made even the strongest stomach turn. Publicly, Captain König spoke highly of the *Deutschland*'s seakeeping qualities. But the truth was another matter.

She was an awful sea boat. She rolled like a bottle, was almost impossible to get under in a really heavy sea, and ventilation was almost nil. Clothing mildewed, mold formed on the bulkheads, and the men had no water for bathing. Krapohl laughed at the fanciful suggestions made by American reporters that the U-boat might carry passengers. Three days in the *Deutschland* and the passenger would happily opt for an open boat and a pair of oars.

There was a pounding on the hatch at his feet. Krapohl gauged the seas, waited for the next huge wave to pass over them, and stamped on the hatch. It was the signal for Eyring to open it and scramble on deck. In a flash, Eyring and a seaman were through the hatch, which was slammed shut behind them. Jammed in the narrow space atop the conning tower, the four men quickly exchanged information. Krapohl gave the Zeiss binoculars to Eyring and the watch was officially re-lieved. Now all they had to do was wait for an opportunity to open the hatch so that Krapohl and his companion could dive below.[3]

Another wave washed across the boat, the water poured from the conning tower, and the hatch was flung open. The seaman dropped through, hardly touching the ladder. Krapohl was right behind him. The hatch slammed shut.

Krapohl assumed his place in the command central, relieving Captain König, who left to inspect the ship. The lieutenant would stand a four-hour watch in the command central and then grab four hours' sleep. Then it was back to the conning tower for another wet four hours. Eyring was on the same schedule, and Klees stood watches in the engine room and on the conning tower. Only the captain was exempt from regular watch standing. But he had plenty to do.[4]

Captain König stood the noon to 1600 watch in the control central, and the midnight to 0400 watch. He was also atop the conning tower whenever the *Deutschland* left or entered port, sighted another ship, or was in sight of land. Whenever the boat was submerged he was in the command central. The rest of the time he prowled around the ship, checked the navigation, ate, and tried to sleep. The heavy seas had made the latter almost impossible. On the seventh day out, another problem associated with the heavy seas made sleep absolutely impossible.

The *Deutschland* was rolling badly, her crewmen being tossed from one side to the other. There were plenty of bruises, but luckily no broken bones or serious wounds. Suddenly there was a tremendous crash forward. The first impression was that the boat had hit something other than just a wave. But what? Then a second crash jarred the U-boat.

"Captain to central."

The call was unnecessary, König was already hurrying forward. As he did, another resounding thud rattled the hull. The captain stepped into the crowded central, and looked at Lieutenant Eyring for an explanation.

"The anchor has broken loose, sir," Eyring reported, his voice calm. "I have Humke and a party forward now trying to resecure it."

The bow pitched upward and the anchor crashed into the hull.

"Any damage reported?"

"Not yet, sir."

König nodded. "I'll be forward," he shouted, ducking his head as he stepped into the next compartment.

Captain König hurried through the narrow companionway that passed through the cargo hold, the officers' quarters, the crew quarters, past the spares locker, the forward diving plane motors and to the forepeak. As he entered the forward compartment he saw water in the bilges.

"The anchor's started some of the plates," Humke said. His report was accompanied by a falling sensation as the bow dropped into a deep trough. There was a deafening crash followed by a violent shudder, and almost immediately a heavy blow on the starboard side. "We'll have her under control just as soon as we get the cable brake repaired."

"How long will that take?"

"In this sea," Humke paused to consider, "maybe an hour." The bow plunged into another wave, slamming the anchor against the hull. "It's awful wet in there." He shouted, gesturing toward the forepeak. "And we're being tossed around like marbles in a box. There's nothing to hang on to." He was shouting to be heard.

König knelt to examine the plates over the bilge. Normally the steel hull below the plates was dry, but now there was water several inches deep. He examined the pressure hull at the forward transverse bulkhead. Water was seeping in along the seam. That was probably where the anchor was pounding the hull like a battering ram. Fortunately, most of the blows were being absorbed by the outer hull. He stood up.

"Get it done quickly," he said, and turned away.

As he made his way aft, he stopped and looked down at the deck. Beneath his feet were two huge batteries, each with one hundred and forty cells. If we get seawater back here, he thought, we will have a boat full of chlorine gas. Is that what happened to *Bremen?* Another bone-jarring crash caused him to cast a glance forward. Better hurry, Humke, he thought, and then turned toward the control central.[5]

Two hours later the anchor was again secured, but water still seeped through the started plates in the bow. The flow was easily handled by the pumps—so long as the *Deutschland* remained on the surface. But if she were forced to dive, the increased pressure would force water through the openings like a fire hose. And there was no chance to repair the damage in this storm.

The storm continued for four days. Several times Captain König wished he could dive to escape the relentless pounding, an idea every member of the crew heartily endorsed. But the damaged bow prevented that, and, in any event, the seas were so rough that König doubted the *Deutschland* could safely submerge even if her bow were not damaged. To ease the rolling and pounding, he ordered the U-boat slowed to where they could just maintain steerage.

On 21 October, the storm passed and the seas began to settle down. The sky cleared, allowing the captain the first opportunity in five days to fix his position. He was shocked. Since 16 October, the *Deutschland* had made good just one mile.

For the next ten days, the *Deutschland* charged ahead at full speed, trying to make the lost time. She had left Germany with one hundred and fifty tons of fuel and needed only about half of that to reach the United States. Knowing that he could buy more in New London, Captain König was not terribly concerned about fuel economy at that point. What he was concerned about was the damage to the *Deutschland*'s bow. That had to be repaired before he reached the United States coast, where he planned to dive and wait for dark before going in.

Chief Engineer Klees and Boatswain Humke worked around the clock to repair the damage, the captain standing Klees's conning tower watches. By 26 October the temporary repairs were completed, the flooding was stopped, and the bilges were dry. But would the patches hold when the U-boat dove? Five days later they got the answer.

On 31 October, at 1500, Captain König spotted the American coast through the haze. Swinging his glasses along the horizon to his right he saw a large ship with four funnels proceeding out to sea. The ship was too far away to identify, but he assumed it was a British cruiser. He watched the ship to be sure she was heading away from the *Deutschland* and then turned his attention back to the coast.

His experience upon leaving Baltimore had made him doubly cautious. He was certain that if the British suspected he was off the coast, there would be fishing boats waiting to call down the cruisers on him. In fact, the British did know he was there, and had already told the American press that the *Deutschland* was due to arrive in New London on 1 November.[6]

Apparently, Captain Hinsch and the other members of the Eastern Forwarding Company either did not read the papers or did not believe what they read. Because the *T. A. Scott Jr.*, a tug they had leased, had been recalled from her position offshore a week earlier. No one, not even the Germans, waited for the *Deutschland*.

At 1600 the captain cleared the bridge. Taking a last look around he pressed the klaxon alarm and dropped through the hatch. The *Deutschland* slid beneath the surface and turned south toward the entrance to Long Island Sound.

It was dark when she surfaced and Captain König, aided only by a chart published in 1860, entered the Sound without a pilot.[7] Apparently his concern about Americans being in the service of the British extended to the harbor pilots, a concern that very nearly brought the second voyage to an abrupt end.

Just before midnight the river dredge *Atlantic* was proceeding down the Sound as the *Deutschland* was proceeding up. Both ships were displaying the proper lights, but the U-boat's navigation lights were so low on the water that the dredge's skipper had a hard time recognizing them. He could faintly see the U-boat's green starboard light, which told him that the *Deutschland* was passing across his bow from left to right. The dredge had the right of way, but there was no problem because the crossing vessel was moving fast enough to clear the dredge. At least that is how it looked to the dredge's skipper.

Captain König saw and recognized the lights on the dredge. But he interpreted them to mean that the oncoming vessel would pass him port side to. But the pass would be close. Maybe too close. In his mind, prudent seamanship dictated that something be done to avoid an obviously dangerous passing situation, and Captain König ordered the *Deutschland* to change course slightly to the right. That would take him well clear of the oncoming vessel, or so he thought.

When the U-boat made her slight turn to the right, both her running lights came into clear view. The dredge skipper suddenly realized he was looking right up the keel line of an oncoming vessel. Sounding one short blast, he spun the helm right.

The deep blast of the dredge's horn came just as König realized what was really happening. He was looking at the broad bow of an enormous dredge bearing down on him.

"Hard astarboard! Ahead full!" he shouted into the voice tube as his hand reached for the horn. The *Deutschland*'s higher-pitched horn sounded one short blast as her bow swung right.

"Close the hatch," he shouted to the seaman on watch, his hand already on the collision alarm. The man slammed the hatch shut, spinning the wheel to dog it down tight. If they were rammed König did not want any open hatches to add to the flooding. As the two vessels bore down on each other he shouted down the voice tube, "Close watertight doors," and pressed the collision alarm.

Inside the U-boat twenty-seven men and officers felt their stomachs knot. What the hell was going on? Four watertight doors slammed shut, sealing off the boat in five separate compartments. And then they waited.

The mate standing next to the dredge skipper gripped the brass rail that ran along the forward bulkhead of the bridge. "He's turning," he said.

"So are we, but it's gonna be close," the skipper said through clenched teeth. "Keep turning, you bastard, keep turning."

Gripping the edge of the conning tower, his arms straight and stiff, Captain König watched the angle on the bow grow. Both vessels were turning away from each other, but they were still closing. The

Deutschland's diesels were pounding as the U-boat gained speed and her rudder bit into the water. Never a particularly maneuverable boat, the *Deutschland* felt like a truck in sand.

"We're turning clear." The relief and jubilation in the lookout's voice was clearly evident.

Captain König said nothing. He was still rigidly gripping the edge of the conning tower when the two ships slid past each other, only a few feet apart.[8]

König was badly shaken. That had been a very near thing, the result of a stupid mistake. The collision with the tug in Bremen had been embarrassing, but at least it had not been his fault. This, on the other hand, would have been a disaster in every respect. He took a deep breath, thanked his lucky star, and looked for a place to anchor. Forty minutes later the *Deutschland* was anchored at the mouth of the Thames River.

In the meantime, the *Atlantic*'s skipper was also heaving a sigh of relief. He had recognized the other vessel as a submarine as she slid past so close he could have stepped aboard. But it was not an American boat. He saw plenty of those coming and going from the submarine base at New London. The boat he had nearly hit was too big to be an American. Then it dawned on him. That must have been that German boat, the *Deutschland.*

A few minutes after the near miss, the *Atlantic* came up to the Eastern Forwarding Company's small workboat, the *Efco*. She was apparently waiting for the *Deutschland* to arrive, but had not seen the U-boat go by. Either they were asleep or in the wrong place. The *Atlantic*'s skipper told the *Efco* about the U-boat, and the *Efco* sped off to investigate.[9]

At 0035 on 1 November, the *Efco* came alongside the anchored U-boat and put Captain Hinsch and Health Officer Walter Chipman aboard. Chipman inspected the boat, waived the usual quarantine regulations, and told Captain König to move his vessel to the State Pier.

At 0235, the *Deutschland* docked under her own power, and without assistance.[10]

CHAPTER THIRTEEN

NEW LONDON,

1–17 NOVEMBER 1916

A small crowd, not more than a hundred people, clustered along the railroad tracks that led onto the State Pier. It was a disappointed crowd. The people, mostly reporters, had come to get a look at the *Deutschland*. Instead, all they saw was a solid, corrugated-metal fence twenty feet high, above which protruded the *Willehad*'s funnel.

There was no high ground near enough to give the watchers a view over the fence, and no pile driver such as had been available in Baltimore. A few enterprising souls had used their pocket knives to bore holes in the fence to peek through, but that small success came to an abrupt and painful end when New London Police Department's "one-man strong-arm squad," Officer Nelson Smith, showed up just after 0800. But even if Officer Smith had not shown up, the hole-boring enterprise was doomed. From inside the already formidable fence came the sounds of hammering. The Eastern Forwarding Company was erecting another fence inside the first one.[1]

And chartering a boat to get a look from the water was also a waste of time. The *Deutschland* was enclosed in a box formed by the L-shaped State Pier, the steamer *Willehad,* and a twelve-foot-high floating fence. Outside the floating fence the *Efco* kept curious boaters at a distance, while inside an army of private guards kept an eye on the American workers. It would be interesting to know who was watching the guards.

The short leg of the L-shaped pier was formed by a large warehouse. The fence patrolled by Officer Smith ran parallel to that

This exceptional photo shows the brief glimpse the crowd got of the *Deutsch-land* every time the gate to the State Pier was opened. A wagon load of lumber is being delivered for construction of the interior fence. The *Willehad*'s funnel juts up above the fence. (National Archives)

building. The long side of the "L" was the three-hundred-foot pier to which the *Deutschland* was made fast. Another warehouse ran the full length of the pier.

At the point where the leg and the foot of the "L" joined was a huge double gate. It was there that the crowd gathered, because the hole borers had reaped an unexpected dividend. Having not antici-pated the need to build an inner fence, and having no building materials on hand, the Eastern Forwarding Company had to order boards and posts from a nearby lumberyard. But the large order required several wagon loads to fill, and every time a wagon arrived or departed, the gate was swung open, allowing the crowd a brief view of the big U-boat.

The Germans' insistence on security was understandable, but overdone. Keeping people off the pier and away from the *Deutschland* made sense because there was a real threat of sabotage by British agents or sympathizers. But denying people even a distant view of the boat was silly, and was due entirely to Captain Hinsch's loathing for the press. In fact, nearly all the security measures, especially those that protected the *Deutschland* from view, were directed at the press.

The press can be a pain in the neck under the best circumstances, and a huge pain if they put their minds to it. But one of the *Deutschland*'s primary roles was to develop American sympathy for Germany's efforts to break the British blockade. Therefore, maintaining good press relations should have been a high-priority item. But fences, armed guards, and open hostility did not accomplish that. As a result, the *Deutschland*'s second visit to the United States was characterized by bad press.

In all fairness to Captain Hinsch, not all the *Deutschland*'s bad press can be attributed to his attitude toward reporters. Many of the problems resulted from German insensitivity, and the first example cropped up on the day she arrived.

Early in the morning on 1 November a hand-picked crew of seventy-five black stevedores arrived from Baltimore, and were taken immediately to the State Pier where they started unloading the U-boat's cargo. Though the news did not appear in the nation's newspapers until the next day, it was the sole topic of conversation in New London that day.

Local white dockworkers, angry that the Germans had given their jobs to a bunch of black outsiders, were threatening violence. And local residents, convinced that their town was on the brink of a crime wave, were demanding to know why the Germans had brought in all those blacks. Looking back over seventy years, the incident is interesting because it shows how racism was taken as a matter of faith by all concerned.

The last thing the Germans wanted was a picket line across their gate, and an outraged community. But they needed those black stevedores, or so they thought. Clearly, something had to be done, and fast. The answer was a 1600 press conference held in the Mohican Hotel.

Speaking to a large and attentive crowd of reporters, Captain König explained that the blacks were the same crew that had been used to unload and load the cargo in Baltimore. They were hired in July and were being used again in November for security reasons. It was well known, the captain said, that blacks had little power of observation and were unlikely to recognize anything important. Even if they did, poor communications skills would prevent them from giving anyone an accurate description of what they had seen.

The crowd bought that explanation. And the local community was relieved to learn that the blacks would be working all day and most of the night, leaving them little time to wander the streets. As an additional security precaution, the stevedores would be berthed aboard the *Willehad.*

Faith is a powerful thing, and Captain König's explanation neatly fit the white community's views of black people. Everyone was happy, especially the British. Because one of those black stevedores was a British spy.[2]

Having finished his prepared statement, Captain König asked if there were any questions. There were. Did he expect any difficulty in evading the British blockade as the *Deutschland* left the United States coast? The captain could have used the same propaganda line that had been used in Baltimore to answer the same question. Instead he dropped a bombshell.

Recalling the visit by *U-53* in October, he told the press that he would not be surprised if the *U-57* met him off the coast to provide escort through the blockade. The implications were enormous and Germany's campaign to gain American support suffered a staggering setback. In less time than it would take to snap your fingers, the issue of the *Deutschland*'s status reappeared. Was she really just a commercial vessel?

The State Department immediately ordered Commander Yates Stirling to conduct an inspection of the boat to determine her status.[3] At the same time, the *Deutschland*'s radio was sealed by the navy, over Captain Hinsch's loud protests. He pointed out that in Baltimore the government had waited more than ten days to take action. Furthermore, British commercial vessels that docked in American ports for brief periods were not subject to the same treatment.[4]

The following day, 2 November, Commander Yates Stirling and twelve other officers went aboard the *Deutschland* at 1400.[5] Their exhaustive inspection covered every detail about the boat and resulted in two separate reports totaling eighty-one pages, typed single space on legal-size paper. Included in the reports were detailed drawings of the boat's hull, layout, machinery, and specialized equipment. But the most interesting part of the report was found in Commander Yates Stirling's conclusions.

Concluding that the *Deutschland* was at the time an unarmed merchantman, the commander added:

> The vessel could be quickly converted into a commerce raiding subma-
> rine by the mounting of several guns on the non-watertight superstruc-
> ture housing within the superstructure; a certain amount of stiffening
> would be required. The vessel could also be readily converted into a
> mine-laying submarine, launching the mines from the superstructure
> deck; the watertight hatches are large enough to pass a mine suffi-
> ciently large to do considerable damage.

That was a substantial change from the conclusion drawn after the
inspection in Baltimore. But the next point was even more revealing.

> Furthermore, the *Deutschland* could act to a limited extent with its
> present equipment as a tender for several submarines. The cargo space
> inside the pressure hull could be utilized for the stowage of spare parts
> and supplies. In addition to 150 tons of fuel oil carried in the fuel
> tanks, several hundred more tons of fuel oil could be carried in one or
> more of her ballast tanks. The *Deutschland* could act, therefore, in the
> capacity of a supply ship for war submarines within the limit of its oil
> capacity, thereby permitting war submarines to remain a longer time
> on operating grounds than they could remain with supplies and oil
> ordinarily carried by themselves.[6]

Mounting large deck guns and taking mines aboard was out of
the question while the U-boat was in the United States. But she could
easily take aboard spare parts, supplies, and fuel oil. In fact, on
1 November seventy-five tons of diesel oil were pumped into her from
the *Willehad*. Two days later another twenty-five tons were pumped
from a tank car that had been rolled onto the pier. The government
got nervous.

According to the Germans, the *Deutschland* carried a normal fuel
supply of one hundred and fifty tons. That claim was supported by
the inspections made in Baltimore and New London. That amount of
fuel gave the boat an operating range of about 7,200 nautical miles,
not quite enough for a round trip.[7] The Germans always told the
press that she had plenty of fuel for the return trip, but they preferred to top off with the higher grade American product. In part
that was true.

Chief Engineer Klees told the navy inspectors that the *Deutschland*
burned about four tons of fuel per day while under way.[8] That was an
average figure that varied with speed and sea conditions, and it may
or may not have been accurate. If Klees was telling the truth, the
Deutschland could steam for thirty-seven days and twelve hours on her
normal fuel supply. That was enough time to make a round trip under

nearly perfect conditions. But nearly perfect conditions had not pre-vailed on the first trip, nor the second.

The first round trip had taken thirty-nine days. Using the four tons per day figure, the *Deutschland* would have come up six tons short had she not refueled in Baltimore. Still, she arrived home with a lot more fuel than she needed, and it is safe to assume that the balance went into an outbound war boat.

When he arrived in New London, Captain König told everyone that they had left Bremen on 10 October. If that was true, the crossing had taken twenty-one days. But it was not. The *Deutschland* had de-parted from the Jade on 8 October, so the crossing had really taken twenty-three days.[9] At four tons per day she had used ninety-two tons of fuel, or 61 percent of her normal supply.

Actually, the figure was closer to one hundred tons. That is why on 3 November she took aboard another twenty-five tons from the tank car. The extra fuel was needed to top off her tanks. But the German propaganda line about not really needing to refuel, plus the conclusions drawn by Commander Yates Stirling, made it look like the Germans were planning to use the *Deutschland* as a "milk cow."

Why did the Germans insist on issuing misleading information about so mundane a matter as the boat's fuel consumption? Certainly her puny 400-horsepower engines were nothing like the 2,200-horse-power giants being installed in the war boats then under construc-tion.[10] There were no secrets to give away.

The best explanation is probably pride and propaganda. They wanted the world to believe that the British blockade was totally ineffective against a fleet of U-freighters—even if the United States should refuse to sell fuel to the boats. They also wanted to impress the world with the strength of German technology. What they accom-plished instead was a growing doubt that the *Deutschland* was the simple merchantman she was reported to be.

To many people the refueling underscored Commander Yates Stirling's warning that the *Deutschland* could be used to resupply war boats at sea. And that raised a pair of questions. If the *Deutschland* joined up with the *U-57*, did the freighter give up her rights as a merchantman? The answer was yes. Under international law the con-voyed vessel took on the character of her escort. That meant that the *Deutschland* could be sunk on sight.[11]

But suppose she did act as a tender beyond the three-mile limit, would that compromise United States neutrality? After all, the fuel and supplies would have been obtained in the United States. It was

substantially the argument the British had forwarded in Baltimore—
submarines are almost impossible to control. The State Department
avoided the implications involved and said, no, American neutrality
would not be compromised if that happened.[12] But there was official
doubt.

They had only been in port two days and already Captain König,
his crew, and his boat were taking on the appearance of shady char-
acters. So far the public's negative attitudes were the result of German
official policies, statements, or actions. But in the early morning
hours of the third day, the actions of two crewmen added fuel to the
growing anti-German feeling.

The two sailors had been drinking in the Knickerbocker Restaurant on Bank Street. Both had become drunk, loud, and belligerent.
In the minutes after 2 November had become 3 November, one of the
sailors made a move on a woman who was in the bar. She turned him
down and he grabbed her. There was a noisy, ugly scene as the woman
struggled to break away and the sailor continued to force himself on
her.

The lone waiter on duty, Lloyd Blanchard, tried to intervene
while the few bar patrons watched. Lloyd was accustomed to dealing
with obnoxious drunks, which is why he worked the late shift. But he
was not prepared for the knife. The brawl was short, violent, and
fortunately not fatal.

Grabbing the sailor by the shoulder, Lloyd jerked the man away
from the woman. The sailor crashed into the bar stools, slipped, and
grabbed the bar. When he came off the bar, at Lloyd, he had a six-
inch sheath knife in his hand. The two men faced each other for only
a moment before the sailor slashed at the waiter, laying open his
forearm.

Badly cut, Lloyd retreated looking for something with which to
defend himself. At the sight of blood most of the customers decided
it was time to leave by the nearest exit. Among the fleeing patrons
was the woman Lloyd had been protecting. A noisy nuisance had
suddenly become vicious, a fact that became obvious to the other
sailor. Rushing forward, he wrestled his shipmate, pinning his arms
to his sides. Before anyone developed the belated nerve to get involved, he hustled his companion out the door.

A few hours later, Lloyd Blanchard and the police were waiting
at the gate to the State Pier. Lloyd's arm was heavily bandaged, and
he was mad. Receiving an urgent summons from the night watchman,

Captains Hinsch and König hurried to the gate where they were confronted by the injured waiter, the police, and a mob of reporters.

Sensing that this was not the time to enforce the no visitors rule, the two captains asked Lloyd and the policemen to step inside the gate, which was closed firmly behind them. The reporters were left outside wondering what was being said inside.

When the gate opened and the Americans came back out, Lloyd "was in a much better frame of mind." The whole thing was a mistake, he now said. It was not a crewman who had cut him, and the weapon was a harmonica, not a knife. In fact, the wound really was not bad at all, just a scratch.[13] It is amazing what fifty dollars in cash could accomplish in 1916.[14]

The situation and the outcome were surprisingly similar to what had transpired between the *Deutschland* and Simon Lake in Baltimore. The victim vowed prosecution, the boat was threatened, and the Germans bought him off. The press reported the satisfactory resolution to both problems, but there the similarity ended. The public was happy over Lake's financial arrangement, but not at all pleased with the sordid outcome to the midnight brawl.

Circumstances that otherwise would have caused the Germans little concern were being brought together by a series of events. Some of the events were so minor, even petty, that they might have passed unnoticed were it not for the fact that the press was becoming increasingly irritated over being denied all access to the *Deutschland*. One of those minor events happened on 4 November.

Reporters had by then dubbed Hinsch the "bane of reporters."[15] His no-press-visitors rule particularly angered them as their daily vigil outside the gate dragged on. It seemed that anyone who was not a reporter could get in. That was not really true, but the stream of official visitors made it look that way. And there was at least one unofficial visitor.

On Saturday, 4 November, a photographer joined a group of visitors and slipped past the guards. He was busily snapping pictures when he was discovered. His film was ripped from the camera, thrown in the water, and the photographer was thrown bodily out the gate. As he was getting to his feet, a touring car with Pennsylvania license plates stopped in front of the gate.

The passenger in the rear seat turned out to be Mrs. George L. Adams of Brooklyn. The wealthy, attractive woman was not an official visitor, but she wanted to see Captain König anyway. Wealthy, attractive women are rarely denied their wishes, and the guard hurried away to fetch the captain. The reporters moved closer.

In a moment Captain König came through the gate, went to the car and spoke to the unexpected visitor. She talked about her summer home in Pennsylvania, gave him a box of cigars, and asked to see the *Deutschland*. Without hesitation the former Lloyd skipper extended his hand, helped the lady from her car, and escorted her through the gate. The reporters closed in on the driver. Who was the lady, they asked? Where is her husband?

An insignificant event became a petty scandal. Reporters suddenly recalled that the captain had frequently dined with ladies while he was in Baltimore. Of course, he was always with a large group on those occasions, but it did seem that he had an eye for a pretty face. Now one had simply shown up at his front door and had been taken aboard the U-boat. No one actually accused him of being a womanizer, it was not necessary—the suggestion was enough.

By the week of 6 November, the Germans' image was badly tarnished, and people were ready to believe just about anything bad that was attributed to them. There was already a rumor going around New London that the *Willehad* was making nightly radio contact with a vessel offshore. The rumor grew in part from the suspicion that the *Deutschland* was really a U-boat resupply ship, and in part from a deliberately planted British intelligence leak.[16]

The radios on both German ships had been "sealed," a term that meant the radio had been rendered inoperative by cutting out the brushes in the motor generator and disassembling the tuning set. The outer panels were then replaced and a government seal was taped across the edges. Periodic inspection ensured that the panels had not been opened, a condition that would have been made apparent by the broken seals.[17]

Despite those precautions, the British heard from their stevedore spy that the *Willehad*'s radio might be operational. The man, who was allowed to roam the *Willehad* with few restrictions, had not seen anything that looked like a radio, except in the radio room. And he learned that a part of the radio known as the "machine" had been sent to New York for repairs. But, he reported:

> The wireless operator on the *Willehad* made the remark that he could rig up instruments to take the place of the wireless, but they could only send messages and could not receive any.

The *Willehad* served as a barrier to onlookers, and provided quarters for the *Deutschland*'s crew and the black stevedores. The floating wall that screened the U-boat from the river is on the left side of the picture. In the background on the right is the house that British Intelligence thought contained a German transmitter. (National Archives)

And there was another possibility:

North of the warehouse on the State Pier is a high embankment on which stands a frame house. The house is the assistant engineer's office. East of the house is a telegraph pole. Wires come from the house to this pole and from the pole to the warehouse at the corner of the dock. This wire runs to the northeast corner of the warehouse. Another wire runs from the southeast corner to the upper deck of the *Willehad* right over the lifeboats. This might be a means of communication. There are no wireless aerials.[18]

It was not much to go on, and there is nothing in the documents to show that the British ever picked up a message sent by the Germans in New London. But there was enough there to plant a story in the press that made the Germans look even more sinister. Sending the "machine" to New York for repairs had just been a trick "to throw investigators off the track." In fact, on Wednesday and Thursday nights, it was reported, the *Willehad* had sent messages to a vessel off Fishers Island in Long Island Sound. It was darkly hinted that the vessel receiving the messages was a U-boat.[19]

The State Department was starting to feel very uneasy about the *Deutschland*. The *U-53*'s visit was still fresh in everyone's mind, and the implied threat had not been forgotten—especially after it was so dramatically underscored by five sinkings within sight of land.

On 9 November, amid growing doubts about the *Deutschland*'s real purpose, the State Department asked the Treasury Department to deny clearance to the *Deutschland* until the clearance was approved by the State Department. Approval would depend on the results of an inspection to be made after Captain König submitted his request for clearance. Even after the inspection was made, the boat was to be kept "under close surveillance" until she departed, to ensure that no additional supplies or materials were taken aboard."[20]

Doubts about the *Deutschland*'s true character had been growing even before she arrived in New London. The disappearance of the *Bremen* had a lot to do with that. According to one German source, most Americans did not believe the "private company ownership story. Especially after the millions lost on the *Bremen*."[21] To dampen those doubts, Captain König told the press that the *Deutschland*'s cargo was worth at least ten million dollars. The true value was really closer to three million, but he wanted to assure the American people that the German Ocean Navigation Company was making a profit. How else could it stay in business, unless it was really a government operation?

And there was the nagging question about the crewmen. How was it that so many young men of service age were available to man the *Deutschland?* Especially young men who knew how to operate a submarine, but had never served in the Imperial German Navy.

Back in July, while the boat was in Baltimore, Captain König had told reporters:

> It's foolish to believe that any of my men have come from the German submarine service. They have had their training in the shops of Ger-

A rare view from inside the pier showing the *Deutschland* well hidden in her pen. (National Archives)

maniawerft in Kiel, where Krupps are making Diesel engines. The crew occupies the same relative position as the civilian experts in American submarine plants who continuously run the trials of their boats until they are turned over to the navy.[22]

The reporters did not challenge the captain then, and they missed their chance four months later when Alfred Lohmann told a group of foreign reporters in Bremen, "They have been released to us until the end of the war. Their training was done exclusively on the *Deutschland* after she was launched in March."[23] Hints, partial admissions about previous military service, and outright contradictions were completely overlooked or ignored. Why?

The failure by the press to expose the truth was due largely to poor communications. What was said on the Continent rarely reached the United States in time to be of any value, because the transatlantic cables were cut and everything reaching the United States went through the British censors. And local news was literally here today and gone tomorrow.

In this age, we have become accustomed to instant computer recovery of archival information. That did not happen in 1916. Information recovery depended on tedious hand searches aided by the reporter's memory of what he had seen and heard. And that added to the problem, because the reporter who covered the story in Baltimore might not be covering it in New London. In short, there was little opportunity for recall and rapid comparison of specific statements.

In any event, few people really believed the *Deutschland* was purely a private venture. Most assumed that the German government had a hand in it, and that the crew may have been in the German navy at one time. But they seemed to have been satisfied that at the moment they were not. Nevertheless, the Germans carried on with the charade that the boat was paying its own way by trying to secure a mail contract with the United States.

Actually, there was more to getting a mail contract than merely making it appear that the *Deutschland* was being operated for profit. The Germans needed a reliable, fairly frequent, and secure method of communication between their embassy in Washington and the Foreign Office in Berlin.

In April the British had announced that from that point forward ships carrying mail between the United States and Scandinavia would be taken into port for a thorough search. If contraband goods—at that time just about anything was contraband—were found hidden in letters or packages, they would be seized.[24]

The new policy put a serious crimp in Germany's ability to send communications between Berlin and Washington. Sending coded radio transmissions was forbidden by the Americans, the transatlantic cables had been cut, and the British were already intercepting nearly all the mail sent by ship. Letters sent to safe addresses in neutral countries took three to four months to reach Berlin—if they got there at all. Now, letters sent to dummy post boxes in Norway and Sweden, or disguised as official correspondence of one of those countries, were going to be seized.

Sending official mail aboard the *Deutschland* could be done without a contract since it would be sent under diplomatic privilege. That was how the new code book entered the United States. The code book was among dispatches in six bags carried under diplomatic seal by Lieutenant Krapohl to Washington on 2 November. So the mail contract was not really necessary, but it did provide good cover. And if some additional income resulted, so much the better.

The idea of securing a mail contract came up while the *Deutschland* was in Baltimore. At the time, the suggestion resulted from public demands for a means of postal communication between the United States and Germany. Many German families were represented by members in both countries, and nearly all of them had been without news for two years. When the idea arrived at Alfred Lohmann's desk he turned it down.

"We can't carry mail for a fee except on regular mail routes," he said. Then referring to diplomatic mail he continued, "Some speciality mail will be carried. We are in the business to help the Vaterland, and then make a profit."[25]

But the pressure for a means of postal communication increased. Why not establish a regular mail route, and carry both private *and* diplomatic mail? Early in October 1916, in anticipation of the *Bremen*'s arrival in New London, negotiations were opened with the United States.

From the start both countries agreed on a once-a-month contract, with the first-class mail limit set at eight hundred pounds. There was little agreement on any other point. The United States was willing to pay the going steamer rate of eighty cents a pound. The Germans wanted eight dollars a pound and wanted the mail hermetically sealed in special bags. The Americans said no. The Germans dropped the special bag demand and raised the rate to ten dollars a pound. The Americans said no. Finally both sides agreed on a dollar per pound.

Assuming that the two governments agreed to the deal hammered out by the negotiators, the mail run was to start in January 1917. Events prevented that from happening.

Negotiating the mail contract may have eased a few doubts, and it certainly was good propaganda. Americans objected strongly to

Completely empty, the *Deutschland* rides well above her marks, showing off her enormous beam. Shortly after this picture was taken, the U-boat took on 25 tons of fuel from the tank car standing on the pier, causing many people to wonder if she was really a U-boat supply ship. (Naval Historical Center)

interference with their mail, especially by a foreign government, and the negotiations publicized the fact that American mail was being interfered with by British warships. Small matter that relatively few Americans ever sent a letter overseas. What mattered was the principle of the thing, and if the Germans could get the mail through in a U-boat, so much the better.

The small gains in prestige made by the Germans with the mail agreement were given a slight boost by the incoming cargo. Over three million dollars in securities were entered, along with some semiprecious stones for industrial use. The bulk of the cargo was, again, dyestuffs. But this time there was not even a hint of price gouging, the entire load being consigned to three major American firms.

Among the pharmaceuticals she brought was a drug believed to be effective against infantile paralysis. No one was sure that the drug would be effective, but the hope it represented went a long way toward polishing the *Deutschland*'s tarnished image.[26]

The generally negative tone evident in news reports about the *Deutschland* substantially reduced enthusiasm for the boat's visit. As a result, the sort of hoopla that attended her visit to Baltimore never materialized in New London. Even events hosted by German-American clubs and societies were few. And that was a significant setback for German propaganda.

The Germans needed those demonstrations of public support by German-Americans to show other Americans how widespread German influence was in the United States. But in New London, there were only three such demonstrations, two were so small as to have no meaning, and none received much publicity.

The news coverage of the largest official banquet was relegated to page twenty-one, and the articles about Captain König's induction into the Sons of Hermann, and the honorary membership bestowed upon him by the Harvard German Club, ended up with the want ads.

The biggest gathering was on Thursday, 9 November, when two thousand people attended a banquet at the New London Municipal Building. Mayor Ernest E. Rogers presented Captain König with a gold watch, engraved with the city seal, and each crewman received a silver match box and a pen. The city-sponsored event stemmed from a comment made by the president of the New London Chamber of Commerce, A. T. Minor.

"The *Deutschland* has done more for New London in a week, than the Chamber of Commerce has done in a year."[27]

He was referring to the number of tourists who poured into New London in a vain attempt to get a look at the big U-boat. Every shop in town benefited, and several temporary souvenir shops sprang up, including one run by the American Relief Committee for German Widows and Orphans. Using their inside connection, they obtained twenty tons of pig-iron ballast from the Eastern Forwarding Company and turned it into souvenir *Deutschland* medals.

On 15 November, the day the *Bremen* was officially listed as lost, Captain König told James T. McGovern, collector of customs, that he would be requesting clearance the next day. The *Deutschland*'s outward foreign manifest showed she was loaded with over one thousand tons of rubber, metal, and oil. Included in the metal were 6.2 tons of silver valued at $140,000.00.[28]

Unlike the gold that had gone aboard in Baltimore, the silver was openly declared. It had arrived in New London on 7 November by train from San Francisco, and was transported through town in five horse-drawn wagons. The wagons, open and unguarded, looked like any other freight wagon delivering goods to the State Pier.[29]

König told McGovern that the *Deutschland*'s tanks were full, and there was a sixty-day supply of food and stores aboard. She was in every respect ready for sea.

That night the U-boat was inspected by navy and customs representatives. McGovern informed the State Department that everything was in order, and he was told to issue the clearance.[30] Clearance in hand, Captain König waited through the day and half the night of 16 November before leaving. During the afternoon he met one more time with the press.

It was the expected: what will you do if you meet enemy ships? König gave the expected reply. Then a reporter asked him what he would do with the *Deutschland* after the war.

"Well," König laughed, "it wouldn't be any use to carry freight under water if you could carry it on top of the waves." He paused a moment, thinking. Then vigorously nodding his head he added, "We'll bring her to America and show her at ten cents a look."[31]

Everyone laughed. Unknown at the time, the joke was amazingly prophetic.

CHAPTER FOURTEEN

COLLISION,

17 NOVEMBER 1916

A light breeze rippled the water as the *Efco* dragged the huge floating gate away from the entrance to the State Pier, the widening opening illuminated by a searchlight from the tug *T. A. Scott Jr.* The *Deutschland* backed slowly, her bulk being set away from the pier by the current. Captain König, bundled in oil skins and a heavy sweater, looked aft as the stern pushed through the opening. The cold night was crystal clear, the river palely illuminated by a half moon. The captain could clearly see the *Scott* waiting for him a hundred yards away. To the right, almost hidden against the shoreline was the dark form of the smaller tug *Cassie*. The time was 0115.[1]

Captain König spoke into the voice tube, "Port ahead one-third. Starboard back full. Port standard rudder."

The U-boat continued to move astern, twisting right, the bow sweeping past the shoreline. As the boat swung at right angles to the opening, the captain again spoke into the voice tube.

"Both ahead one-third. Starboard full rudder."

The *Deutschland* continued to move astern, pivoting along her axis as the propellers dug in. She stopped, the bow swung downriver, and the U-boat moved forward, gaining speed. To her right, the *Scott* also gathered speed, paralleling the U-boat, while the *Cassie* took a station to port. Abreast, the three boats moved downriver toward Long Island Sound.

From the now-empty pier, a group of reporters watched the *Deutschland* leave. Hastily they jotted down all they had seen, especially noting that the beam from a searchlight atop the *Willehad*'s bridge was being directed far down the river. They also noted that the beam was not being played on the water. It was just being pointed toward the Sound. Was it a signal?

Several concluded that it was a signal, and it was being directed toward the waiting *U-57*. But they were puzzled—all three vessels were displaying their navigation lights. Shouldn't they be slipping away with their lights off? Of course, they concluded, the navigation lights were on to aid the *U-57* in spotting the *Deutschland*.[2] Armed with "proof" that the *U-57* was probably operating inside Long Island Sound, they ran to the nearest telephone.

Aboard the *Scott,* Captain John Gurney gripped the wheel. A veteran of many years with the T. A. Scott Company, Gurney knew every inch of New London Harbor and the Sound. It was his responsibility to lead the *Deutschland* to open water—a piece of cake. The only problem tonight was the bitter cold, but at least visibility was good.[3]

Leaning against the base of the deckhouse, Able Seaman Eugene Duzant tried to escape the biting cold. A newcomer to the T. A. Scott Company, he was the only crewman aboard who was not a New London resident. Twenty-three years old and single, Duzant had spent most of his life in fishing boats. He was used to back-breaking work and long hours, but he never had gotten used to the cold. He pulled his collar up higher and watched the large, barrel-chested man standing on the bow.[4]

Captain Hinsch also felt the bite of the cold, but either he was accustomed to it or was more warmly dressed. Scanning the water on both sides he watched for any threat that might appear. He cast a glance aft, beyond the *Deutschland,* spotting the *Cassie*'s running lights. She was well astern of the U-boat—maybe too far astern. If a threat developed off the *Deutschland*'s stern, it was her job to move up and drive the threat away. The *Scott* would handle anything that approached from ahead. Hinsch looked forward. He saw only black water and darkness occasionally pierced by a winking light or the lights of an anchored ship.

In the cramped galley, Cook Clarence B. Davidson brewed a large pot of coffee. He would take a mug up to Captain Gurney, but the new kid would have to come get his own. Beyond making coffee, Davidson had little to do on this trip. They were scheduled to be back in New London just after sunup, and well before breakfast. The crew would eat ashore.[5]

In the boiler room, Fireman Edward Stone shoveled coal into the furnace, slammed the furnace door shut, and threw the shovel on the coal pile. Wiping his forehead with a rag he walked aft to the engine room.

Engineer William A. Caton looked at his gauges, wiped a spot of oil off the engine, and made an entry in the engine log. As Stone stepped into the engine room, Caton motioned him to a small table on which was a deck of cards. Caton sat down, shuffled the cards, and dealt. It was too noisy to talk without shouting, but the two old friends had no need to talk. Their routine was second nature to them.[6]

Franz Krapohl looked at the navigation chart spread out on the table in the control central. There was plenty of deep water once they reached the Sound, a reassuring thought with the British waiting just outside the three-mile limit. If, of course, they *were* outside the three-mile limit.

The new cook, Otto Stephen, squeezed into the control central with two mugs of coffee.

"Coffee, Herr Leutnant," he said handing Krapohl one of the mugs.

"The other one for the captain?" Krapohl asked.

"Yes," Stephen answered, moving toward the ladder. "Coffee and a cigar. Just like aboard the *Schleswig.*"

Lieutenant Krapohl watched the cook climb the ladder, the mug in one hand. His movements were awkward, like a cripple. But not a drop was spilled. Krapohl chuckled. Knowing the old man, the cook could just as well have left the coffee behind on a night like this. It was the cigar that the captain wanted.

Actually König was glad to get both. He was crazy about cigars, the bigger and blacker the better. But the hot, black coffee was equally welcome tonight. He lit the cigar, took a deep drag, and looked forward.

The *Scott* was four hundred feet ahead and forty-five degrees off the *Deutschland*'s starboard bow, the *Deutschland* slowly gaining on the tug. There was no other traffic. This departure was quite different from the one in Baltimore, König thought. Probably because of the late hour and the cold. Just as well. He looked aft expecting to see the *Cassie* about one hundred yards astern. Instead she was nearly a mile back, apparently having a hard time keeping up. Oh well, no matter. It doesn't look like we will need her anyway, he thought.

The small convoy was pushing across Long Island Sound. Ahead and a little to the left was Fishers Island, the Race Rock Light flashing off its western end. To the right, some distance away, was Gull Island. Between the two islands was the Race, through which the three ships would pass as they bore left toward the Atlantic. The *Cassie* was still a mile astern, but no one was concerned. In fact, at this point Captain König felt he could dispense with the *Scott* too. Visibility was still good, there were no boats to be warned off, and the *Deutschland* had a clear shot at the Atlantic.

They were nearing Race Rock, which lies just off the end of Fishers Island. At 0228 Race Rock bore one-and-a-half points, about seventeen degrees, off the *Deutschland*'s port bow, a half mile away. The tide runs with exceptional force through the Race and was at maximum flood as they approached the rock.

Captain König was unfamiliar with the conditions in those waters and was relying on Captain Gurney's local knowledge. Suddenly the full force of the tide slammed into the *Scott,* swinging her to port against her helm. As the *Scott* swung to port she turned bow on to the full force of the flood tide. It was as though a giant hand was pressed against the tug's bow. The engine continued to drive the three-blade propeller, the helm remained steady as the water streamed across the rudder, but the *Scott* came to a dead halt.

On deck Hinsch and Duzant felt the tug shudder, gripped by the rushing water, and watched with growing horror as the *Deutschland* bore down on them. In the galley Clarence Davidson was probably unaware that anything had gone wrong. For Engineer Caton and Edward Stone, the situation was nothing unusual; they continued to play cards.

Hinsch yelled at Gurney to "ring her up"—go to full speed. But to Hinsch's horror, Gurney responded by ringing just one bell— engine stop. Seeing the *Deutschland*'s steel bow bearing down, Hinsch ran to the wheelhouse ladder.

The *Deutschland* was moving forward at eight knots when the *Scott* made her turn and shuddered to a halt dead ahead. Captain König reacted at once. Bellowing down the voice pipe to put the rudder over hard astarboard and go full astern, he slammed his hand down on the collision siren button. Howling like a banshee, the *Deutschland* surged forward as her propellers stopped, and went astern.

At 0229 the *Deutschland*'s bow smashed into the *Scott*'s portside, just twelve feet forward of the stern, rolling the tug over. The eighteen-hundred-ton U-boat continued to plow through the tug, shearing off the stern and passing over the rapidly sinking wreck. Only Hinsch survived.

When the *Deutschland* rammed the tug, Captain Hinsch, one foot on the second rung of the wheelhouse ladder, was thrown into the water. Struggling to stay afloat he saw the *Scott* disappear beneath the surface as the *Deutschland* slid past him. Weighted down by his heavy clothes, Hinsch sank beneath the surface. He struggled out of his coat, boots, and heavy sweater, gasping for air each time he surfaced.

While Hinsch fought to stay alive, the *Deutschland* ground to a halt and started to back, her collision siren still howling, her crew spilling out on deck. Two searchlights swept the water from her conning tower, joined quickly by a dozen damage-control lanterns from the deck.

A mile astern, the *Cassie*'s crew heard the siren, saw the running lights on both ships come together, and knew at once what had happened. Going forward at full speed, the *Cassie* rushed toward the scene. On deck, Albert Mix, chief superintendent for the Scott Company, ordered the tug's boat readied for lowering.

Hinsch was in trouble. Worn out from his struggle to stay afloat, and chilled by the frigid waters, he knew he would not last much longer. He had hoped to find a piece of wreckage to hang on to. There was none. The *Deutschland* was too far away, and the searchlights were being used in the wrong place. He had all but given up when the *Cassie* arrived.[7]

By sheer luck, her searchlight's beam was pointed squarely at Hinsch's thrashing form. Leaping into the now-lowered boat, Albert Mix told his crew to pull away as he scrambled into the bow. Seeing that Hinsch was about to go under, Mix hurled a life ring at the man. His aim was right on. Hinsch grabbed at the ring, caught it, and clutched it to him. In moments the boat was alongside, and Hinsch was hauled aboard.

For an hour and a half the *Deutschland* and the *Cassie* remained on the scene looking for survivors. In a short time they knew that what they were actually looking for were bodies. None were found. At 0530 the *Deutschland*, her stem warped and twisted, returned to her berth at the State Pier. The *Efco* pushed the floating gate closed behind her, and a worried, upset Captain König waited for morning.

By sunup the word about the disaster had reached every home in New London. The residents were devastated. Captain Gurney and

Engineer Caton left widows and orphans. Ed Stone and Clarence Davidson were bachelors, but had many friends. Only the deck hand, Eugene Duzant, was an outsider, his home in Rhode Island.

Outside the offices of the T. A. Scott Company the American flag was raised to the mast top and then lowered to half mast. A crowd of reporters, thrill seekers, and mourners gathered at the company gate.[8] The rumors started at once.

Oddly, most of the rumors favored the *Deutschland.* It was reported that a boat had sped out of the dark in an attempt to ram the U-boat. Forced to take evasive action, the *Deutschland* had collided with the *Scott,* causing the boiler to explode and giving the tug's crew no chance to abandon ship. The *Deutschland*'s crew was credited with rescuing Captain Hinsch.[9]

A variation of the same story had the *Scott* cutting across the U-boat's bow to intercept a mystery boat that threatened the *Deutschland.* Unable to stop or turn in time, the *Deutschland* struck the *Scott* in the engine room, causing the boiler to explode. Captain Hinsch was saved when he grabbed a life ring from the *Scott* just as the tug went under.[10]

The reported boiler explosion produced another rumor. The mystery boat had been captured and the man aboard arrested after he was found to be carrying explosives. He told his unnamed captors that he intended to put the explosives aboard the *Deutschland.*[11]

All the rumors were dispelled before noon that day. But not before they had been widely reported as fact in the nation's newspapers.

In Germany, the navy and Alfred Lohmann learned of the collision from Reuters, getting more details—inaccurate—from press reports that relied on the early rumors. The problem was that the Germans could not separate fact from fiction because they had no way of getting direct, timely information from their people in the United States. To say that the German authorities were frantic for accurate information is to understate their concern.

Captain König was also concerned. A collision, any collision, is a serious matter. One that results in the loss of life, the total destruction of the other vessel, and threatens to become an international incident is even more serious. The captain had every reason to be concerned. And there was another angle. Despite their merchant seaman's clothing, company hat badges, and claims of being released from service, every man of the *Deutschland*'s crew was a member of the Imperial German Navy. And that included the captain.

At 1000 that morning inspectors William Withey and Harry Rankin inspected the U-boat's damaged bow. That afternoon a preliminary hearing was convened in the customshouse in New London. Reporters watching the principals arrive described Captain König.

"He seemed as though his nerves were entirely unstrung. His face was pale and his eyes were deep circles."[12]

The preliminary hearing was short and inconclusive, largely because the only survivor from the *Scott*, Captain Hinsch, was in no shape to testify. Only the bare facts, the sequence of events, were established. But on 22 November the portly captain was well enough to give his statement. Combined with a certified copy of the *Deutschland*'s log, Hinsch's statement became the sole basis for the inspectors' exoneration of the *Deutschland*.

In the meantime, a number of legal firms were getting into the act. Blodgett, Jones, Burnham and Bingham, a Boston law firm, represented the T. A. Scott Company. On the 22nd they demanded copies of any testimony that had been taken.

George Uhler, supervising inspector general, turned them down, citing legal restrictions and general policy. But he did promise to send them a copy of the final report.

Not happy with the answer, the lawyers sought help from their congressman, James A. Galvin. Pointing out that the matter "involved deceased American citizens" while the other party was a "foreign boat that may never return," Congressman Galvin asked Uhler to overlook procedure. Uhler refused.[13]

In the meantime, a portable forge was brought to the pier, and the rubber stored forward between the hulls was stacked on the deck. The after ballast tanks were flooded, raising the damaged bow out of the water, and crewmen started removing the twisted plates. The time needed for repair was estimated at one week. But now a new problem surfaced.

Two days after the collision, C. Hull, partner in the New York law firm, Hull, McGuire, and Hull, filed suit against the *Deutschland*. Acting on behalf of the T. A. Scott Company and the five crewmen, Hull libeled the boat for $200,000.00. That day two federal agents boarded the *Deutschland*, nailed a Writ of Libel to the wooden deck, and ordered the crew off.

For two days, Captain König and his crew stayed aboard the *Willehad*, allowed to go aboard the *Deutschland* only on "urgent business." König found several pieces of urgent business that needed to be done and sent small groups aboard. But they could stay only a short while, and were not allowed to work on the damaged bow.

Frustrated and depressed, the Germans spent most of their time watching the lone guard reclining on the *Deutschland*'s deck near the Writ of Libel. Things looked bleak.

But the Hilkens and Captain Hinsch were not standing idly by waiting for something to happen. They had retained Charles W. Field, a Baltimore lawyer, who was busy trying to arrange bond for the boat. He accomplished that on 20 November when the Maryland Casualty Company agreed to post the bond. The following day, a company representative posted $97,230.00, less than half the face value of the libel. The bond was accepted, and the *Deutschland* was free to go.

At that point an interesting decision was issued by a federal court. The court told Hull, McGuire, and Hull, that they had not shown that the *Deutschland* was completely owned by the Deutsche Ozean Reederei. The law firm had named the German company and the Eastern Forwarding Company in the suit. But the court's decision let both companies off the hook. That was probably just as well, since one had no assets in the United States and both were dummy operations, so the plaintiffs would never have collected a dime from them anyway.[14]

But there was another issue the decision raised that was completely overlooked. If the Deutsche Ozean Reederei did not own the *Deutschland*, who did? Had the question been asked, and answered, the *Deutschland* would have lost her merchantman status. As things worked out a few months later, that would not have made any difference anyway.

While repairs were being made on the bow, there was speculation about who was at fault. The early support for the *Deutschland*'s innocence in the matter evaporated, and was replaced by the lawyers' legal opinion.

It was pointed out that Captain König had not taken a pilot aboard, though he had paid the required pilot fees. Actually, he was not obliged to take a pilot, and had not taken one because he did not want to stop to let the pilot off. That was certainly his right, but it did not help his case.

The fact that the *Deutschland* was the overtaking vessel was also brought up. On that point the law was clear—and still is—the overtaking vessel is burdened. The fact that he was unfamiliar with the waters and had refused to take aboard a pilot made that point even more significant to the detractors. They argued that Captain König had not allowed himself enough room between the *Deutschland* and the *Scott* for the conditions he faced.

But the lawyers' opinions went out the window when Withey and Rankin released their report on 20 December. Classified "investigated and dismissed," the report concluded:

The collision was due to a mistake in the bell signals given to the engineer by Captain Gurney at a time when the vessels were in such position that this mistake proved to be a fatal error.[15]

The next day, the *Köln Tagesblatt* reported that the *Scott* had been found at fault. According to the report "the cause was the inaccurate flag signal given by Captain Gurney."[16] Something had been lost in the translation, but at least the essence was there.

Despite the negative report, the civil case was settled out of court on 22 August 1917, four months after the United States had entered the war against Germany. The announcement of the settlement was not released, but the Germans did pay restitution to the families and relatives of the five men.

The day she was freed from state and federal custody, new clearance papers were issued and a date for departure was set. Late that night, the crew completed the repairs, restowed the cargo, and pumped out the after ballast tanks. The *Deutschland* was again ready for sea.

On the day the clearance papers were issued, 20 November 1916, Foreign Minister Gottlieb von Jagow was replaced by Arthur Zimmerman. The change would have a profound effect on the *Deutschland* and the country whose name she bore.

She departed New London in the afternoon of 21 November. There was no fanfare, a fact noted by the *Kriegspresseamt* (War Press Office) in a report that said, "the second departure from America was without the jubilation of the first departure from Baltimore."[17] The *Kriegspresseamt* report attributed the lack of American enthusiasm to several things: the *U-53*'s actions after her October stop in Newport; the use of black stevedores; the sinking of the *Scott;* and the growing American opinion that the *Deutschland* was not really a private venture, but a part of the Imperial German Navy. The conclusion was that the *Deutschland* had lost most of her propaganda value in the United States. The assessment was correct.

Her image was further tarnished by the message Captain König sent to Hinsch after the *Deutschland* cleared the three-mile limit. *AUSFAHRT GEGLÜCKT.*[18] Listeners interpreted the message to mean that the *Deutschland* had linked up with the *U-57.* In fact, all König had told Hinsch was that the *Deutschland* had successfully gotten away.

The belief that the *Deutschland* was being escorted by a war boat was underscored later that day and the next. The American freighter SS *Saratoga* broadcast GERMAN ARMORED SUBMARINE MAY BE ANYWHERE IN ATLANTIC. TAKE EVERY PRECAUTION.[19]

Captain König noted that the steamers seemed to have shifted to a more southerly track. He attributed that to the fear caused by the *U-53* and the belief that he was being escorted. Beyond that short entry and the discovery of a new cruiser line off Kirkwall, Orkney, Captain König saw nothing unusual on the trip home. On 7 December he was warned about a new line of nets strung between Kirkwall and Udsire, to a depth of ten meters.[20] He passed them safely. In fact, had it not been for a startling event just off the mouth of the Weser, the second trip home would have been totally uneventful.

CHAPTER FIFTEEN

LIMBO,

9 DECEMBER 1916–31 JANUARY 1917

The horizon was barely distinguishable between the lead grey sky and the grey-green sea as the *Deutschland* pushed southward toward Helgoland, now only hours away. But except for an occasional snow flurry, visibility on the morning of 9 December was generally good. Lieutenant Eyring and a seaman were in the conning tower, only their binoculars protruding from the scarfs, wool caps, and turned-up collars that protected them from the cold. Both men knew what they were looking for. Out there ahead of the U-boat was a German picket boat, an ex-ferry, that bore the unlikely and high-sounding name, SMS *Kaiser Wilhelm*.

"Look there," Eyring said, pointing to a dark spot on the water. "Is that the picket?"

The seaman trained his glasses on the spot. "Looks like it."

Eyring leaned over the speaking tube. "Picket boat in sight," he shouted, "two points off the starboard bow." The *Deutschland* held her course while the two men in the conning tower continued to watch the vessel ahead and to the right of the U-boat. Quickly, the vessel's lines became more clearly recognizable: straight stem, pronounced shear, box-like superstructure topped by a high pilothouse. It was the *Kaiser Wilhelm*.

"Right ten degrees of rudder." Eyring resumed his place, peering through his binoculars, his elbows propped on the conning-tower rim. He heard someone coming through the hatch, and knew that the captain had come to the conning tower.

"Is it the *Kaiser Wilhelm*?" König asked, taking Eyring's binoculars.

"The ferry, not the battleship," Eyring chuckled, referring to the 12,000-ton battleship commissioned in 1900.

"Better signal him to identify, just to be sure."

Three signal flags soon snapped in the stiff breeze above the *Deutschland*'s conning tower. The boxy-looking vessel answered.

"That's her," König said. "We'll let her lead us in, just in case there are mines in the area."

"Right," Eyring said, motioning the seaman to hank on the signal.

At 1100 the tiny *Kaiser Wilhelm* sent: SMS KAISER WILHELM IN CONTACT WITH DEUTSCHLAND, 147 GAMMA. An hour and fifty-six minutes later the *Deutschland* broadcast, DEUTSCHLAND, 147 GAMMA. Those were very nearly the last position reports ever sent about the *Deutschland*.[1]

What follows is based on sketchy information provided by J. Y. Buck, an American diplomat stationed in Bremen. But even though the information is sketchy, it is believed to be factual. During the third week in January 1917, Adolf Stadtländer, a director for Norddeutsche Lloyd, hosted a dinner for Paul König at the Hotel Beermann in Bremerhaven. During the dinner, Captain König told the guests an astounding story.

Shortly before the *Deutschland* reached the fortified island, Helgoland, the U-boat developed engine trouble. The nature of the trouble was not described except that both diesel engines abruptly stopped and could not be restarted. At the same time she started to settle by the stern. Fortunately, due to the cold weather, the deck hatches were closed and only the watch was on deck, both men in the conning tower.

The boat settled steadily, and fairly quickly, causing the two men in the conning tower to retreat below, slamming shut the hatch, and dogging it down. Despite efforts to restart the diesels, and blow the after tanks, the boat continued to sink by the stern until the depth gauge read twenty meters, and the down angle by the stern was forty-five degrees.

König told his stunned listeners that the hull plates near the stern bulged inward as the boat hung by her bow from the surface. The *Deutschland* had been built to withstand pressure to fifty meters, about one hundred and sixty-five feet. Yet, at the time her stern was probably no more than one hundred and fifty feet below the surface. Why was the hull collapsing inward?

The captain did not offer any explanation for the cause of the accident, and he did not explain why he could not bring his boat to the surface. He did say that the crew tried for ten hours to get the boat under control without success. As time dragged on, the crew "despaired of success, and messages were written and placed in bottles for release." They were even preparing one man for an attempt to leave the boat and swim to the surface.

At the critical moment, the eleventh hour, "the boat suddenly began to move, reached the surface, and continued on to Bremerhaven without further mishap."[2]

The next day, 10 December 1916, the *Deutschland* passed the Rotesand light at 1400, and broadcast that her ETA to Bremerhaven was 1700 or 1800.[3] She entered the Weser at 1535 on a Sunday, but there were no cheering crowds waiting.[4] In fact, her return was a closely guarded secret. The boat went directly to a dock in Bremerhaven that was well hidden, and her crew was put aboard a receiving ship.

According to Captain König, the next forty-four days were spent repairing the boat—a job made bigger by the fact that no one seemed to agree on what had caused the problem.[5] And there were other problems.

Because the experts could not agree on what was wrong, nearly the entire "mechanical interior" of the boat was torn out and ordered rebuilt. But the work could not be done in Kiel where the Krupp technicians and engineers were available, because of the fear of spies. Instead, the boat remained in Bremerhaven, and all new parts had to be assembled there. To further confound the dreaded spies, orders for replacement parts were not placed with a single firm. Instead the orders were farmed out to several firms throughout the country, resulting in delivery delays, and parts that often did not fit.

While the repairs were being carried out, preparations went ahead for the boat's third trip to America. American consulates throughout Germany sent copies of invoices to the American Embassy in Berlin, for transmittal to Washington. Most of the invoices listed dyestuffs, chemicals, and pharmaceuticals. But one invoice showed that the Bergmann Elektrizitäts Werke, AG, was sending 1,050 meters of twisted copper cord to Emil Mayer in Tuckerton, New Jersey. The value was set at 12,714.50 Reich Marks, or about $3,000.00.[6]

The invoice caught everyone's attention because there was a critical shortage of copper in Germany. So short was the supply that the government had already seized private stocks and was requisitioning household items that contained copper. Aluminum was being substituted in many products, the meager copper supply on hand being reserved for specific products in which the substitute was totally unacceptable.[7] Under normal circumstances a thousand meters of copper wire was an insignificant amount. In December 1916 it was a lot of wire.

Despite the shortage, the raised eyebrows, and bureaucratic interference, the shipment was approved by the *Kriegsamt* for delivery in the United States. The shipment may have been made to provide an American manufacturer with materials needed to build parts for Germany, since it included electrical insulation of the type used on equipment installed in U-boats. That would be the sort of scheme, coupled with the plan to build U-boats in cooperation with the Lake Company, that the *Etappendienst* would have come up with.

In addition to chemicals and dyestuffs, the warehouse in Bremerhaven became a storage place for tons of mail. Thousands of Germans were eager to send letters to America, even at the high rate being charged. Included in that group were collectors and dealers who saw large profits in stamps canceled with the *Deutschland* logo.

Across the ocean, preparations were being made to receive the *Deutschland* in New London. On 5 January 1917, an advance force of twenty-five black stevedores, part of the crew that had handled the cargo on the two previous trips, arrived by train from Baltimore. This time their arrival hardly caused a stir, in part because of their small number, and in part because the New London residents were now accustomed to the Germans' security measures.[8] It would be interesting to know if the British spy was among the twenty-five.

But things were happening in Germany that would soon put an end to those preparations.

The blockade was slowly paralyzing the German economy. By December 1916 Germany was experiencing its first "turnip winter," a term coined for the only food that was available in large quantity. Fifty percent of the potato crop had failed that year, grain harvests were badly reduced by fertilizer shortages, and the nation's livestock were starving on the hoof.

At the front the soldiers' daily meat ration—when there was one—had been cut to six ounces. That was usually horse meat. It was sometimes mixed with dried vegetables, but more often with nettles, and served as stew. In fact, gathering nettles was a daily chore for frontline soldiers. Their bread was made from ground turnips, mixed with sawdust, and flavored with a turnip paste called "Hindenburg fat."[9] The situation was not much better at home.

The huge offensives of 1916 had failed to break the stalemate. And it was obvious to nearly everyone that if the war of attrition continued, the Entente powers would probably win. In fact, the outlook was so grim in November 1916 that General von Ludendorff asked a conservative deputy, "How on earth is this going to end?"[10]

Since October 1916 the Germans had been conducting a U-boat campaign according to the prize rules. But they were not sinking enough tonnage to cripple the British, and they were losing U-boats to armed merchantmen and Q-ships. Even when they eased the rules and adopted what they called "restricted" U-boat warfare, they failed to achieve the necessary results. There was a growing opinion among civilian politicians, the public, and the military that the answer lay in a return to an unrestricted U-boat campaign.

Since December 1915, a year earlier, the U-boat faction had been forwarding figures claiming that the U-boats could win the war—and quickly. They said that if 631,000 tons of shipping were sunk each month, Britain would be beaten in six months.[11] To accomplish that, the U-boats had to be allowed to attack without warning.

The U-boat faction acknowledged that an unrestricted U-boat campaign would bring the United States into the war as a British ally. But that was not a problem, because the Americans could not get themselves organized quickly enough to play a role before the six months were up. By then Britain would be out of the war.

General Hindenburg and Ludendorff supported the plan, but were waiting until certain military situations had been resolved before they gave their blessing. As 1916 ground to a close, there was increasing pressure on the kaiser to give the nod to the U-boat faction. At the same time, Chancellor Bethmann-Hollweg and his civilian supporters were trying to block the plan while working for a negotiated peace.

Two days after the *Deutschland* had arrived in Bremerhaven, Bethmann-Hollweg had started to put out peace feelers in Washington. On 18 December President Wilson opened his own bid for a negotiated peace, and the Germans responded with a suggestion for a peace conference. Four days later, the French, replying on behalf of the Entente powers, insisted that the Germans give "restitution, reparation, and guarantees."[12]

The peace charade dragged on for a few more weeks with neither the Germans nor the Entente powers playing the game seriously. In

the meantime concrete moves toward a renewal of unrestricted U-
boat warfare were taking place.

On 16 December 1916, the navy ordered four of the *Deutschland*'s
sister ships converted to war boats.[13] They had been under construction since June, but were still on the stocks. Since they were still a
long way from being completed, now was a good time to start their
conversion. The hulls selected were located at Reiherstieg in Hamburg, and Flensburger in Flensburg. The three Hamburg hulls were
designated *U-152, U-153,* and *U-154*. The lone hull in Flensburg became *U-151*.[14]

On 22 December the U-boat supporters issued a new estimate
that showed Britain could be beaten in just five months. The required
destruction figure was reduced to 600,000 tons per month, but it
would also be necessary to "scare off" 1,200,000 tons of neutral shipping.[15] Hindenburg and Ludendorff agreed with the plan and began
to put more pressure on the kaiser.

Eighteen days later they met at Supreme Headquarters in Pless
and put their plan before him. Bethmann-Hollweg and his backers
vigorously opposed the idea, pointing out that America's entry into
the war would be Germany's ruin. The navy again discounted the
threat, saying that the war would be over before the Americans could
set foot in Europe. The kaiser agreed with the military, and unrestricted U-boat warfare was scheduled to resume on 1 February 1917.

On the day of the Pless decision, the Germans were still intending
to send the *Deutschland* to America on another trip. They knew that
after 1 February the American position might be dramatically
changed, but they were hoping to forestall her entry into the war
despite the resumption of submarine warfare. How successful their
efforts might be, was, at best, a guess. But if the American entry into
the war could be postponed long enough to get the *Deutschland* into
New London and out, that would be enough.

The dinner for König at the Hotel Beermann was held around
17 January; the exact date is not recorded. After the dinner, the
American diplomat, Mr. Buck, overheard Paul König talking to Director Stadtländer in German. König was a bit tipsy and speaking in
exaggeratedly hushed tones that carried halfway across the room.

"Bis jetzt," he said leaning forward to speak in the director's ear,
"haben wir keine Passagiere mitgebracht. Aber das nächste Mal kommt
einer mit." He straightened up, looking the director in the eye. "Sie
wissen das wohl, Herr Stadtländer, und wen ich meine." (Until now we

haven't taken a passenger. But the next time we will bring someone back with us. And you know very well, Herr Stadtländer, who I mean.)[16]

Herr Stadtländer glanced to his right, saw Buck listening, and signaled König to shut up. Captain König's head snapped around, his face reddening. Casting a weak smile at the American, König nodded his recognition, turned, and walked away. Buck returned the embarrassed greeting, finished his drink, and strolled away to join the other guests.

Buck had absolutely no idea about whom König was talking, and the conversation seemed unimportant. In fact, so unimportant that he did not report any of the things he heard that evening until eleven months later.

Who did the Germans intend to bring back on the *Deutschland*? My guess is that it was Captain Hinsch. He was an important operative in the United States, in regular contact with a host of German agents. Most of the other big names had diplomatic status, and would be sent home when the United States went to war against Germany. But Hinsch was the skipper of a naval auxiliary and had no diplomatic standing. Events after 6 April 1917 support that opinion.

At the same time, the Hilkens were telling the press that they expected the *Deutschland* to arrive in New London during the week of 18 January. Either they were basing their estimate on a previously established timetable, or they were just blowing hot air. In all probability, they were acting on the last information they had and really did expect the *Deutschland* in mid-January.

But they were blowing hot air when they added that a second boat had left Bremerhaven at the same time as the *Deutschland*. The second boat was reportedly a giant, twice as large as the *Deutschland*. Though they claimed the two boats had left Germany at the same time, the Hilkens were not sure which boat would arrive first.[17] In fact, neither would arrive.

Sometime before 20 January, the *Deutschland* made a trial run in the Weser. Everything was in order, the repairs seemed to be working as planned, but the boat was a bit overloaded. She returned to her berth, off-loaded part of her cargo, and was declared ready in every respect for sea.[18] At that time there was no operational reason to cancel her third trip. But on Saturday, 20 January, Berlin ordered the U-boat held until further notice.[19]

In the meantime, the Hilkens' press release had created a storm of rumors in the United States. The first one popped up on 29 January, claiming that the *Deutschland* had left Bremerhaven on 4

January and had been captured. The report was attributed to two merchant captains, one American, the other British, who had heard it from a Royal Navy officer. The capture had taken place in the North Sea said one, while the other said it had happened off the Irish coast.[20] It was a rerun of the stories that had filled the newspapers about the *Bremen*. But the next rumor was even sillier.

The next day, American newspapers carried a wild story, attributed to eyewitnesses, that a German U-boat had snuck into New London under cover of darkness and had resupplied from the *Willehad*. It was obvious to everyone that the mystery boat was the *Deutschland*'s escort, and the cargo U-boat would arrive at any time.[21]

The same day Captain Hinsch was cornered by the press and asked if the *Deutschland* had been sunk or captured. Certainly not, answered the captain. Then they asked him if she had started from Germany. Showing his true feelings about the press, Hinsch answered, "Now what's the use of asking me such a question? You know I won't answer you."[22]

Captain Hinsch probably did not know what was happening with the *Deutschland*, and he may have been seriously worried about her nonappearance in New London. He certainly could not show his concern, but neither could he answer the press's questions. At the moment, he was suffering confusion and doubt about the *Deutschland*'s next assignment, but events were about to eliminate all that.

Anticipating America's entry into the war, Germany's foreign minister, Arthur Zimmerman, embarked upon a plan to pit Mexico against the United States. On 16 January 1917 he sent a coded message via Sweden to von Bernstorff in Washington. The German ambassador was to pass the message on to Germany's representative in Mexico, Heinrich J. F. von Eckhardt.

The message promised Mexico the return of the land she had lost to the United States in exchange for her alliance against the Americans. It was not an unreasonable offer from the Germans' point of view, and certainly one that might appeal to the Mexicans. The problem was that the plan later became a red flag to the American bull.

The message was sent from Berlin to Washington in the new code 0075 that had been delivered by the *Deutschland* in November 1916. The problem was that only one code book had been aboard the U-boat. That meant that von Bernstorff could receive the new code, but he could not use it to send the message on to his man in Mexico.

The British had intercepted the message in code 0075 and had partially decoded it by the 17th. At that point they were stuck because they could not fill in the missing pieces of the message. But when von Bernstorff re-sent the message to Mexico on 19 January, using the old code 13040, the British had what they wanted. The British had broken 13040 in 1915, and could read it easily.[23]

The final act was played out on 31 January when the Germans notified the Americans that on 1 February unrestricted U-boat warfare would be resumed.

CHAPTER SIXTEEN

SHUTTING DOWN THE PROGRAM,

1 FEBRUARY–6 APRIL 1917

T he small band was playing *Prussia's Glory* for the seventh or eighth time that evening, two barmaids were delivering mugs of Schultheiss beer to the tables, and the multiple conversations were happy and noisy. In bars all over Berlin, the news that unrestricted U-boat warfare had again started was being heartily celebrated. The men gathered in the Alte Krug, a popular restaurant and bar in the affluent district of Dahlem, were especially happy about the news.

These were the men who collectively formed the backbone of the German economy, and the news they were celebrating represented the salvation of that economy. And the economy needed salvation, because at the moment it was in serious trouble. There was more at stake than just winning or losing the war. A faltering economy, the seemingly endless casualty lists, and the growing food shortage threatened to unleash social unrest. And with it would come changes these men did not want.

The military had promised that an unrestricted U-boat campaign would end the war by summer, and these men believed it. Not just because they wanted to, but because they had faith in von Hindenburg and von Ludendorff. And faith was something these men no longer had in the kaiser, his ministers, the chancellor, or the Reichstag deputies.

Outside the smoke-filled, noisy bar, the number 40 streetcar rattled by, its pale yellow headlamp casting a weak beam on the snow-covered street. The car was packed with people returning to their homes from the stores and offices in Steglitz, all of them clutching a newspaper with the banner headline U-BOAT WAR RESUMED.

Among the people on the number 40 there was an air of expectation and optimism. Like the men celebrating inside the Alte Krug, the people on the streetcar had faith in the General Staff. Every time the streetcar ground to a rattling, screeching halt, a few passengers got off and quickly scattered, each hurrying home to a private celebration.

Far across town, in the working-class district of Spandau, August Götze sat hunched over a bowl of watery soup. His wife was brewing a cup of coffee made from a mixture of burned acorns and used coffee grounds.

"At last," he said, "the generals are going to run the war."

"Do you really believe it will be over in five months?" his wife asked as she poured boiling water over the mound of ersatz coffee.

"Now that the U-boats have been unleashed, with no more asinine restrictions put on them by the politicians, it will end quickly." He stared directly into his soup bowl as he spoke, spooning up the colorless, nearly tasteless fluid.

"I hope you're right," she said, pouring the black liquid into a thick-walled mug. "The war has gone on too long."

"You're sounding like the Bolsheviks in the factory," he warned. "Do you want us to just stop fighting?"

"No." She set the mug next to him and sat down at the table. "It's just that every time they have a plan, it's supposed to end the war. But what do we have to show for all their grand plans?"

"We occupy most of Europe, the Western Front is stable, and we are advancing in the East. With Hindenburg and Ludendorff in charge the war will end quickly. Britain can't go on." He reached for the coffee mug.

"Neither can we, if we starve," she said, her voice tired.

"Now you do sound like a Bolshevik," he said without reproach. "It's the sort of thing they're spreading in the factory."

"I'll tell you something, my dear husband," she said picking up the newspaper. "If this U-boat campaign fails, the Bolsheviks won't just be in the factory. They'll be in the streets."

While the German people celebrated, Chancellor Bethmann-Hollweg and his supporters in the Foreign Office waited for the American reaction to the announcement. It came three days later. On

On 3 February 1917, the United States broke diplomatic relations with Germany. Count von Bernstorff, his wife, and daughter are seen here leaving Washington, D. C., to return to Germany. One week later the German navy officially ended the cargo U-boat program. (National Archives)

3 February 1917, the United States broke diplomatic relations with Germany. In Washington the German Embassy was closed, and Count von Bernstorff packed his bags. In New London a mysterious fire destroyed the Eastern Forwarding Company's machine shop on the State Pier.

That same day the *New York Times* reported that the *Deutschland* had sailed from Bremerhaven on 16 January. The report was a follow-up to a rumor that the *Deutschland*, laden with a thirty-million-dollar cargo, was due at any time. The question was: now that diplomatic relations had been broken, what would happen when she arrived?

She had not sailed on 16 January, and she was not laden with a thirty-million-dollar cargo. On 3 February 1917 she was still tied up in Bremerhaven, but her future was no longer in doubt. Three days earlier, the decision had been made to convert the *Deutschland* and the two remaining cargo boats, still under construction, into war boats.

The *Deutschland* was designated *U-155,* the other two were *U-156* and *U-157.*[1] On 4 February 1917, stevedores started unloading her cargo.

In New London twenty tons of cargo were removed from the Eastern Forwarding Company's warehouse and sent to Hoboken, to be stored in a warehouse belonging to Norddeutsche Lloyd.[2] The *Etappendienst* would have to find another way to get it to Germany. That same day Captain Hinsch disappeared.

On 10 February the navy officially ended the merchant U-boat program.[3] Captain König was again placed on active duty with the Imperial German Navy, returned to the rank of Kapitänleutnant, and took command of the blockade breaker, SMS *Rio Negro.* Lieutenants Krapohl and Eyring remained aboard the *Deutschland* as merchant officers.[4]

Meanwhile, in the United States the rumor mill was working overtime. On 8 February, the White Star liner, SS *Lapland* docked in New York with 199 passengers aboard. The trip across had been a bad one, taking eleven days instead of the usual nine. The delay was caused by repeated U-boat scares that forced Captain Bradshaw to spend long hours following a zig-zag course. One of those scares produced one of the most colorful rumors of the war.

According to R. N. Smith, a wealthy Canadian passenger, the *Lapland* was in the North Sea when a U-boat was sighted. Suddenly a British plane appeared, spotted the U-boat, and attacked it. While the passengers lined the rail to watch, the plane dove to four hundred feet and released its bomb.

The bomb struck the U-boat squarely, resulting in a tremendous explosion that blew the German apart and flipped the airplane over on its back. While the passengers watched in horrified fascination, the British pilot and his observer tumbled from their cockpits and fell into the sea. There was, however, a happy ending. The British airmen survived and were rescued by the *Lapland.*

But that was not the point of the story. What made R. N. Smith's tale worth telling was that the U-boat he had seen blown to pieces was the *Deutschland.* How did he know? Smith said he recognized it by its huge bulk when the pieces erupted from the sea in the explosion.

A better story would have been an explanation of how the two British airmen survived a four-hundred-foot fall into the sea. Miracles are rarely witnessed by over two hundred people, and a story like that would be worth at least a small headline. But in their eagerness to print the destruction of the *Deutschland* the press overlooked the apparent miracle. The fact that only Smith recalled the event may have had something to do with it.[5]

Three days later a new rumor contradicted Smith's claims about the *Deutschland* being blown to pieces. She had been captured. This time the source was absolutely unimpeachable—he was Dr. Nicholas Murray Butler, president of Columbia University.

Speaking at a banquet at the William Penn Hotel in Pittsburgh, Doctor Butler told his audience that the *Deutschland* was among eighty-five captured U-boats. He added that the Germans were trying to hide the fact by painting the name *Deutschland* on another boat. But Doctor Butler was not fooled. He knew she was in British hands, he assured his very attentive audience, because a friend who had seen the boat had told him so.[6]

Within a week Doctor Butler's claim was supported by an eyewitness account. William Palmer, second engineer aboard the SS *Mongolia,* told reporters in New York that he had seen the *Deutschland* in Plymouth. She was chained inside a huge floating pen that held 187 captured U-boats. And that was just a part of the 400 U-boats the British had captured. The sighting had been made while the *Mongolia* was discharging cargo in Plymouth between 14 and 27 January 1917. At least William Palmer claimed to be an eyewitness.[7]

By 15 February it became evident that something had happened to the *Deutschland,* or at least there had been a change in plans. On that day a notice appeared in the *New York Times* stating that mail for delivery to Germany aboard the *Deutschland* would no longer be accepted.

In Germany, an American journalist, Carl W. Ackerman, had firsthand knowledge that the plans were changed. Ackerman had posted several postcards to friends as souvenirs, but on 15 February all the cards came back. Several of his business friends also had letters returned with notices that they would be given a refund on the postage.[8]

Three days later the German navy officially took over the *Deutschland* and the two remaining sister ships.[9] The transfer of ownership, really only a paper shuffle, was a closely guarded secret. At the moment nothing changed outwardly. The boat was still tied up in Bremerhaven, Krapohl and Eyring were, at least on paper, still merchant officers, and no work was being done on the boat.

At this point there was no diplomatic development that could alter the *Deutschland*'s fate. So when on 24 February the British turned over to the State Department a decoded copy of the Zimmermann

This photo was taken in London after the war when the *U-155* was on display. The wide gun deck that replaced the narrow walkway is clearly seen, as is the opening that was cut into the rear of the conning tower. (U. S. Army Military History Institute)

telegram to Mexico, it was simply icing on the cake. The American government made the telegram public on the 28th, and the text appeared in the nation's newspapers the following day. The American people were outraged, but by that time the Germans did not care.

On the day the contents of the Zimmermann telegram were released to the public, the Eastern Forwarding Company was dissolved. The *Willehad* was released from her lease, and the remaining cargo stored on the State Pier was moved to a half dozen other locations along the eastern and southern seaboards.[10] The Hilkens, both American citizens, did not go into hiding, but they faded from the scene. It was not a good time to be doing business with the Germans.

That same day, in Bremerhaven, Emil Eyring was recalled to the navy, returned to the rank of Oberleutnant zur See, and assigned as the second officer aboard the *U-155*.[11] That night, with most of the men aboard who had been her "civilian" crew, she proceeded toward Wilhelmshaven for conversion to a war boat.[12]

The recoil from the two 150-mm guns splintered the wooden deck panels, loosened the metal plates, and caused the ready-ammunition lockers to leak. An officer is inspecting a pair of ready ammo storage tubes. (U. S. Army Military History Institute)

On 8 March a swarm of workmen started converting her. Two days later Franz Krapohl shed his disguise as a merchant officer, donned the uniform of an Oberleutnant zur See, and became the *U-155*'s executive officer. Their new skipper, Kapitänleutnant Meusel, arrived the same day.[13]

The *Deutschland* was the first of her class to be converted. The other six were still in their stocks in various stages in construction, and the first two would not be launched until April. There would be two more launchings in May, one in July, and one in September. Once the boats were in the water they would be towed to Wilhelmshaven where the conversion work would be completed. From that point they would be put into service at the rate of one per month, starting in July 1917. The last boat, *U-154* would be commissioned in December 1917.

Of all the boats, the *Deutschland* was the most quickly converted, the job being completed in less than fifty-three days. The most notable outward change was the addition of two 150-mm guns mounted fore and aft of the conning tower. The big deck guns had been taken

The original 150-mm guns were taken off an old cruiser. They were replaced after the first cruise with these monsters built for torpedo boats. These guns were on the *U-151*, turned over to France after the war. The *U-151* was identical to the *U-155* in outward appearance. (U. S. Army Military History Institute)

from the SMS *Zähringen*'s secondary battery after she became a training ship for boilermen in 1916.[14]

In order to mount the huge guns, the deck had to be reinforced and made larger. As a cargo boat, the raised wooden deck atop the pressure hull had been 8.3 feet wide. A new deck 20.8 feet wide, extending thirty-two feet aft, was added. The deck, made of steel plate and wood panels, was pierced with watertight ports through which the 150-mm ammunition could be passed. Forward and aft of the wide gun deck was a narrow wooden deck, 7.9 feet wide, extending to the bow and the stern.[15]

The other boats were being equipped with two torpedo tubes in the bow. That was possible because at the time their conversions were started, they were still unfinished. The *Deutschland,* however, was a completed boat, and tearing her apart to install bow tubes would have been too time consuming and costly. Instead, she was equipped with six exterior tubes, four in the bow and two in the stern.[16] All six were mounted between the pressure hull and outer hull in the space that had previously been used to stow wet cargo. All six tubes were angled fifteen degrees away from the hull, and could only be reloaded while the boat was on the surface.[17]

In an attempt to increase the boat's speed, two larger propellers were installed. The increase in speed was marginal at best, and the boats remained relatively slow. As a war boat the *U-155*'s top speed on the surface was officially reported as 12.4 knots. Submerged was 5.2.[18] In reality, the speeds were much lower.

While the *Deutschland* was being transformed into a long-range U-cruiser, Germany's U-boats were carrying out the renewed unrestricted U-boat campaign with vigor. One hundred and thirty-four ships were sunk in February, totaling 540,000 tons. In March the world shipping losses rose to 593,000 tons, still short of the Germans' 600,000-ton goal. But among the March losses were four American ships.

Three were sunk on 18 March, and the other on the 21st. All were sunk according to the prize rules with no loss of life.

On 1 and 2 April two more American ships were sunk, again according to the prize rules and without loss of life. But it was too much for the Americans, who had always been closer to Britain and her allies than to the Central Powers. The renewal of unrestricted U-boat warfare and the publication of the Zimmermann telegram had strengthened that relationship. Now the loss of six American flag carriers was too much to bear. On 6 April 1917, the United States declared war on Germany.

CHAPTER SEVENTEEN

WAR BOAT,

6 APRIL –21 AUGUST 1917

T he idea was brilliant, over two decades ahead of its time, and sure to be effective. Predictably, it was rejected out of hand. Kommodore Hermann Bauer, Führer der U-boote, had suggested in early April that the *U-155* be used as a radio command boat. Stationed in the southwestern approaches to the British Isles, the *U-155* would analyze enemy radio traffic, plot the approach and course of convoys, note the shifting of routes and the strength of escorts, and direct the movement of U-boats in a coordinated attack. He was proposing the wolf-pack tactic.[1]

The *U-155,* with her great size and range, was ideally suited to the role of providing close tactical direction, a feature that was notably lacking in U-boat operations. At the same time, she could have provided coordination for the Flanders and North Sea flotillas in their U-boat blockade of the British Isles. But the Admiralty Staff wanted a long-range U-cruiser to disrupt shipping carrying goods from the United States to the Mediterranean. So the wolf-pack leader idea was scrapped in favor of a lone war patrol around the Azores.

The Admiralty staff, anxious to try its U-cruiser concept, ordered the *Deutschland*'s conversion to be rushed. And it was. By 20 April, just forty-four days after conversion was started, she was undergoing speed trials outside Wilhelmshaven.[2] Ten days later she was assigned to the Kiel School for trials as a war boat. By the 23rd she was ready for sea and her first war patrol.[3]

The officer selected to command the *U-155* on her trial effort,

Kapitänleutnant Meusel, was an interesting personality. He was a good officer, competent, and concerned about his men and his mission. He was also a humanitarian who set out on his assignment intending to conduct his operations according to the prize rules.[4] He was reliable, rock solid under pressure, and, above all, tenacious. But if Meusel had a fault, it was his propensity to complain about his boat to anyone who would listen. He was not a whiner. His complaints were legitimate, well founded, and accurate. But he griped to everyone—even the enemy.[5]

When he left Kiel on 23 May, escorted by *V-160*, he was probably optimistic. And why not? After all, his boat had made two trips to the United States and back without serious problems, and she had just undergone a major refit in the German navy's largest yard. His optimism suffered its first setback on 24 May, one day out.[6]

At mid-morning the motor that drove the main compressor stopped. The failure was a major problem because without the main compressor, pressure could only be developed with two small auxiliary compressors that operated directly off the diesel engines. Running those compressors all the time put an extra strain on the diesels that caused them to overheat. That, in turn, revealed a shortcoming in the design of the cooling system on the diesel engines and the air pumps.

While the engineering staff worked to repair the problem, a message was received that a convoy was in the area. Captain Meusel immediately altered course to intercept the convoy. Throughout the next day he worked to place his boat in position, stopping occasionally to examine Swedish fishing boats that he came across.

At 0820 on the 26th a lookout spotted a steamer. As the crew went to battle stations the starboard diesel engine sputtered, coughed, and died. Limping forward on one engine the *U-155* was unable to keep up with the steamer, much less catch her. The ship vanished in the mist.

Frustrated, Captain Meusel heard from his chief engineer that the starboard engine had shed an exhaust valve. A hurried examination had shown that seawater had somehow entered the valve, which operated at a temperature of 400° C. The contact with the cold seawater had demolished the valve.

It was soon discovered that the mechanical system for closing the various openings in the hull was poorly designed. All were operated by hand and involved a series of wheels, cables, and pulleys. The

The interior of a *Deutschland*-class U-boat, modified to a war boat, was cramped and poorly lighted. With the exception of the *U-155*'s forward torpedo room, all the boats had the identical interior layout. This picture was taken aboard the *U-151* and shows the passageway through the former after cargo hold. (Naval Historical Center)

system was simply too slow, so that when the boat dove, some of the openings were still partially open as she went under. That is how the water got into the exhaust valve.

The explanation was doubly aggravating to Meusel because he had pointed that out to the job engineer in Wilhelmshaven. But nothing had been done. The job was so rushed that there was no time to make the obviously needed modification.

The *U-155* now had only one operating diesel, and Meusel quickly felt the loss of the starboard engine. Even running on the surface the boat used electrical energy to power many of her systems. That represented a battery drain that required three hours of daily charging to recoup. The problem was that battery charging was done with a diesel engine that was not connected to a propeller. But with only one engine Meusel had to make a choice: drive the propeller or charge the battery. The result was that for three hours each day, the lone diesel was disconnected from the shaft and put to work charging the battery. During those three hours the boat was dead in the water.

There was another decision to make. Captain Meusel had intended to pass through the Shetland-Faeroes channel, the shorter route around Scotland. It was also more dangerous because there were more British patrols along that route, which meant that the *U-155* would have to dive more often. It also meant she would have to remain on the move and keep her batteries fully charged. With only one engine she could not meet those requirements, so Meusel was forced to take the longer route around the Faeroe Islands.

He was only four days out and already he was facing serious problems with his boat. What he did not know was that on 27 May he came very close to having all those problems permanently resolved when he was nearly torpedoed.

The *U-155* was running on the surface at one-engine speed, about 5.5 knots, when she was spotted by the *U-19*, commanded by Kapitänleutnant Johannes Spiess. The sea was calm, weather misty, when the dive alarm sounded board the *U-19*. The time was 1645.

Captain Spiess hurried to the conning tower as his boat dropped below the surface. His crew, experienced, well trained, and battle hardened, were already preparing to attack the target.

"Up periscope."

"Torpedo tubes ready."

Spiess swung the tube around, the target filling the lens. "Now I wonder if we will get a shot in?" he said studying the target. "He must be making high speed, well over 15 knots." The estimate was wildly inaccurate.

"Down periscope." He stepped back a half step as the tube slid downward. "That must be the Britisher who lies near Utsire. He shot *U-36* a while back."

The hum of the electric motors filled the conning tower. Spiess looked at the rating who operated the periscope, nodded, and said, "Up periscope."

Peering through the lens he continued to talk out loud. "Engines half speed. Good God, what a mob of men there are on deck." He studied the target carefully. "Engines slow. Down periscope."

Command central, shown here in the *U-151*, looked the same in the *U-155*. The periscope, covered with a heavy coat of grease, is just right of center, and the two chains to the far right are part of the periscope hoist. The original periscope was 6 meters long, but it was replaced with one 7 meters long after the first war patrol. Periscope depth for the *Deutschland* was 42 feet, and after the new periscope was installed, periscope depth increased to 45 feet. (National Archives)

Stepping back he folded his arms, dropping his chin in thought. "We'll pass ahead of him," he spoke to his torpedo officer. "A stern tube will be fired."

The officer gave the necessary orders.

"Up periscope."

Spiess watched his target carefully to be sure that he had set up the problem correctly. But something was wrong. He was puzzled by the two huge guns on deck, and more confused because the tubes were painted black. All German U-boats had black tubes. Was it a German boat? He had certainly never seen anything like it.

"Hold the stern tube," he said, stepping back. "Down periscope."

The men in the conning tower were puzzled by their captain's actions. Why had he held the shot?

"Watch officer and helmsman to the periscope," Spiess said.

The two men quickly came forward.

"Up periscope." Spiess gestured toward the lens. "Take a look and see what you think. Is she German or British?"

The two men took turns studying the strange submarine that was closing quickly. "German. *Deutschland* class," they both said. Spiess took another look, and agreed.

"Surface."[7]

Alongside one another the two captains exchanged information. Spiess told Meusel that there were no steamers or sailing vessels in the North Sea, and warned him to stay away from the coasts where there were "only destroyers and cruisers waiting for convoys." He also told the outbound skipper that the *U-19* had found little use for its deck gun. They had carried out torpedo attacks against ships in convoy, but only after having severe difficulty working in close enough to get a shot.

The following day another problem caused by the hurried conversion was discovered. The *U-155* had submerged to avoid a British patrol boat, but had been seen as she went under. Speeding to the place where the U-boat had disappeared, the patrol boat dropped two depth charges. Both exploded very close to the *U-155*, rattling her hull and the crew. Luckily for the German, the patrol boat skipper ran down the wrong bearing, dropping two more depth charges that exploded harmlessly in the distance.

Several hours later the U-boat rose to the surface, and unclutched her electric motors preparing to cut in the one working diesel. But when the main induction valve was opened, water poured into the engine room. The valve was quickly closed, and for several hours the only air source for the diesel engine was through the conning tower hatch and a small air shaft in the after part of the boat.

At first the engineering staff was at a loss to explain the cause of the problem. But later that day, while the *U-155* was waiting for a boarding party to return from the SS *Arundo,* they located the cause. The metal tube that passed between the outer hull and the pressure hull had collapsed. A close examination showed that the damage was due to faulty workmanship and not the depth charging.

Regardless of the reason for the failure, there was no way for the crew to repair or replace the section of pipe. So it was cut away and thrown over the side. But that left the U-boat with only one watertight closure for the main induction valve. With a deficiency that serious, many captains would have returned to port for repairs. Meusel pressed on.

His decision reflected his tenacious character and his commitment to his duty as he saw it. It was, nevertheless, a tough decision to make, but one that was soon rewarded by the report that the starboard diesel was back on line. For the next six days it looked like the *U-155* was over her bad luck.

During that time Meusel stopped three Dutch steamers, inspected their papers and cargoes, and released them. Though his boat was behaving well, the stops were not entirely problem free. On 31 May, while the SS *Texel* was being examined, the after 150-mm gun went off. The firing was unintentional, totally unexpected, and very nearly fatal for two crewmen who were standing on deck near the muzzle. Stunned, dazed, and probably scared witless, the two sailors were carried below. Both recovered.

On 1 June a storm started to build. Soon the seas were breaking across the *U-155*, tossing her about, and reducing her surface speed to less than 3 knots. At noon a lookout spotted a large ship with four stacks just 4,000 meters away, but the boat's motion was too violent to man the deck guns. Captain Meusel, concluding that the seas were also too violent to use torpedoes, dove and waited for the ship to pass.

The following day the seas had moderated enough for the guns to be manned, and the *U-155* had her first victory. That morning the U-boat stopped the Norwegian steamer SS *Hafursfjord,* found contraband aboard, and sunk her with gunfire and bombs. But there was a damper on the occasion.

Captain Meusel found that not only did heavy weather reduce his boat's surface speed to a snail's pace, but it also was about to rip out the torpedo tubes. Again, both problems were due entirely to the haste with which the conversion work had been done.

The torpedo tubes had been mounted on short struts that were welded to the flat tops of the various fuel and lubricating oil tanks. Large slots cut in the hull at the bow and the stern allowed the torpedoes to leave the tubes and pass through the outer hull. In heavy weather, tons of water surged through the bow slots, poured across the tubes, and slammed into a heavy steel bulkhead that ran athwartships behind the tubes. The volume of water being forced into the space between the hulls was too great to be carried quickly through other openings cut in the hull, causing a number of things to happen.

A tremendous strain was put on the bow tubes as the water surged in through the slots. That strain was increased by the violent motion of the water trapped between the hulls. Under strain, the tubes and the heavy torpedoes worked on the short struts that were

The *U-155* seen from the deck of one of her victims. This scene occurred in less than half the U-boat's attempts to stop her target, because she was too slow to catch most Atlantic steamers. (National Archives)

welded to the tank tops. The least that could happen was that the tubes and the struts would separate at the weld joints. Though bad, that was better than the other possibility.

Captain Meusel's big concern was that the tubes would literally pull the struts out of the tank tops. The metal there was very thin, and the struts tearing away would rip open the tanks, causing leaks the *U-155*'s crew could not fix.

There was another problem with the arrangement that had not yet become evident, but soon would. The *U-155* had been issued only six torpedoes; one for each tube. There were no reloads. Those six torpedoes had been loaded in Kiel before she left, and were intended to remain in the tubes, fully immersed in seawater until they were fired. It was expected that the torpedoes would be periodically serviced while the boat was at sea. In practice, however, the service schedule could not be kept.

The biggest obstacle to servicing the torpedoes was the location of the tubes. In order to work on them the torpedomen had to crawl between the hulls and work in water up to their chests. That might not have been too bad for short periods in a warm climate, though even in a warm climate, long periods of immersion are hard on people. They are also hard on torpedoes.

Despite the difficulties, the torpedoes were serviced whenever possible. The first opportunity came on 14 June, and three were found to be in "generally poor condition." The problems were mainly with faulty motors, but one was found to be losing compressed air, and another had a damaged rudder. Two weeks later all six were inoperative, and Meusel had to shut down for three days to repair torpedoes. Working ten-hour shifts in chest-deep water, the torpedo-men were able to get four back on line.

Related to the torpedo-tube problem was the boat's loss of surface speed in any sea condition other than flat calm. She had been rated at 12.5 knots, but experience showed that 9.5 knots was about the best she could do under normal conditions. At that low speed just about any freighter in service at the time could outrun her. And they did, regularly. The problem was the athwartships bulkhead above the torpedo tubes.

The bulkheads had been put there to support the gun deck on which sat the two 150-mm guns. The after bulkhead was not such a problem, but the forward one was. It acted like a dam, interrupting the free flow of water aft. Just as a rudder that has been put hard over acts as a brake, slowing the vessel, so did that bulkhead. The difference was that a rudder spent most of its time amidships, while the bulkhead was always at a right angle to the water flow.

The loss of speed was attended by an increase in fuel consumption and a corresponding drop in range. Captain Meusel estimated that his range was half the yard's estimate of 25,000 nautical miles. Though the yard's estimate was wildly optimistic, the reality, 12,000 nautical miles, came as a shock. And the captain added that his estimate was based on a "conservative speed of three knots."

Those were the problems that caused Captain Meusel to complain about his boat. And complain he did. From 10 June forward, his daily war-log entries record his growing frustration, disappointment, and anger. By the end of his cruise, the list of problems had grown much longer, and in many cases more serious. At the same time that his successes were mounting, they were irritatingly overshadowed by a lengthening list of lost opportunities and failures. All were caused by the boat's slow speed, equipment failures, and another problem that was about to appear.

On 10 June he intercepted the British SS *Scottish Hero*, en route to Sydney, Australia, from Le Havre. Opening fire at 7,000 meters, Meusel watched the tanker turn away from him and open fire with a 120-mm gun in the stern. Captain Meusel had intended to make a torpedo attack, but decided he had too little faith in them to risk losing the tanker. Now, as rounds from the *Scottish Hero* fell alarmingly close, he wondered if a gun attack might also have been a bad idea.

The *U-155* registered eight hits on the tanker, one round explod-ing in the engine room and another hitting the bridge. After exchang-ing fire for thirty minutes, the tanker was dead in the water, her crew going over the side. Meusel stayed long enough to get the information he needed from the survivors, gave them a sack of provisions, and directions to the nearest land. He then "left them to their fate." Theirs was an unenviable fate.

The weather was turning bad again, and the seas were mounting. Turning away from the sinking ship, the *U-155* cut in both diesels, and hurried away to find calmer water. Along the way they spotted the SS *Armenia*, tried to close on her, but failed because the boat could not move fast enough to catch the target. Frustrated, Captain Meusel broke off the chase. Moments later the starboard diesel shed another valve.

Three days and a valve job later they attacked the SS *Kintuck* with gunfire. The British ship returned fire, turned away, and escaped behind a smoke screen laid from generators on her stern. An hour later, the *U-155* fired on the American steamer, SS *Luckenback*. The American escaped. Later in the afternoon they fired at the SS *Grain-ton*, en route to Bizerte. The British steamer never saw the U-boat, but as soon as the rounds hit the water off her bow, she poured on the coal and disappeared over the horizon.[8]

Captain Meusel now tried to devise a method of operation that would offset his boat's shortcomings. He decided that as soon as a target was spotted he would dive to avoid detection. Then he would run submerged to a point directly in front of the target and across its projected course. At that point *U-155* would surface and man her deck guns.

He was sure that the big, 150-mm guns would deter a merchant skipper from trying to ram the surfaced U-boat. "Nobody in his right mind would try to ram in the face of such fire power," he wrote. At the same time, his position athwart the target's course would allow him to score solid hits whether she turned right or left. He had a chance to try his plan the next day.

Shortly after sunrise on 14 June, a lookout spotted the SS *Ays-garth*, an Admiralty transport proceeding from Hornillo Bay to Glas-gow. She was armed. The U-boat dove and moved quickly into the *Aysgarth*'s path. When the U-boat suddenly appeared on the surface, 7,000 meters away and off the *Aysgarth*'s starboard bow, the transport tried to turn to the left in order to bring a large caliber stern gun to bear. But the *U-155* maneuvered so that she held her position forward of the *Aysgarth*.

Both deck guns opened fire, rounds smashing into the transport's hull and superstructure. The *Aysgarth* returned fire from a 76-mm gun in the bow. During the engagement that lasted nearly an hour, the U-boat fired fifty rounds, scoring fifteen hits. The *Aysgarth* got off just ten rounds in that time, but one caught the U-boat in the port lubricating-oil bunker, blowing it open, and rupturing the neighboring fuel tank. Oil spread quickly across the surface of the water.

The *Aysgarth*'s crew now abandoned their ship and rowed to the U-boat. While a boarding party was sent to the stricken transport, Captain Meusel had the British wounded treated, and a sack of supplies prepared. Soon detonations from inside the *Aysgarth* told the men on the U-boat that the boarding party had finished their work.

With the return of the boarding party, and the consignment of the *Aysgarth*'s survivors "to their fate," the Germans turned to the job of damage control.[9] The lubricating-oil tank had lost 4.5 tons of oil, the fuel tank 10.5. The oil remaining in both tanks was pumped into other tanks, a job that took ten hours. The amount of lubricating oil lost was not significant, according to Captain Meusel, but 10.5 tons of fuel oil was a serious matter.

Late that afternoon, the *U-155* captured the Norwegian tank steamer, SS *Benguela*. He needed the ship as a temporary "hotel" for his prize crews, in order to get "more air and space" aboard the U-boat. He also needed provisions from the prize, and he wanted to use her as a tow boat to conserve the U-boat's fuel supply.

Using the *Benguela*'s crew to operate the ship, the *U-155* was taken in tow at 1700.[10] Throughout the night the two ships proceeded on a westerly course, stopping at noon on the 15th. They had covered just 40 nautical miles, but Meusel estimated that he had saved a half day's fuel.

For the next twenty-two hours the two ships lay side by side while repairs were made to the *U-155* and a temporary radio was hooked up aboard the *Benguela*. Captain Meusel intended to use the *Benguela* as a support ship, and he wanted to be able to stay in radio contact with her. He did not think the prize crews would be captured while he was away, so long as he was near enough to return and torpedo any enemy cruiser. But to ensure that the *Benguela* was not recaptured, he ordered charges set below the waterline.

From 16 to 22 June, the *Benguela* plodded westward, towing the

U-boat, and stopping every twenty-four hours so that the *U-155* could make a practice dive. By 1700 on 22 June, they had covered 365 nautical miles. The *U-155*'s batteries were fully charged, her repairs were completed, and her main compressor was back on line. Captain Meusel was ready to hunt.

The SS *Fernleaf,* under Admiralty charter, was en route to Port Arthur, Texas, when the *U-155* surfaced off her port bow and opened fire. Using the same tactic he had used against the *Aysgarth,* Captain Meusel waited for the steamer to turn away. To his surprise, the *Fernleaf*'s captain did exactly what Meusel had said no man in his right mind would do—he turned toward the U-boat.

The range quickly closed from 8,000 meters to 5,000 meters, the freighter firing steadily at the U-boat with a 76-mm gun mounted in the bow. The *U-155* continued to fire with both guns, scoring three hits on the superstructure below the bridge. At 5,000 meters the *Fernleaf* went about, unmasking a 120-mm gun on her stern that opened fire with surprising accuracy. Two rounds fell very close to the U-boat.

The *Fernleaf* now went to full speed, making smoke, and firing her stern gun whenever there was a view of the target. The *U-155* gave chase, pumping round after round from her forward gun at the fleeing freighter, the gap between them widening. In the U-boat's conning tower, Meusel stared after the freighter and vowed to sink the steamer at any cost.

Three hours and five minutes later, after firing one hundred rounds, all misses, Meusel broke off the chase. The *Fernleaf* was far out of range and continuously broadcasting an SOS, giving the U-boat's position, course, and speed. The time had come to clear the area before help arrived.

That evening he made two observations in his war diary. He complained that the *U-155* had too much freeboard, making her too easily seen at a distance. The outer hull, he wrote, was much too large, and should be cut down so that it is closer to the pressure hull "as in modern war boats."

The second observation had to do with tactics. Based on his recent experience with the accuracy of the *Fernleaf*'s 120-mm gun, he modified his surface-in-front-of-them plan. It was still a good plan, especially for a boat as slow as the *U-155*. But, he wrote, "you should first approach the target submerged to see what kind of armament it's carrying."

The *U-155* as she appeared on her first war patrol. (National Archives)

For the last two weeks his boat had been behaving reasonably well. The torpedoes were still unreliable, the fuel consumption was too high, and the boat was losing targets almost daily because she was too slow. But nothing had broken down since 10 June. That was about to change as another design flaw became evident.

On 28 June, the chief engineer reported that the starboard, after lubricating-oil bunker had run dry. The loss was about five tons. He also reported that the fuel bunker below the lubricating-oil bunker was leaking. There were two possibilities for what caused the leaks: the two near misses scored by the *Fernleaf* or the vicious recoil of the 150-mm guns.

A near miss may have been the culprit in the case of the leaking oil tanks, but the guns' recoil was definitely beating up the outer hull. Every time the guns were fired the decks worked, and in turn that worked the steel struts that bound the outer hull to the pressure hull and the tanks. The strain was simply passed down the line, doing damage as it went. And the damage was clearly evident.

Steel deck plates and watertight closures were loose. The outer lids on the watertight ready-ammunition storage tubes were so loose that the tubes had filled with seawater, destroying forty rounds of 150-mm ammunition that had to be thrown over the side. Wooden deck panels were broken and splintered. In one instance the steel flap covering the port-bow torpedo tube had fallen into the sea when the forward gun was fired. And there were leaks in the pressure hull.

Describing the situation in his war diary, Meusel wrote, "The recoil is an eternal well for failures."

On 29 June Captain Meusel closed the first phase of his cruise by sinking the SS *Benguela*. Her crew and the crew of a sailing ship he had stopped that same day were now put aboard the Spanish freighter, SS *Joaquim Mumbru,* for return to England.

While the *Benguela* had been acting as his support ship, Meusel had several conversations with her skipper, Captain Hansen. The two men may not have become good friends, but they certainly shared a professional interest in the sea, and the British merchant officer was particularly interested in what Meusel was telling him.

Captain Meusel had been about as talkative to the *Benguela*'s captain as the *Deutschland*'s crewmen had been to the citizens of Baltimore. He had told the Norwegian about his boat's problems, and showed him the damage done by the recoil. He had also talked about the nightly radio messages from Germany, the quality of Zeiss periscopes, and German plans to send three large U-cruisers into the Atlantic. The Norwegian captain was an attentive listener.

Just before the Norwegian crewmen went aboard the Spanish ship, Meusel called the Norwegian officers aside. He had a document he wanted them to sign. It was an agreement promising that for the rest of the war they would not serve aboard a vessel that was an enemy of Germany. It was a ridiculous idea, one that many officers would have refused to sign. Not so the Norwegians. Captain Hansen had valuable intelligence to deliver to the Royal Navy, and he wanted no delays getting it to them. He signed, and so did the others.[11]

With the departure of the *Joaquim Mumbru,* Meusel's experiment using a prize as a support ship ended. During the two weeks he had the ship, he had only one success, the sailing vessel *Siraa* on the 29th. Most of the time had been spent making repairs and training. He had spotted several ships during that period, but his boat's shortcomings had prevented him from attacking them.

The following day he opened a period of independent operations that was to last until the end of his cruise. The technique proved to be much more practical and successful than using a support ship, and during this period the *U-155* made a strong impression on Allied naval planners. But his successes were still outnumbered by his setbacks, and another setback occurred that day. He had gone to Ponta Delgada in the Azores to torpedo a couple of ships that he hoped were anchored in the harbor. They were there, but were masked by the huge stone mole. Disappointed, Meusel turned away, and as he did, his lookout spotted a steamer just five miles out. Meusel immediately took up the chase, intending to stop the ship when they were out of sight of land. Instead, the ship was soon out of his sight, and he gave up the chase.

Compared to the *U-155* in the previous picture, the *U-35* had a much lower silhouette. Captain Meusel regularly complained that the *U-155*'s great size made her too easy to see, even at long distances. (National Archives)

In his war diary he wrote, "If this boat's surface speed had been a little faster, I would have chased her."

He was now thirty miles south of Ponta Delgada. His batteries were fully charged, and he decided to return for another try at the anchored ships. As he approached the harbor, he submerged, came to periscope depth, and moved toward his target. Suddenly the bow broke surface, and plunged down as the stern rose up. It was impossible to hold the boat at periscope depth as she porpoised through the water toward the harbor entrance.

Coming about, he took the boat deep and set about to correct the trouble. The electric motor that powered the after horizontal planes had burned out. Without it, the planesman could not hold the boat steady at depth.

There were no spare motors aboard, so one had to be taken from somewhere else. After all, holding the boat steady at depth was absolutely necessary, especially at periscope depth. The answer was to unship the main rudder motor and hook it up to the after diving planes. That meant the main rudder had to be worked by hand, and could only be put over 10° to either side. That worked out to a turning circle of about 1,000 meters. But at that point, Captain Meusel felt that depth keeping was more important than surface maneuverability.

Following the disappointment at Ponta Delgada, Captain Meusel got his chance to fire a torpedo on 7 July, a stern shot at the SS *Coblentz* bound from Genoa to London. The torpedo left the tube and disappeared, apparently sinking to the bottom like a rock.

Captain Meusel knew something had gone wrong when he did not see the torpedo's wake streaking away toward the target. He concluded that the torpedo had gone bad while it lay in its tube beneath the port diesel exhaust pipe, where the wide fluctuation in temperature between the hot exhaust and the cold water had ruined it. He knew the torpedo had been reconditioned on 2 July, so the damage had been done in just five days.

The *U-155* surfaced and opened fire on the *Coblentz*, which now turned away, making smoke and zig-zagging. Despite the fact that she could only make ten knots, the freighter escaped. In part, she escaped because Meusel had adopted the practice of opening fire at extreme range. He wanted to avoid being hit, and was hoping that his heavier guns would damage the target sufficiently to force her to stop. The plan only worked occasionally.

The American intelligence summary prepared in April 1918 had this to say:

> The *Deutschland* is of slow speed, 11 knots as a maximum, a rate hardly greater than that of the transatlantic freighters. She is very prudent, holding herself at the extreme limit of her range. Her fire, moreover, is slow and not very accurate. A number of vessels less heavily armed than herself were able to escape from her. Several others might have escaped as well if they had shown a little more tenacity.[12]

He finally made two successful torpedo attacks, one on the 8th and the other on the 11th, followed on the 14th by another success when he stopped one of the less tenacious skippers and sank the freighter with explosives. But his string of successes was interrupted for three days when water was found in the starboard engine's exhaust and the boat's cooling system broke down. Temperatures inside the hull rose to 45° C (113° F), and the batteries were so hot he could not recharge them.

The repairs made, he went on to sink six ships during the next four days. He would have had a seventh, but the torpedo he fired missed. Despite the miss, Meusel had reason to feel things were looking up. That is until the starboard diesel went lame again and the cooling problem again became a crisis. This time the lubricating-oil temperature in the tanks located in the electric motor room rose to 65° C (149° F), forty-five degrees above normal. Repairs took another five days, during which the boat was virtually immobilized.

On 26 July, the U-boat spotted a freighter 8,000 meters away, and opened fire. In a scene that the German sailors were finding boringly repetitious, the freighter turned away, made smoke, and returned fire with a stern-mounted gun, the rounds falling very close to the *U-155*. One in fact exploded so close alongside the port number-three ballast tank that the seams opened. The *U-155* struggled along after the fleeing freighter, her rounds falling wide of the mark while the distance between the two ships steadily grew. Frustrated, Captain Meusel watched his victim disappear over the horizon. In his war diary he bitterly wrote, "By best weather, flat sea, and no fog or rain we can only make 7.5 knots." And that was not all.

Franz Krapohl, his first officer, told him that the deck guns were in bad shape. In fact, they were wobbly. An examination of the guns had disclosed that the muzzles could be pushed to the right or left of the line of sight by as much as 21°. That explained the growing inaccuracy.

Up to that time the forward gun had fired 453 rounds, the after gun 288. That was not a great deal, normally. But when the guns had been installed aboard the *U-155*, their mounts and training gear were too lightly built. The vicious recoil that was beating the boat apart had also taken its toll of the light mounts.

They tried to tighten the training gear by driving in lead stops. It helped, but made the guns very difficult to turn, and was not expected to last very long. Meusel's war diary entry summed up the situation.

"In any event, the guns have ceased to be precision weapons."

While the guns were being jury-rigged with lead stops, the torpedoes were being inspected. The findings were not encouraging. One was leaking compressed air, and the other had a damaged rudder. Captain Meusel decided to use them as soon as possible, before they became completely inoperable.

In the meantime, there was a third problem: a port-side fuel bunker was leaking. Using a specially constructed bottle, the bunker was sounded to determine how much fuel had been lost. The bottle was lowered and the top was opened. The depth marker on the line was noted and the bottle was raised. If it was full of water it meant the sample had been taken from below the oil, and samples were then taken at regularly spaced increments approaching the surface. When the bottle came up filled with oil, they knew how full or empty the tank was. The process was time consuming and Captain Meusel complained about the lack of technology for sounding tanks. But at the moment he was more concerned about the leak and the oil loss.

He estimated he had lost about 10.5 tons, or 500 nautical miles of range. At the rate the *U-155* was moving about, that could be two or three days operating time.

Beginning on 31 July the *U-155* enjoyed a short string of successes, sinking four ships and losing another through the usual run, fire, and make-smoke routine. Then on 2 August she picked up a broadcast from the German transmitter in Nauen that a large American transport was expected in the Madeira Islands early in August. Running on two engines, *U-155* headed for Madeira to intercept the American.

On 4 August, after losing one target and releasing another, the port diesel engine gave up, forcing the U-boat to lie dead in the water for two hours while the engineers replaced an injection-pump valve. When they were finished the chief engineer told the skipper that the port engine was about to fall apart. Meusel, no longer surprised at such reports, simply shrugged and ordered the run toward Madeira resumed.

The *U-155* was limping toward Madeira on one engine, barely making five knots, when there was more bad news—the after diving-plane motor was on the fritz again. There was now no hope of reaching Madeira in any shape to carry out an attack. Bitterly disappointed, Captain Meusel laid out a course to a point north of the Azores where he intended to lay up and repair his boat.

The following day the port diesel came back to life and things started looking up again. The situation improved when a freighter was spotted dead ahead, coming toward them, an ideal situation for a torpedo attack. The U-boat dove and moved in for the kill.

Things were going smoothly, the problem was being set up in textbook style, and there was plenty of charge still in the batteries. Meusel was taking periodic, quick looks through the periscope, and was about to take another.

"Up periscope," he said leaning forward, poised to grab the handles as the scope rose to eye level. The tube started up smoothly, rose to half extension, and stopped. The drive motor had broken down. Leaping through the hatch into the Command Central, Captain Meusel ran forward to the second periscope.

Unfortunately, it was not equipped with a motor and had to be raised by hand. It took two men fifteen minutes to crank the periscope up. Meusel was livid. He was even more livid when he tried to use it. In his war diary he described the second periscope as "worthless," pointing out that the conning tower was half out of the water when using the periscope in the Command Central.

Surfacing, the *U-155* brought both her big guns into action, the rounds throwing up geysers on both sides of the freighter. But instead of shooting back at the U-boat, the freighter opened up on another ship that the Germans had not seen. In utter amazement, the Germans watched the two freighters blast away at each other, while making smoke and running in opposite directions. Both ships escaped each other and the U-boat. Disgusted, the *U-155* resumed her trip north. That afternoon the port diesel broke down.

On 7 August, the *U-155* sank the SS *Iran* with a torpedo that struck the freighter in the stern, sinking her in less than ten minutes. That same day the U-boat sank a sailing vessel after stopping it and placing explosive charges in the hold. While alongside the bark, waiting for the boarding party to complete their work, a seaman shouted and pointed toward the water. As far as the eye could see, there was oil all around them on the surface.

Continuing north, Captain Meusel took stock of his boat's condition. Her port diesel was out of commission and the starboard diesel was on its last legs. With only one engine, they could not produce fresh water. The main rudder could only be operated by hand, the after diving-plane motor was unreliable, the periscope motor was burned out, they were losing oil literally by the ton, and the one remaining torpedo was losing compressed air. He estimated it would take eight days to put things right.

From 10 to 15 August, the *U-155* holed up at a small island. The repairs needed would have been impossible to make on a regular U-boat, and they were difficult enough aboard the *U-155*. But she had a complete machine shop aboard, including a six-inch lathe. That made it possible for the crew to completely tear down and rebuild both engines. In fact, the only repair they could not accomplish was to the original diving-plane motor. For the time being, the main rudder would still have to be moved by hand.

His repairs completed, Captain Meusel intended to remain in the area for another six days, but he was getting low on fuel. If, during those six days, he did not find a target for his last torpedo, he was going home. As things worked out his last target was the Japanese freighter *Tobe Maru*, and she got away. But the chase, and the recoil of the 150-mm guns finished the *U-155* as a fighting boat.

Oil was leaking from several tanks, and an auxiliary tank on the starboard side was already dry. The guns were so wobbly for lay and train that Captain Meusel concluded that they were worthless. The next day, 17 August, the port diesel engine blew a cylinder head. Four days later while trying to make a submerged attack against the American tanker *Sun,* the U-boat became unmanageable at periscope depth. She broached several times, was spotted, and broke off the attack. It was time to go home.[13]

CHAPTER EIGHTEEN

THE FINAL YEAR

Heinz Berger flattened himself on the ground, his legs spread in a wide V, his cheek pressed against the stock of his anti-tank rifle. One hundred yards to his front a thirty-ton steel box with rhomboid tracks lurched toward him, machine-gun fire pouring from its sides. Even as Heinz sighted the heavy, 13-mm rifle at the tank, he saw dozens more emerging from the mist of the November dawn. Heinz's stomach knotted, and his mouth went dry with fear.

All along the German line machine-gun and rifle fire erupted, tracers streaking toward the oncoming tanks. Grenades thrown prematurely by panicked troops arched forward, exploding harmlessly. German artillery began to fall among the steel monsters, tearing off tracks, and blowing huge holes in their sides. From the right a pair of 77-mm guns opened up, their flat trajectory rounds whipping across the front of the German line into the steadily advancing tanks. Still they came.

Heinz Berger waited until the tank he was aiming at had come within sixty meters of his position before he pulled the trigger. The recoil was violent, terrifying, and painful. The round had no effect on the tank.

On both sides of him, men were starting to run toward the rear. The din alone was unnerving, but the sight of those apparently unstoppable machines was devastating. Heinz opened the bolt, inserted another round in the chamber, and rammed the bolt home. Machine-gun fire was chewing up the ground around him, and cannon fire was exploding to his rear. Behind the tanks he saw the massed British infantry, bayonets fixed, moving closer.

Heinz simply pointed the rifle at the enemy and fired. There was no attempt to aim. There was no need to; the enemy was nearly on top of him. Terrified, he wanted to run, but he could not. Beneath his prone body the ground shook from the combined pounding of artillery and the tracks of the British tanks. A grenade exploded in the trench behind him, showering him with dirt and stones. Heinz cast a fearful look to the rear, looking for a route to safety, but saw only torn ground, corpses, and smoke.

Leaping to his feet, he raised his arms straight over his head and yelled, "Kamarad."

A burst of machine-gun fire from a tank twenty yards away hit him in the chest, blowing him over backwards.[1]

The British tank attack at Cambrai on 20 November 1917 was the Allies' first full-scale use of the new weapon.

Attacking along a six-mile front, three hundred tanks smashed through the Hindenburg line, and rolled four miles into the German rear area. By noon the massed tanks had shattered two German divisions. In a sense, the British were trying to accomplish with the tank what the Germans had set out to accomplish with the U-boat. Curiously, both were dependent on large numbers to be successful, a condition the British achieved with the tank but the Germans failed to achieve with the U-boat. In the end, neither weapon accomplished the goal of winning the war for its user.

Field Marshall Viscount Montgomery of Alamein summed up the situation later when he wrote: "The 1914/18 war could not be won; it could only be lost in a final failure of endurance by the men of one or the other side."[2] As early as 1917 there were signs that endurance was starting to fail, evidenced by mass refusals among French soldiers to go forward. Even the British had experienced a few problems. The Germans were still gritting their teeth and carrying on, but they were as tired of the war as were the others.

The war had become a slaughterhouse that was consuming nearly an entire male generation of all participants except the Americans. But the Germans had two additional hardships. The first was the economic ruin and near starvation brought on by the blockade, and the second was the demoralizing disappointment caused by the failure of the U-boat campaign to end the war. They had been *promised* that the U-boats would end the war by the summer of 1917. It was now autumn and there was no end in sight.

While Heinz Berger was dying at Cambrai, the *U-155* was in the middle of another major overhaul. Since 6 September she had been in dock 10 in the Germania yard in Kiel undergoing some of the major modifications that had been recommended by Captain Meusel. But Meusel had already been transferred to the *U-152,* and was replaced by Korvettenkapitän Erich Eckelmann.[3]

Under Captain Eckelmann's supervision, the six exterior torpedo tubes were removed and replaced with two bow tubes built inside the hull. The conventional placement allowed the boat to carry eighteen torpedoes, and made it possible to reload whether surfaced or submerged.

The two deck guns were also removed. In their place, following Meusel's recommendation, the yard installed two 150-mm L/45 guns taken from a torpedo boat. The six-meter-long main periscope was replaced with one seven meters long. It was not what Meusel had recommended, it was still too short, but it was an improvement.

The new propellers that had replaced the originals were pulled off, and the original *Deutschland* propellers were put back on. Experience had shown that the old propellers delivered the same speed as the new propellers, but did it at thirty revolutions per minute less. Thirty revolutions per minute for over one hundred days represented a measurable fuel savings.

The yard also added a cable cutter that was mounted on the foredeck. A complicated device something like a bolt cutter, it was designed to be operated from inside the U-boat. The idea was to submerge, drag the bottom until a telegraph cable was found, and then cut it. Despite being unwieldy and complicated, the thing worked and the *U-155* cut three cables on 10 and 11 February 1918 in the Azores.

Another device that was added to the foredeck was a steel net cutter. Essentially a steel triangle with a saw-toothed leading edge, the device was despised by Captain Eckelmann, who felt it was worthless. No nets had been reported in the Azores, his patrol area, and he did not expect to find any on the trip around Scotland. When after an eight-day storm the cutter was found to be twisted and loose, Eckelmann happily had it thrown over the side.

During the week of 13–20 December, the *U-155* completed her post-overhaul trials, tested her armament, and spent forty-two hours on the bottom looking for leaks. There were none.

Her crew was given Christmas and New Year's leave, the last man returning on 7 January 1918. For the next six days they loaded ammunition and provisions, and ran into their first problem. There was not enough room to store provisions for "sixty-six heads for one hundred days" plus all the 150-mm ammunition. Captain Eckelmann ordered the starboard, forward ammo locker emptied and repacked with food. The ammunition was put ashore.

By 14 January 1918, when the *U-155* left Kiel to start her second war patrol, General von Ludendorff had reached the conclusion that Germany must win the war quickly in 1918, or face certain defeat. Totally disillusioned by the failure of the U-boat campaign to achieve victory in 1917, von Ludendorff intended to launch an all-or-nothing offensive in the west. But the victory had to be won before the Americans arrived in Europe in sufficient force to shore up the sagging Allies.

On the plus side, the Russians were now out of the war and the Italians were no threat. Germany could at last concentrate her effort on one front. Enough food to sustain the army could be obtained from the secured areas in the east, though civilian rations would be in short supply.

On the minus side was the dangerous shortage of war materials caused by the now very effective blockade, and the obvious fact that the Austrians were losing their resolve. But probably the biggest threat was the increasing number of American troops arriving in France. And the general knew that it was just a matter of time until his own war-weary troops started to break down.

His plan called for a three-part offensive to be launched in March 1918. The U-boat campaign now became secondary, merely an ongoing operation in another theater. The U-boats were not considered unimportant, they were simply recognized as being unable to win the war on their own. The down-playing of the U-boat campaign does not seem to have dampened Captain Eckelmann's resolve, but it may have reinforced his conservative, careful nature.

The *U-155*'s 14 January to 4 May cruise was nearly a carbon copy of the cruise made under Captain Meusel. The only major difference was that Captain Eckelmann did not complain about the boat's short-comings and problems. In fact, he rarely mentioned them in his war diary. But he did discuss them in the attachments to his final report.

The problems encountered on the second war cruise were almost identical to those experienced on the first. There were torpedo problems, five of eight fired missed, the new periscope jammed, and the engines broke down regularly. Only the new deck guns behaved as

By 1918 General von Ludendorff had become disillusioned with the navy's boast that the war could be quickly won with an unrestricted U-boat campaign. A year had past since the campaign had been reopened, and no end to the war was in sight. These UB boats of the Flanders Flotilla continued to attack British shipping, but their operations had become a secondary theater. (Author's collection)

intended, and the cable cutter performed as planned until it broke beyond repair.

There was really nothing that could be done about the engines. They had not been designed to be power plants in a U-boat, they were to have driven auxiliary generators aboard a cruiser. They had made four trips across the Atlantic without a problem, but they had not been pushed as hard under Captain König as they were under Meusel and Eckelmann. The strains and loads put on them during war patrols that lasted more than one hundred days were just too much.

His boat was still much too slow, and many freighters simply ran away from the U-boat. Despite that drawback he sank ten steamers, seven of them armed, and seven sailing vessels for a total of 50,926 tons—very close to the eleven and eight for 53,262 tons sunk by Meusel. He fired more torpedoes than Meusel, but they both sank three ships with that weapon.

The *U-155* returned to Kiel on 4 May 1918 and received a new captain the next day. Meusel and Eckelmann had not been transferred because of poor performance, or because of their expressed criticism of the *U-155*. Germany was at that time building or planning to build a whole fleet of big, oceangoing U-boats, and the *Deutschland*-class boats provided an opportunity to familiarize new commanders with long-range, U-cruiser operations.

For three months, from 5 May to 9 August, the *U-155* underwent another overhaul. There were no major modifications made this time, just a lot of repairs. On 11 August she was ready for sea, and her last war patrol. Her new skipper was Korvettenkapitän Studt.[4]

Captain Eckelmann's resolve may not have been affected by the war situation in January, but the situation in August appears to have played a role in Captain Studt's operations.

The day before the *U-155* left Kiel on her last cruise, the Allies opened their offensive. General von Ludendorff's three-part offensive had failed, and Germany had no reserves left. Supported by hundreds of tanks and reinforced by fresh American troops, the Allies were again on the move. 8 August, the day the offensive opened, became known as "the black day."

On 27 August a lookout aboard the American steamer SS *Montoso* spotted a wake off the port beam. The man had seen the plume thrown up by the *U-155*'s periscope. At 1800, the *Montoso*'s captain, A. O. Forsyth, set extra lookouts and radioed his escort about the sighting. The steamer then made a radical course change.

Three hours later the *U-155* broke surface 2,000 meters from the *Montoso*'s port quarter, showing four feet of her conning tower. She was again spotted, and this time she was taken under fire by the *Montoso* and her armed steamship escort, the USS *Ticonderoga*. The U-boat surfaced, her gun crews running to their guns.

The American ships turned away, losing contact with each other in the dark, but the *Montoso* continued to fire at the U-boat, her rounds falling short. Unable to see the *Montoso* in the dark, the *U-155* gunners fired at her gun flashes, their rounds falling on both sides of the fleeing steamer.

From that point the duel ended like so many before it: the steamer pulled away, the *U-155* ceased firing and broke off the chase. She was still too slow to catch a fleeing steamer.

The encounter also included the same mechanical problems that had plagued the boat since her conversion. She had broken surface as she approached the *Montoso* because of a breakdown in the after diving-plane motor, making it impossible to maintain periscope depth. Fortunately, the problem was repaired quickly. But the failure of the gunners to hit the target had convinced Captain Studt that his deck guns were unreliable, and the previously unseen escort had come as a nasty surprise. In the future, he would be very cautious about surface attacks and rely more heavily on torpedoes.

He cleared the area, running due north for four days. On 31 August he stopped and sank the schooner *Gamo* in mid-Atlantic. The next day he made a gun attack on a navy tanker, the USS *Frank H. Buck,* an experience that reinforced his dislike of surface attacks.

The weather was clear and windy, the sea choppy when the U-boat spotted the *Buck.* Standing off 14,000 meters, Captain Studt opened fire with both guns. Despite the long range, his fire was fairly accurate, the rounds exploding close alongside the American.

Changing course frequently, the navy tanker returned fire with her two 3-inch guns. For thirty minutes the two ships traded shots, the U-boat closing to 10,000 meters. At that point the American opened up with a 6-inch gun mounted on the stern, and the *U-155* found herself in trouble. The American had her range, and the fire was accurate.

Captain Studt tried to pull away in an attempt to get clear of the American's fire, but still be within the range of his own longer-barreled deck guns. The U-boat was just pulling out of range when it was hit in an after oil tank. Moments later another round hit the water close aboard, just forward of the conning tower.

The *U-155,* her crew, and her captain were extraordinarily lucky. The lubricating-oil tank was a total loss, but not one that caused a serious problem. In fact, the damage was very similar to what Captain Meusel had experienced. The hit forward of the conning tower had showered the deck with shrapnel, punched a few small holes in the outer hull, but had miraculously not caused any casualties among the men on deck. However, the hit and the near miss did convince Captain Studt that the tanker was too tough a target to fool with. *U-155* broke off the attack.

On 2 September 1918 he successfully torpedoed the Norwegian

The American vessel SS *Lucia* was torpedoed by the *U-155* on 17 October 1918 near the Azores. The *Lucia* was the *U-155*'s last victim to be sunk under Erich Eckelmann's command. (Naval Historical Center)

SS *Shortwind* in the same general area where he had fought with the *Frank H. Buck*. As soon as the sinking was confirmed, he set out for the North American coast. Along the way he chased and lost the steamer SS *Monmouth* and sank the sailing vessel *Sophia*.

During the next six and a half weeks, the *U-155* sank five ships, three with torpedoes. The other two were sailing vessels that were boarded and sunk with timed charges. She also laid mines off Nova Scotia and cut a cable in the same area. The five ships she attacked with gunfire fought back and escaped, one scoring a hit on the *U-155* that did not seriously damage her.

Her last success occurred on 17 October when she torpedoed the American transport USS *Lucia,* bound for Marseille. The *Lucia* was in convoy with several other vessels, but without escort, when a torpedo exploded in the engine room, killing four men. Having fired the single torpedo, Captain Studt turned away and left the area. The presence of other ships kept him from surfacing to finish off the target with gunfire, something he would normally have done.

The *U-155* now headed back toward the Azores to attack shipping there. At home, the front was collapsing. On 26 September, the Americans had attacked at Argonne against stiff German resistance. But the German will to continue the war was ebbing fast, and by 4 October they were being driven back all along the front. On that day the Germans requested an armistice. But while the negotiations were

going on the fighting continued, and by the time the *U-155* was approaching the Azores, the Germans had been thrown out of western
Belgium and were almost out of France.

On 21 October, with the end clearly in sight, the *U-155* received
a radio order to return home. She arrived in Kiel on 15 November,
four days after the armistice had been signed.

Her final war patrol had not been spectacular. Half the ships she
attacked escaped. But that had also been the case during the first two
war patrols. In fairness to Captain Studt, he had spent seven days
laying mines and cutting a cable, there had been breakdowns, and the
recall shortened his patrol considerably. But his score, four steamers
and three sailing ships sunk, totaling 17,485 tons, was much lower
than Meusel's or Eckelmann's.

There can be no doubt that the situation at home when the *U-
155* departed on her cruise affected the captain and crew. Morale was
good aboard the *U-155*, but the men were not optimistic. The fact that
gun attacks were opened at ranges up to 14,000 meters indicates
greater caution than was exercised by Meusel and Eckelmann, both of
whom were noted for opening fire at extreme range.

The generally unreliable boat contributed to the crew's cautious
nature, and Captain Studt must have been influenced by the information he received from the two previous skippers. That information
told him his boat was too slow to catch anything faster than eleven
knots, the guns were inefficient and did as much damage to the U-
boat as they did to the enemy, and his torpedoes were literally a hit-
or-miss proposition. None of it was very encouraging.

There had been no joyous return, no band, no dockside crowds,
and no welcome-home speeches. The revolution that the German
middle class and aristocracy had feared had happened. But it had not
started in the Spandau factory where August Götze worked, nor in
the trenches at the front. The revolution started in Kiel among sailors
of the German navy. The kaiser was a fugitive in Holland, Berlin was
in the hands of the revolutionists, and the *U-155* was to be surren-
dered to the British. The war was over.

On 24 November 1918, the former *Deutschland* was handed over
to the Royal Navy at Harwich.[5]

EPILOGUE

Following the entry of the United States into World War I, came a wave of mass paranoia focusing on the imagined threat of German spies and saboteurs. Hundreds of Germans were rounded up and packed off to internment camps, military prisons, and local jails. Anyone with a German name or the hint of a German accent, and who was not an American citizen, was in real trouble. Citizens experienced only slightly less difficulty.

The coast was guarded and seaports were closed to anyone suspected of being German. German nationals who were living in designated barred zones were relocated or sent to the camps. Many lost their homes. At one point it was suggested in Congress that the barred zone be extended 100 miles inland.[1]

The fear was occasionally justified; a few saboteurs were arrested, tried, and convicted of plotting to blow things up. But for the most part the fears were unfounded and at times had outrageous results. Probably the best example of the extremes created by the fear appeared in a *New York Times* headline on 14 December.

MEXICAN ARRESTED IN POUGHKEEPSIE AND BROUGHT TO NEW YORK CITY ON CHARGE OF BEING AN ENEMY ALIEN.

Axel Bergos, the man arrested, was hardly an enemy alien, and certainly not a German. But he did have an accent.

The scope of anti-German feeling and fear is evident from a sampling of page-one headlines that appeared through December 1917.

194

195
EPILOGUE

H. F. BABEL INTERNED AT FT. DOUGLAS FOR BOASTING ABOUT GERMANY[2]

REV. S. SEIBERT ARRESTED AT CARMI FOR DISLOYAL UTTERANCES[3]

M. EISNER, COLLECTOR OF INTERNAL REVENUES, SUGGESTS THAT ENEMY ALIENS BE TAXED AT A HIGHER RATE THAN CITIZENS[4]

GERMAN INTRIGUE SUSPECTED AS CAUSE OF EXODUS OF NEGROES TO NORTH.[5]

The last allegation of German perfidy did not mean that they were trying to cause social upheaval in the North, though the headline certainly made that a possibility. No, the German plot struck more deeply at the ability of the United States to wage war on the Germans. According to the article, the blacks were being sent north to cause a decrease in the production of naval stores. The Germans were not that clever.

The roundups had been going on since 7 April, but one of the most sought-after subjects of the federal action, Captain Hinsch, had escaped. He had been in hiding since 28 February, most of that time spent in New York, his location protected by friends who were actually *Etappendienst* agents. But after the United States entered the war, federal agents hunting Hinsch began receiving information from his girlfriend.[6]

She appears to have been playing both sides, giving the federal authorities accurate information at times, but which was offset by delayed information and carefully prepared misinformation. She gave up some of his friends, told federal agents his whereabouts in New York a week after he was gone, and fed them an outright lie about his escape from America.

Early in July she told federal agents that Hinsch had sailed from South Amboy aboard the schooner *Wanola* and, together with three friends, had gone to Baltimore. She thought that had happened four weeks ago. By now, she added, Hinsch was either at sea headed for Germany or he had already rendezvoused with a U-boat.

She said that Hinsch had bought the *Wanola* in Boston several weeks before the United States entered the war. The purchase was made through third parties, allegedly for "Dutch interests."[7]

Her story sounded good. Records showed that a schooner *Wanola* had been sold in Boston in March 1917. The purchaser was reported

The war was over and the allies met to split the booty. Among their prizes were the five surviving *Deutschland*-class boats. (National Archives)

to be the Luna Ship Company, an American firm, but possibly an-other front like the Eastern Forwarding Company. By the time the federal agents found that the sale, the company, and the *Wanola* were in no way connected with Hinsch, he was long gone.[8]

He had left New York in June and had gone to Baltimore. While he was there, federal agents, acting on information supplied by the girlfriend, raided the New York apartment where he had been staying. They were a week late. By that time Hinsch was on his way to El Paso, disguised as a laborer. Luckily for him no one questioned his heavy German accent, or he would have been snapped up by zealous Ger-man-hunters, so it is probably safe to assume he had someone with him who spoke English well. He crossed into Mexico from El Paso on 14 July 1917.[9]

The other players in the Eastern Forwarding Company, Henry G. Hilken and his son Paul, dropped out of sight. They were American citizens, associated with German business interests, and strongly sus-pected of being German agents. Their close association with Hinsch, described in the press as "a dangerous German loose on American soil," did not help them.

Despite their widely publicized association with the *Deutschland,* Hinsch, and German interests in the United States, the Hilkens avoided arrest—at least on sedition charges. However, Paul again became a public figure for a brief time in November 1917 when a New York court issued a warrant for his arrest.

He had been having an affair with his secretary, Frances Billings. The problem was, she was Mrs. Frances Billings, and her husband, Guy, caught them.

Guy filed suit against Paul for $50,000.00, charging alienation of affection. Since Paul was a wealthy man with business interests in Milwaukee, Guy thought his wife's lover might go there to escape the suit. He expressed those fears to Judge Goff, adding that Paul was a known German sympathizer, and recounting his association with Hinsch. Despite objections by Paul's attorney, Edward A. Brown, Judge Goff issued a warrant for Paul's arrest, setting bail at $2,000.00.

The resulting divorce trial was front-page news for weeks, detailing a lurid tale of lust, passion, and deceit. The readers loved it, and it may have been the best thing that happened to the Hilkens. So much attention was focused on Paul's love life, the Billings's scandalous background, and the revelations about her parents' marital problems, that people forgot the Hilkens were supposed to be German agents.[10]

A shadowy figure who appeared briefly in the early stages of the *Deutschland* operations had gone home with Ambassador von Bernstorff. Dr. Heinrich F. Albert was the man who bought most of the cargo, especially the nickel, for the Germans. He was a member of the diplomatic staff in Washington, and had immunity from arrest. Because of his activities in the United States, he was known as "Germany's leading bagman and blockade runner."[11]

On his return to Germany, Albert was made the trustee of enemy property. In that capacity he managed the disposal of property, goods, and securities in the captured areas. He has been described as a "brilliant man of business, a commercial colossus, and somewhat of a mystery."[12] The former statements may be a bit overdone, but the last one is absolutely correct. After the war his name disappeared from the press. But he remained active in the government, where his superior understanding of international business made him a valuable member of the *Etappendienst.*

Dr. Albert's civilian counterpart, Alfred Lohmann, spent the rest

The *Deutschland*'s last commander was Lieutenant J. A. Blackburn, RN, shown here with his crew aboard the U-boat in London on 4 December 1918. (U. S. Army Military History Institute)

of the war directing much of Germany's centralized procurement program. The war proved costly to him, and the postwar financial setback may have contributed to his early death in 1928.[13]

Paul König remained a Kapitänleutnant until the end of the war. He commanded in succession the auxiliary minesweepers, *Rio Negro, Dania, Wigbert,* and *Rio Padre,* and commanded a Half Flotilla of the Minesweepers Group (*Halbflottenchef der Sperrbrechergruppe*). In 1920 he was promoted to Korvettenkapitän in the reserves.[14] By that time he had rejoined Norddeutsche Lloyd, but not in command of a ship. He became a division director, rising to chief clerk.

During 1931 and 1932 he toured the United States giving lectures on his wartime experiences. By that time interest in the *Deutschland* had waned and the talks were poorly attended. They received little or no press coverage.

In January 1932, at the age of sixty-five, he was retired from Norddeutsche Lloyd, and died twenty-one months later on 8 September 1933.[15] There is no mention of his wife or children having seen him or even having corresponded with him since the start

Port side, looking aft across the gun deck, clearly shows many of the modifications made when the *Deutschland* was converted. The forward periscope has been strengthened, the conning tower enlarged, and the deck widened and elevated. This picture was taken in London after the war. (Naval Historical Center)

of the war. It may have been that the intense animosities developed during the war, and postwar conditions prevented that from happening.

Franz Krapohl became ill in September 1917 and was sent to a military hospital in Wiesbaden where he stayed until 11 October. From there he went back to the U-boat school to take a pre-command course. From March 1918 until the end of the war he commanded in succession the *UB-92* and the second *U-52*. He was released from service on 31 December 1918.[16]

He probably spent the years between the wars working for Norddeutsche Lloyd, because on 26 August 1939 he was recalled to active duty in the navy and given command of a nearly completed supply ship.[17] The ship was the *Ermland*, a 12,000-ton supply ship built to sustain a raider at sea.

Korvettenkapitän Krapohl was sixty years old when he went aboard, a veteran of World War I, and thirty years at sea. He was the only skipper the *Ermland* had during her short career, commanding her during both phases of Operation Berlin.[18]

For nearly four months, the *Ermland* was the resupply and support ship for the *Scharnhorst* during her operations west of the British Isles (25 December 1940–4 January 1941) and west of the Azores (25 January–23 March 1941). For Franz Krapohl Operation Berlin must have seemed like a step back into the First World War.

On 27 May 1941 the *Ermland* was sent out to take the damaged *Bismarck* in tow after the pocket battleship's rudder had been damaged by attacking British aircraft. The rescue attempt was aborted when the *Bismarck* was reported lost.

In September 1942, Captain Krapohl saved his ship from sinking after hitting a mine off the French coast. Good seamanship, quick damage control, and good fortune brought the *Ermland* into Nantes, France. She never left that port. On 10 September 1943, she was blown in two by heavy bombers, and sank at the dock.

Captain Krapohl returned to Germany and was again taken ill. Age and the rigors of war were taking their toll. A year and a half later on 1 April 1945, he was again certified fit for duty and given command of the *Ermland*'s sistership, the *Franken*. It was the shortest, and last, command he held.

The war was nearly over, the battle for Berlin was being savagely waged, and thousands of Germans were fleeing the wrath of the avenging Soviet horde. Many of the fleeing Germans, civilian and military, were trapped in the East Prussian ports of Pillau, Danzig, Gdingen (Gotenhafen), and Kolberg trying desperately to get aboard a ship—any ship.[19]

On 8 April 1945 the *Franken* was steaming toward Gotenhafen when she was attacked by Russian bombers. At 1240 a solid hit amidships broke her in two, sending her to the bottom with most of her crew. Captain Franz Krapohl was among those who went down with her.[20]

Emil Eyring remained aboard the *U-155* until the end of the war. He was released from service on 16 December 1918, and dropped out of sight. But somewhere along the line he turned in his seaman's jacket and donned the blue-grey uniform of the Luftwaffe. By the time World War II had started in Europe, he had moved up one service grade to Hauptmann, equivalent to the navy rank of Kapitänleutnant.

The British carefully examined the *U-155* before deciding she had no out-standing features they wanted to copy in future designs. In this picture part of the gun deck has been removed in the lower right corner. (U. S. Army Military History Institute)

He was recalled to active duty on 25 August 1939 and assigned to an antiaircraft unit. He was fifty-three years old. On 15 September 1942 he was promoted to major and given command of a heavy antiaircraft group in Bavaria, where he spent the rest of the war trying to beat back the Allied bombers that came in increasing numbers.[21]

Rumors about the *Deutschland* continued to crop up after the war. Some found their way into "factual" accounts and are still being repeated seventy years later. The most ridiculous postwar story was still being told as late as May 1919. According to that account, the big U-boat had been rammed and sunk in June 1917 while operating in the Mediterranean. Supposedly, a Captain John Thompson had earned a £1,000.00 reward and the sobriquet of "Deutschland Thompson" for sinking the U-boat.

Captain Thompson was reported to have had a run in with a German U-boat skipper on an earlier occasion in 1915. Reportedly

The *U-155* alongside the former Q-ship HMS *Suffolk Coast* in St. Katherine's Dock, London. December 1918. (U. S. Army Military History Institute)

his unnamed ship was stopped, searched, and declared to be carrying contraband. The accusation so angered Thompson that he decked the German officer with one blow. Miraculously, Thompson was not killed on the spot. Instead, the German drew his sword—hardly the weapon of choice for a boarding officer—and cut Thompson's face. We must assume that the German, having taught the Englishman a lesson, let him go, because in 1917 Thompson is again in command of a British merchant vessel. That is the beauty of fiction; anything can happen.

That set the stage for Thompson's 1917 encounter with the *Deutschland*. According to the tale, he spotted the U-boat on the surface, but being unarmed he had no choice but to ram her.

> For more than an hour the two ships circled around each other, mutually intent on gaining the advantage. The German submarine fired several shots, which did very little damage. Finally, the English ship managed to steer straight at the submarine and cut it in two.[22]

It was a wonderful story, but would have been much better if the British ship had been named the SS *Mongoose*.

The final humility, put on display as a private show for 10 pence a look. Stripped of her guns, engines, and all other machinery, she was towed from port to port around Great Britain. (Bibliothek für Zeitgeschichte, Stuttgart)

In a way, all those rumors from 1916 and 1917 about the *Deutschland* having been captured and put on display did come true. On 2 December 1918 she was taken to London and put on public display as a war trophy. On 10 January in the new year she went to the Firth of Forth, back to Harwich, and then on to Rosyth. Late that month she was sold to a private businessman.[23]

Her guns gone, engines removed, and a huge DEUTSCHLAND painted on both sides of the hull, amidships, she was towed from port to port as a show attraction. For 10 pence you could go aboard the famous blockade runner turned showboat.

The situation was awfully close to the answer Paul König gave the press just before his departure from New London. He said that after the war they would tow the *Deutschland* to America and show her off for ten cents a look. Only the place was different. Growing rusty and decrepit through neglect, the battered U-boat drew progressively smaller crowds. By 1921 she could not earn enough to pay her way, and she was sold for scrap. The selling price was £200.00.[24]

On 17 September 1921 she was in the Birkenhead yard of Robert Smith and Sons being dismantled. It was a Saturday, a regular work day in 1921, and five seventeen-year-old apprentices were using

Her sisters all went to either France or Britain. This is the *U-151* in Cherbourg in January 1919. (National Archives)

torches to cut her up. Suddenly a tremendous explosion ripped the boat. Flame and black smoke billowed into the air as shock waves rolled across the yard, rattling windows in the surrounding buildings.

The cause of the blast was never determined. But most thought that one of the boys had cut into a fuel tank and ignited the vapors. One thing was certain, however—all five apprentices were dead.[25]

Her sister ships met similar ends, going either to the breakers or being sent to the bottom by gunfire. As war booty they were not useful for anything else. The Germans had developed several bigger and better U-boats that the victorious Allies wanted to study, and the five surviving *Deutschland*-class boats were already dinosaurs, slow, underpowered, and unreliable.

But were the *Deutschland* and her sisters forerunners of a new class of cargo-carrying submarines? The idea, and even the application, will not die. In 1939, Simon Lake patented a design for an all-welded boat capable of diving to 500 feet. She was intended to carry 750 tons of cargo, plus 200 passengers at a submerged speed of ten knots. An unusual design feature was a telescoping conning tower that when raised acted as a snorkel.[26]

During World War II the Germans, Italians, and Japanese built submarines designed to deliver cargo, and the United States had three large submarines that filled that role. They were the USS *Argonaut*, famous for her part in the raid on Makin in August 1942, and two similar boats, the USS *Narwhal* and USS *Nautilus*. All three were built during the 1920s, and the *Narwhal* and the *Nautilus* were actually inspired by the German U-cruisers. Conceptually, the *Deutschland*-class boats might have contributed to their design, but the *Narwhal* and the *Nautilus* designs were really products of the *U-142* through *U-150* U-cruisers. But the most interesting World War II attempt to build a cargo submarine took place in San Francisco.

Hal B. Hayes, a local cement contractor, had designed and built a ferrocement prototype of a cargo submarine that he said would replace the C-2 Liberty ship. He claimed his design could be built in less time, and use 90 percent less steel than a C-2 Liberty ship, and it could be done with unskilled labor.[27]

A quarter-size model, 125 feet long and with a seven-foot beam, was launched in the Richmond, California, harbor on 3 August 1943. Powered by two Ford V-8 engines, the *Lektron* was demonstrated on 5 August to representatives of the navy and the Maritime Commission. Plowing around a course laid out in Richmond Shipyard No. 4, the *Lektron* did reasonably well, considering that the demonstration was the first time Hayes had ever operated the craft. But despite his claims of surface speeds up to "80" knots, and the ability to carry cargo in enormous quantities, the navy rejected the idea. They just were not ready for a cement submarine.[28]

Since the war there has been more discussion about unusual and specialty submersible designs for all kinds of ships, including an aircraft carrier.[29] And shades of Simon Lake, the design calls for a retractable conning tower. The point is, given the proper technology and materials, anything is possible. Fully submersible designs for cargo vessels are considered workable solutions for a wide variety of military problems, including the delivery of heavy equipment.[30] If those designs become a reality, the *Deutschland* shall have been their progenitor.

NOTES

CHAPTER ONE

1. The boarding account is taken from E. Keble Chatterton, *The Big Blockade,* 228–32.
2. Ibid., 172.
3. Gordon A. Craig, *Germany, 1866–1945,* 354.
4. Louis Guichard, *The Naval Blockade, 1914–18,* 266–70.
5. Chatterton, 151.
6. Ibid., 150.
7. Guichard, 264–65, 269.
8. Ibid., 78–79; and Chatterton, 150.
9. Chatterton, 149.
10. John Ellis, *Eye Deep in Hell: Trench Warfare in World War I,* 125–29.
11. Craig, 371.
12. Guichard, 273–74.
13. Craig, 347.
14. Ibid., 342.

CHAPTER TWO

1. The details about the source of the nickel are found in: Roll 660 PG 75197; *New York Times* 11 November 1916; and ADM/1262, Rice to Foreign Office, Radio Message Nr. 2159, 14 July 1916.
2. Information on the *Etappendienst,* its organization and purpose, was obtained in discussions with Dr. Charles Burdick, Dean, School of Social Sciences, San Jose State University; and Dr. David Abenheim, Naval Postgraduate School and the Hoover Library for War, Revolution, and Peace, Stanford, California, during the winter of 1986–87.

3. Philip K. Lundeberg, "The German Naval Critique of the U-boat Campaign, 1915–1918," 112.

4. Eberhard Rössler, *Geschichte des deutschen Ubootsbaus*, 96.

5. Arthur Bremer, *Die kühne Fahrt der Deutschland*, 36; and Otto Weddigen, *Das erste Handels-Unterseeboot, Deutschland, und sein Kapitän, Paul König*, 45.

6. James H. Belote, "The Lohmann Affair," 31–38.

7. Roll 631 PG 67344, "von R. M. A. erhaltene Angaben über *Deutschland*," 15 July 1916.

8. Rössler, 97.

9. Ibid., 97; and Wilhelm Ehlers, "*U-Deutschland*," 266.

10. Ehlers, 266; Rössler, 96; and Roll 95 PG 62024.

11. Roll 631 PG 67344, "von R. M. A. erhaltene Angaben über *Deutschland*."

12. Ibid.

13. Fritz Brustat-Naval, "Das *U-Deutschland* Unternehmen," 236.

14. Roll 631 PG 67344, "von R. M. A. erhaltene Angaben über *Deutschland*."

15. Ibid.

16. Paul König's biography and his military record are taken from: File 00423, Zentrales Staatsarchiv, Potsdam; Personalunterlagen, Deutsche Dienststelle (WASt), Berlin; and Certified Copy of Entry of Marriage, General Records Office, London.

17. Personalunterlagen, Deutsche Dienststelle, Berlin.

18. Ibid.; and Dieter Jung, et al., *Tanker und Versorger der deutschen Flotte, 1900–1980*, 163–66.

19. The *Deutschland*'s dimensions are taken from scale drawings, and are also found in Erich Gröner, *Die deutschen Kriegsschiffe, 1815–1945*, 359.

20. Roll 659 PG 75196 and 75197; Roll 660 PG 75197 (cont'd.).

21. Jung, et al., 166.

22. The Baltimore property was bought from Colin McLean, and was a former tannery. It was located near the Baltimore Yacht Club, and about a quarter of a mile from the place where Simon Lake's *Argonaut* made its first dive in 1897. *New York Times*, 18 November 1916.

23. Roll 659 PG 75197.

CHAPTER THREE

1. When maneuvering in tight places where the ability to reverse quickly was needed, the electric motors were clutched in, and both diesels were kept running to power the generators. The *Deutschland*'s clutch system allowed for a fairly speedy switch from electric to diesel drive. Office of Naval Records and Library, "German Merchant Submarine *Deutschland*," 14 November 1916.

2. Getting under way from Kiel is described in both versions of Paul König's book *Voyage of the Deutschland*, 16–19, and *Fahrten der Deutschland im Weltkrieg*, 21–23.

3. Records of the Department of State, Roll 179, Gerard to Secretary of State, 14 July 1916.

4. Roll 658 PG 75195, König to Admiralstab, 28 August 1916, typed report of the trip over and back.

5. Bremer, 17.

6. Cryptanalysis played an even larger role in British intelligence successes than did the captured code books. The HVB code was replaced early in 1916 and the SKM code in May 1917. König relied heavily on the SKM code. Patrick Beesly. *Room 40: British Naval Intelligence, 1914–18*, 3; and Alberto Santoni, "The First Ultra Secret: British Cryptanalysis in Naval Operations of the First World War," 99–101.

7. Roll 658 PG 75195.

CHAPTER FOUR

1. König, *Voyage of the Deutschland*, 69–72.

2. Office of Naval Records and Library, John Rodgers, "Conversation with Captain König," 24 July 1916. Nine years after his conversation with Paul König, Commander John Rodgers led the Navy's attempt to make a nonstop flight from San Francisco to Hawaii. He was killed in a crash in 1926. See Dwight R. Messimer, *No Margin for Error*, Naval Institute Press, 1981.

3. The action and quotes are taken from three sources; König, *Voyage of the Deutschland*, 24–25; König, *Fahrten der U-Deutschland im Weltkrieg*, 20–23; and Roll 658 PG 75195, König to Admiralstab, 28 August 1916.

4. König, *Voyage of the Deutschland*, 24.

5. Ibid., 31.

6. Roll 658 PG 75195, König to Admiralstab, 28 August 1916.

7. Ibid.

8. Ibid.

9. König, *Voyage of the Deutschland*, 49.

10. Ibid., 50–52.

11. Office of Naval Records and Library, Yates Stirling Jr., "Examination of German Submarine *Deutschland*," 3 November 1916.

12. König, *Voyage of the Deutschland*, 55.

13. Ibid., 58.

14. Ibid., 59.

15. Roll 658 PG 75195, König to Admiralstab, 28 August 1916.

16. König, *Voyage of the Deutschland*, 117.

17. Ibid., 109–20.

18. Ibid., 116.

19. Ibid., 91–97.

20. Ibid., 95–96.

21. Alfred Noyes, *Mystery Ships: Trapping the U-boats*, 59–61.

22. Roll 658 PG 75195, König to Admiralstab, 28 August 1916.

23. United States Naval Institute *Proceedings:* "Is there any Defense Against

the Submarine?" (Mar./Apr. 1915), 575; "Protection Against Submarines," (March 1917), 605; and "The Gun as an Answer to the Submarine," (September 1917), 2144–45.

24. R. H. Gibson and M. Pendergast, *The German Submarine War, 1914–18,* 104.

25. Ibid., 148–49.

26. David D. Lewis, *The Fight for the Sea,* 53–54.

27. Gibson, 19–20; and Noyes, 3–10.

28. Gibson, 19–21.

29. Ibid., 38–39.

30. The information is taken from several newspaper articles found on Roll 659 PG 75196 and 97; and Roll 660 PG 75197 (cont'd.).

31. United States Naval Institute *Proceedings,* "The German Commercial Submarines," (June 1917),1240.

32. Roll 658 PG 75195, Lohmann to Toussaint, 7 July 1916.

33. Roll 658 PG 75195, Lohmann to Toussaint, 28 June 1916.

34. Roll 658 PG 75195, Lohmann to Toussaint, 8 July 1916.

35. Roll 631 PG 67344.

36. *New York Times,* 1 July 1916.

37. Records of the Department of State. Roll 179, British Embassy to State Department, 3 July 1916.

38. König, *Voyage of the Deutschland,* 122–23.

39. Roll 658 PG 75195, König to Admiralstab, 28 August 1916.

40. Ibid.

41. *New York Times,* 9 July 1916.

42. König, *Voyage of the Deutschland,* 128–29.

43. *New York Times,* 9 July 1916.

CHAPTER FIVE

1. Today the *Deutschland*'s berth is included in the Locust Point Marine Terminal, Maryland Port Administration. If the Eastern Forwarding Company's office were still standing, it would be directly beneath Interstate 95, at the foot of Andre Street. Office of Naval Records and Library, J. H. Klein, "Report on German Merchant Vessel SS *Deutschland,*" 10 July 1916.

2. Ibid.

3. Roll 658 PG 75196, *New York American,* 10 July 1916.

4. Roll 658 PG 75196, *The Evening Telegram,* 10 July 1916.

5. *New York Times,* 10 July 1916.

6. Records of the Department of State, Roll 179, British Embassy to State Department, 3 July 1916.

7. Ibid., Ferriday to Department of State, 9 July 1916.

8. Ibid., Ryan to Secretary of the Treasury, 9 July 1916.

9. Ibid., various correspondence 9–22 July 1916.

10. Ibid., Joint Neutrality Board to Secretary of State, 14 July 1916.

11. Office of Naval Records and Library, J. H. Klein, "Report on German Merchant Vessel SS *Deutschland*," 10 July 1916.

12. Ibid.

13. *New York Times,* 11 July 1916.

14. Ibid.

15. Office of Naval Records and Library, Letter, Fisher to Grant, 14 July 1916.

16. Records of Department of State, Roll 179, Hobbin to Polk, 12 July 1916.

17. Ibid., Joint Neutrality Board to Secretary of State, 14 July 1916.

18. Ibid., Spring-Rice to Secretary of State, 18 July 1916; and Whillis to Polk, 9 July 1916.

CHAPTER SIX

1. *New York Times,* 10 July 1916.

2. Roll 659 PG 75196.

3. Ibid.

4. Roll 659 PG 75196, *New York Tribune,* 7 July 1916.

5. Records of the Department of State, Roll 179, Lake Torpedo Boat Company to State Department, 10 July 1916.

6. Roll 659 PG 75196, *New York Tribune,* 23 July 1916; and Philip K. Lundeberg, "Undersea Warfare and the Allied Strategy in World War I," Part I, 6.

7. Roll 659 PG 75196, *New York Tribune,* 11 July 1916.

8. Ibid., *New York Sun,* 13 July 1916.

9. Records of the Department of State, Roll 179, Spring-Rice to Secretary of State, 18 July 1916.

10. Ibid., Whillis to Polk, 19 July 1916.

11. Ibid., Adee to Belter, 26 August 1916.

12. Ibid., Grey to Spring-Rice, 18 July 1916.

13. Roll 711 PG 75019, "Weekly Report on General Conditions in Germany During the European War," 30 October 1915.

14. Information on dyestuffs was taken from several sources on three microfilm rolls: Roll 659 PG 75196; Roll 631 PG 67344; and Roll 711 PG 75019.

15. No two sources agree on the cargo figures. The spread is: rubber 348 to 401 tons; nickel 343 to 376 tons; and tin 83 to 93 tons. The British pegged nickel at 400 tons. Francis Duncan "*Deutschland*—Merchant Submarine," 72; Hans-Georg Rieschke, "Handels U-boot *U-Deutschland*," 149; Rössler, 64; and ADM137/1262.

16. ADM137/1262, Decypher 201, 15 July 1916.

17. *New York Times,* 12 July 1916.

18. Rumors about a fleet of cargo U-boats already under way may have been started by the Germans. At various times boats with names *Bremen,*

Oldenburg, Hansa, and *Amerika* were reported in the press. Only the *Bremen* and *Oldenburg* existed, and only the *Bremen* was launched as a cargo U-boat other than the *Deutschland.*

19. The Hamburg yards were Reiherstieg and Stülcken, in Flensburg it was Flensburger, and in Bremen it was Atlas. Gröner, 359; and Rössler, 64.

20. Roll 659 PG 75196, *The Baltimore Sun,* 27 July 1916.

21. Ibid., *The Evening Telegram,* 11 July 1916.

22. Roll 631 PG 67344, Chef des Admiralstabs to kaiser, 25 July 1916.

23. Roll 659 PG 75196, *New York Tribune,* 27 July 1916.

24. Ibid., *New York American,* 20 July 1916.

25. *New York Times,* 13 July 1916.

26. Ibid., 16 July 1916.

27. Ibid.

28. Weddigen, 71.

29. *New York Times,* 16 July 1916.

30. Records of the Department of State, Roll 179, Blakeman to Lansing, 18 July 1916.

31. Roll 659 PG 75196, 17 July 1916.

32. Ibid.

CHAPTER SEVEN

1. ADM137/1262.

2. Ibid.

3. Roll 659 PG 75196, *New York American,* 23 July 1916.

4. Brustat-Naval, 237.

5. *New York Times,* 20 July 1916.

6. Roll 659 PG 75196, *The Baltimore Sun,* 20 July 1916.

7. On 21 July, Captain König and eighteen crewmen attended a bazaar hosted by the Austrian Red Cross Society. 10,000 people attended. Roll 659 PG 75196, *The Baltimore Sun,* 22 July 1916.

8. Ibid., *New York American,* 19 July 1916.

9. ADM137/1262.

10. Ibid.

11. Ibid.

12. Ibid., and *New York Times,* 20 July 1916.

13. Roll 659 PG 75196, *New York American,* 22 July 1916.

14. Ibid., *New York American,* 19 July.

15. König, *Voyage of the Deutschland,* 140–41.

16. Roll 659 PG 75196, *New York American,* 20 July 1916.

17. Ibid.

18. Ibid., *New York American,* 23 July 1916.

19. From the conning tower rim to the bottom of the keel measured 9.25 meters, or 30.35 feet. But the housed periscope protruded 1.9 feet above the rim, making the total measurement 32.25 feet. Gröner, 359 and measurements made by the author.

20. Roll 659 PG 75196, *New York Tribune,* 25 July 1916.
21. Records of the Department of State, Roll 179, Ryan to Halstead, 24 July 1916.
22. Ibid.
23. Roll 659 PG 75196, all recorded newspaper entries for 27 July 1916.
24. Ibid., 26–27 July.
25. Ibid., 27 July.
26. Ibid.
27. Records of the Department of State, Roll 179, Bernstorff to Polk, 21 July 1916.
28. Ibid., König to Ryan, 29 July 1916.
29. Ibid., Polk to Secretary of the Treasury, 29 July 1916.
30. Roll 659 PG 75196, *New York American,* 2 August 1916.
31. Ibid; and König, *Voyage of the Deutschland,* 165. König gives the departure time as 1520, but that is incorrect.
32. Roll 658 PG 75195, König's report to the Admiralstab.
33. Ibid.

CHAPTER EIGHT

1. Records of the Department of State, Roll 179, Deutsche Ozean Reederei to Ryan, 15 September 1916; and König, *Voyage of the Deutschland,* 183–90.
2. Roll 658 PG 75195, König's report to Admiralstab; and König, *Voyage of the Deutschland,* 183–90.
3. Roll 631 PG 67344, Lohmann to kaiser, 1 August 1916; and Lohmann to Admiralstab, 1 August 1916.
4. Ibid., Admiralstab to Kiel, 19 August 1916.
5. Ibid., Lohmann to Toussaint, 31 July 1916.
6. Ibid., Lohmann to Hochseekommando, 14 August 1916.
7. Ibid., Helgoland to Stapelfeld, 14 August 1916.
8. Telegramme der Deutschen Ozean Reederei, Bremen, an den Reichskanzler und umgekehrt, und Zeitungsartikeln über den Kapitän Paul König, Juni-Oktober 1916. File 00423.
9. Ibid.
10. Ibid.
11. The search was made for me by Ken Thomas, a research agent recommended by Public Records Office. Thomas to author, 17 June 1986.
12. Roll 658 PG 75195, König's report to Admiralstab.
13. Ibid., Admiralstab to Kiel, 15 August 1916.
14. König, *Fahrten der U-Deutschland im Weltkrieg,* 147.
15. Ibid., 151.
16. Roll 658 PG 75195, *U-200* to Helgoland, 22 August 1916.
17. Ibid., SMS *Senator Sachse* to Kiel, 23 August 1916.
18. Ibid., Helgoland to Kiel, 23 August 1916.
19. Ibid., Helgoland to Kiel, 24 August 1916.
20. Ibid., Wilhelmshaven to Kiel, 24 August 1916.

CHAPTER NINE

1. Franz Eichberger was my father-in-law. The material on public reaction, opinions, and attitudes is taken from conversations with my family over a thirty-year period, and from letters and photographs.
2. König, *Voyage of the Deutschland*, 225–26.
3. Ibid., 227–28.
4. Telegramme der Deutschen Ozean Reederei, etc., File 00423.
5. Roll 658 PG 75195, kaiser to König, 25 August 1916.

CHAPTER TEN

1. Telegramme der Deutschen Ozean Reederei, etc., File 00423; and Personalunterlagen, Deutsche Dienststelle.
2. *New York Times*, 25 August 1916.
3. Ibid.
4. Ibid.
5. Roll 658 PG 75195, Agent W.29c to Admiralstab, 20 September 1916.
6. Ibid., Lohmann to Toussaint, 14 September 1916.
7. Records of the Department of State, Roll 179, Inspector of Customs to Secretary of State, 15 September 1916.
8. *New York Times*, 30 August 1916.
9. Roll 658 PG 75195, Agent W.29a to Admiralstab, 30 October 1916.
10. Ibid., 2 October 1916.
11. Ibid., 25 October 1916.
12. Ibid.; and Gibson, 110–11.
13. Gibson, 19.
14. Office of Naval Intelligence, "Report of Inspection, German Naval Submarine *U-53*," 6 November 1916.
15. Gibson, 20.
16. Roll 658 PG 75195, Attaché, Stockholm to Admiralstab, 29 & 30 October 1916.
17. Ibid., Attaché, Oslo to Admiralstab, 6 December 1916.
18. Ibid., W.29e to Admiralstab, 20 January 1917.
19. Ibid., W.29c to Berlin, 13 January 1917.
20. Ibid., Attaché, Oslo to Admiralstab, 24 March 1917.
21. Ibid., Lohmann to Admiralstab, 25 March 1917.
22. Ibid., Generalstab des Feldheers to Admiralstab, 3 April 1917.
23. Ibid., W.29c to Admiralstab, 27 April 1917.
24. Ibid., Madrid to Berlin.
25. By the end of 1916, the Germans had lost twenty-two boats, sunk, stranded, and captured.
26. Duncan, 72.
27. Ernst Hashagen, *U-boote Westwärts!*, 26–34.

CHAPTER ELEVEN

1. August Götze is the author's great-uncle.
2. Guichard, 289.
3. Craig, 374.
4. Mann, 317.
5. Roll 658 PG 75195, Deutsche Ozean Reederei to Toussaint, 29 August 1916.
6. Ibid., Nachrichten Abteilung to Toussaint, 1 September 1916.
7. Records of the Department of State, Roll 179, Assistant Secretary of State to Collector of Customs, 7 September 1916.
8. Ibid., Sauner to P. Ryan, 8 September 1916.
9. Ibid., Deutsche Ozean Reederei to Ryan, 15 September 1916.
10. Ibid., Ryan to Secretary of the Treasury, 15 September 1916.
11. Ibid., Lansing to Scott, 26 August 1916.
12. Ibid., Memorandum (unsigned copy), 31 August 1916.
13. Ibid., Deutsche Ozean Reederei to Ryan, 15 September 1916; and Ryan to Secretary of the Treasury, 15 September 1916.
14. Roll 658 PG 75195, Lohmann to Admiralstab, 31 August 1916.
15. Ibid., Bernstorff to Reichschatzamt, 16 September 1916.
16. Records of the Department of State, Roll 179, Taintor to Secretary of State, 13 October 1916.
17. Roll 658 PG 75195, Falk to Admiralstab, 1 September 1916.
18. Records of the Department of State, Roll 179, Macado to Lansing, 27 July 1916.
19. Ibid., Department of State to embassy, Berlin, 12 July 1916; consul, Bremen, to Secretary of State, 14 July 1916; and Department of State to embassy, Berlin, 26 July 1916.
20. Roll 658 PG 75195, Lohmann to Toussaint, 25 September 1916.
21. Ibid., Lohmann to Admiralstab, 16 September 1916.
22. Beesly, 207–8.
23. Roll 658 PG 75195, Lohmann to Berlin, 2 October 1916.
24. Ibid., Lohmann to Admiralstab, 6 October 1916; and Admiralstab to Wilhelmshaven, 7 October 1916.
25. Ibid., Wilhelmshaven to Kiel, 8 October 1916.
26. The SKM code remained in use until May 1917. Santoni, 101.

CHAPTER TWELVE

1. The stormy crossing is described in König's report to the Admiralstab, and in his comments to reporters in New London. Those items are found in several entries in Roll 658 PG 75195 and Roll 659 PG 75196.
2. Ibid.
3. The conning tower hatch was inclined so that it could be opened in almost any weather without causing a deluge below.

4. *New York Times,* 1 November 1916.

5. See note 1 above.

6. Captain Guy Gaunt, RN, British naval attaché in Washington, told the press on 27 October to expect the *Deutschland* on 1 November. Clearly his information had come from British Intelligence and was based on radio intercepts. *New York Times,* 28 October 1916.

7. *New York Times,* 2 November 1916.

8. The estimated distance between the two vessels varies with the reporter—from "a few feet" to over 100 feet. König described it as "passed close aboard." (*sehr nah vorbei gefahren*). Roll 658 PG 75195, König's report to Admiralstab.

9. The *Efco* used in New London was a different vessel from the one used in Baltimore. In fact, *Efco* may not have been the correct name for either vessel, though everyone used that name for both tenders. They had the letters E.F.C.O. painted on the smoke stack, but had no other name. *Efco* probably stood for Eastern Forwarding Company.

10. Records of the Department of State, Roll 179, Malburn to Secretary of State, 1 November 1916.

CHAPTER THIRTEEN

1. Unless otherwise cited, all information for the following account came from several newspaper entries found in Roll 660 PG 75197.

2. He was undoubtedly the same man who had filed the reports in Baltimore and reported gold among the cargo.

3. Records of the Department of State, Roll 179, Lansing to McAdoo, 1 November 1916.

4. Ibid., résumé of telephone messages, 1 November 1916.

5. Office of Naval Records and Library, "Examination of German Submarine *Deutschland,*" 3 November 1916; and "German Merchant Submarine *Deutschland,*" 14 November 1916.

6. Ibid., "German Submarine *Deutschland,*" 14 November 1916.

7. As a cargo boat, the builders estimated the range at 12,000 nautical miles at 10 knots, but as a war boat they estimated the range to be 25,000 at 5.5 knots. Reality was far less dramatic. Gröner, 359.

8. Office of Naval Records and Library, "German Merchant Submarine *Deutschland,*" 14 November 1916.

9. Roll 658 PG 75195, Wilhelmshaven to Berlin, 8 October 1916.

10. *U-63, U-64,* and *U-65* were equipped with dual engines developing a total of 2,200 horsepower. Gröner, 348.

11. Roll 660 PG 75197, *The World,* 5 November 1916.

12. Ibid.

13. Ibid., *Providence Journal,* 3 November 1916; and *New York Tribune,* 3 November 1916.

14. The *New York Tribune* said the payment was only $10.00. Roll 660 PG 75197.

15. Unless otherwise noted the account that follows is based on newspaper accounts found in Roll 660 PG 75197. It was the *New York Times* that called Hinsch the bane of all reporters.

16. ADM137/1262, message 914, 17 November 1916.

17. Records of the Department of State, Roll 179, Stirling to State Department, 3 November 1916.

18. ADM137/1262, message 914, 17 November 1916.

19. *New York Times,* 9 November 1916.

20. Records of the Department of State, Roll 179, Peters to Lansing, 9 November 1916.

21. Roll 660 PG 75197, Kriegspresseamt, 6 January 1917.

22. Roll 659 PG 75196, *The Baltimore Sun,* 12 July 1916.

23. Ibid.

24. Chatterton, 264.

25. The mail contract negotiations are from several newspaper accounts and a lengthy report written by the Kriegspresseamt found in: Roll 659 PG 75196; Roll 660 PG 75196 (cont'd.) and 75197; and Roll 658 PG 75195.

26. *New York Times,* 1 November 1916.

27. Roll 660 PG 75197, *New York Tribune,* 10 November 1916.

28. Records of the Department of State, Roll 179, 16 November 1916.

29. *New York Times,* 8 November 1916.

30. Records of the Department of State, Roll 179, McGovern to Lansing, and reply, 16 November 1916.

31. Roll 660 PG 75197, *World,* 16 November 1916.

CHAPTER FOURTEEN

1. Unless otherwise noted, the basis for the events leading up to the collision, and the collision, are taken from Records of Department of Commerce, Steamboat Navigation Service Correspondence, 1905–23, File 73301.

2. *New York Times,* 18 November 1916.

3. Ibid.

4. All the newspaper accounts said that Hinsch was standing on the stern when the vessels collided, but the official report places him on the bow. Records of Department of Commerce, File 73301.

5. *New York Times,* 18 November 1916.

6. Ibid.

7. Ibid.

8. Ibid.

9. Roll 660 PG 75197, *New York Journal,* 18 November 1916.

10. *New York Times,* 18 November 1916.

11. Roll 660 PG 75197, *Petit Parisien,* undated, typed German translation.

12. *New York Times,* 19 November 1916.

13. Records of Department of Commerce, File 73301, correspondence 22 November–9 December 1916.

14. The legal battle is taken from newspaper accounts found in Roll 660 PG 75197.

15. Records of Department of Commerce, File 73301, Final Report, 20 December 1916.

16. Roll 660 PG 75197, *Köln Tagesblatt*, 21 December 1916.

17. Ibid., Kriegspresseamt, 16 January 1917.

18. Roll 658 PG 75195, *Deutschland* to *Neckar*, 21 November 1916.

19. Ibid., König's report to Admiralstab, 12 December 1916.

20. Ibid.

CHAPTER FIFTEEN

1. Roll 658 PG 75195, *U-200* to Helgoland, 9 December 1916.

2. The reported near loss of the *Deutschland* is taken entirely from a report written by J. Y. Buck to the State Department found in Records of the Department of State, Roll 179.

3. Roll 631 PG 67344, *Deutschland* to Deutsche Ozean Reederei, 10 December 1916.

4. Ibid., Deutsche Ozean Reederei to Kiel, 10 December 1916.

5. Records of the Department of State, Roll 179, Buck to Lansing, 26 November 1917.

6. Records of the Department of State, Invoice 350, 15 December 1916.

7. Guichard, 266–70.

8. *New York Times*, 6 January 1917.

9. Ellis, 129.

10. Mann, 318.

11. Gibson, 81–82; and Lundeberg, 114.

12. Francis A. March, *History of World War I*, 732.

13. Rössler, 67.

14. Ibid., and Gröner, 359.

15. Gibson, 120.

16. Records of the Department of State, Roll 179, Buck to Lansing, 26 November 1917.

17. *New York Times*, 18 January 1917.

18. Records of the Department of State, Roll 179, Buck to Lansing, 26 November 1917.

19. Roll 631 PG 67344, Admiralstab to Toussaint, 20 January 1917.

20. *New York Times*, 29 January 1917.

21. Ibid., 30 January.

22. Ibid.

23. Beesly, 212–13.

CHAPTER SIXTEEN

1. Roll 96 PG 62025, Kriegstagebuch U. I., Band 2.

2. *New York Times*, 6 February 1917.

3. Roll 96 PG 62025, Kriegstagebuch U. I., Band 2.

4. Deutsche Dienststelle, Personalunterlagen.
5. The account is from the *New York Times,* 8 February 1917.
6. Ibid., 11 February.
7. Ibid., 17 February 1917.
8. United States Naval Institute *Proceedings,* "The German Commercial Submarines," June 1917, 1240–41.
9. Roll 96 PG 62025, Kriegstagebuch U. I., Band 2.
10. *New York Times,* 28 February 1917.
11. Deutsche Dienststelle, Personalunterlagen.
12. Roll 21 PG 61710, *U-155* Kriegstagebuch, Meusel's end of patrol report. (Hereafter cited as Meusel Report.)
13. Ibid.; and Deutsche Dienststelle, Personalunterlagen.
14. Gröner, 359.
15. Based on measurements by the author of scale drawings.
16. Roll 21 PG 61710, Meusel Report.
17. Ibid.
18. Gröner, 359.

CHAPTER SEVENTEEN

1. Lundeberg,115; and same, Part II, 62–63.
2. Roll 21 PG 61710, Meusel Report.
3. Ibid.
4. My impressions of Captain Meusel are based on reading his war diary and his final report.
5. His comments to released prisoners are found in Office of Naval Intelligence, "Cruise of the *Deutschland* in the Region of the Azores from 10 June to 16 August 1917," 4 April 1918.
6. Unless otherwise noted, the entire account of the *U-155*'s first war patrol is taken from Roll 21 PG 61710, Meusel Report.
7. Office of Naval Intelligence, Johannes Spiess, 56–57.
8. Added material is from Office of Naval Intelligence, "Cruise of the *Deutschland* . . . ."
9. The entire crew of the *Aysgarth* was rescued by the SS *Highcliffe.* Ibid.
10. Additional information came from Office of Naval Intelligence, "Cruise of the *Deutschland* . . . "; and Office of Naval Intelligence, "I. D. 1181, May 1917 to April 1918."
11. Ibid.
12. Ibid.
13. Roll 21 PG 61710, Meusel Report.

CHAPTER EIGHTEEN

1. Karl Schmidt, *Panzer Vernichtung,* 86–89.
2. Montgomery, 454.
3. Unless otherwise noted, the details of the *U-155*'s second war cruise

are taken from Roll 22 PG 61711, Kriegstagebuch *U-155*, Captain Eckelmann's after-patrol report.

    4. Ibid., Captain Studt's after-patrol report.

    5. ADM137/4220, *U-155* Log.

EPILOGUE

    1. *New York Times,* 17 and 18 November 1917.

    2. Ibid., 20 December 1917.

    3. Ibid., 25 December 1917.

    4. Ibid., 19 November 1917.

    5. Ibid., 11 October 1917.

    6. Ibid., 24 July 1917.

    7. Ibid., 18 July 1917.

    8. The schooner was owned by the Luna Ship Company, which had salvaged her near Boston. At the time the story hit the newspapers, the *Wanola* was headed toward Nova Scotia with a load of sand. Records of the Department of State, Luna Ship Co. to Secretary of Commerce, 19 July 1917.

    9. *New York Times,* 24 July 1917.

    10. Ibid., 23 November 1917.

    11. Chatterton, 273.

    12. *New York Times,* 19 May 1917.

    13. Ehlers, 273.

    14. In this context, *Sperrbrecher* does not mean blockade runner, although that is its literal translation. Here it refers to converted merchant ships used to sweep for mines that the navy's regular minesweepers might have missed. Details of Paul König's service record are found in the Deutsche Dienststelle, Personalunterlagen.

    15. Stadtbibliothek Berlin to the author, 2 October 1986.

    16. Deutsche Dienststelle, Personalunterlagen.

    17. Ibid.

    18. Jung, et al., 321–31.

    19. Before World War I (and again today) Gdingen was called Gdynia. It is north of Danzig and was built after World War I to service the Polish Corridor.

    20. It took an hour for the ship to sink. During that time Captain Krapohl was trapped on the stern. Deutsche Dienststelle, Personalunterlagen; and Jung, et al., 331–32.

    21. Ibid.

    22. United States Naval Institute *Proceedings,* "The Fate of the *Deutschland*," May 1919, 816.

    23. ADM137/3915, *U-155* Log, 20 November 1918–16 January 1919.

    24. United States Naval Institute *Proceedings,* "*Deutschland*—Merchant Submarine," October 1965, 120.

    25. Ibid., "Five Lives Lost in Dismantling of *Deutschland*," November 1921, 1807.

26. "Underwater Cargo Carrier," *Popular Mechanics,* April 1940, 494–95.

27. *Oakland Tribune,* 4 August 1943.

28. For many years the hull was a part of the seawall at the Berkeley, California, public marina. It lay in about eight feet of water next to the Berkeley Yacht Club dock until the 1970s when it was covered by tons of cement and stone during a harbor improvement project.

29. Charles C. Pease, "Sink the Navy," 33.

30. Clark C. Abt, "Submarine Tank Carrier," 140–41.

BIBLIOGRAPHY

BOOKS

Bagnasco, Erminio. *Submarines of World War Two*. London: Lionel Leventhal Ltd., 1977.

Beesly, Patrick. *Room 40: British Naval Intelligence, 1914–18*. London: Hamish Hamilton, 1982.

Bremer, Arthur. *Die kühne Fahrt der Deutschland*. Berlin: Berthold Siegmund and Co., 1916.

Chatterton, E. Keble. *The Big Blockade*. London: Hurst & Blackett, Ltd., 1932.

Craig, Gordon A. *Germany, 1866–1945*. New York: Oxford University Press, 1978.

Ellis, John. *Eye Deep in Hell: Trench Warfare in World War I*. New York: Pantheon Books, 1976.

Gibson, R. H., and Prendergast, M. *The German Submarine War, 1914–1918*. London: Constable and Co., Ltd., 1931.

Grant, Robert M. *U-boat Intelligence, 1914–1918*. Hamden, CT: Archon Books, 1969.

Gröner, Erich. *Die deutschen Kriegsschiffe, 1815–1945*. 2 vols. München: J. F. Lehmanns Verlag, 1966.

Guichard, Louis. *The Naval Blockade, 1914–1918*. Translated by Christopher R. Turner. New York: D. Appleton & Co., 1930.

Hashagen, Ernst. *U-Boote Westwärts!*. Berlin: E. G. Mittler & Sohn, 1941.

Jung, Dieter; Maas, Martin; and Wenzler, Berndt. *Tanker und Versorger der deutschen Flotte, 1900–1980*. Stuttgart: Motorbuch Verlag, 1981.

König, Paul. *The Voyage of the Deutschland*. New York: Hearst International Library, 1916. This American edition is not a translation of the German edition listed next. Slanted toward the American audience, it differs substantially from the German version.

————. *Fahrten der U-Deutschland im Weltkrieg.* Berlin: Ullstein, 1916. The German version was re-released by Ullstein in 1937 at the direction of the Ministry of Propaganda. Both editions are identical in text.

Lewis, David D. *The Fight for the Sea.* New York: Collier Books, 1961.

Mann, Golo. *The History of Germany since 1789.* Tr. Marian Jackson. New York: Praeger, 1968.

March, Francis A. *History of World War I.* Philadelphia, Chicago, and London: United Publishers, 1919.

Montgomery, Field-Marshall Viscount. *A History of Warfare.* New York: World Publishing Co., 1968.

Navy Department. *German Submarine Activities on the Atlantic Coasts of the United States and Canada.* Washington: GPO, 1920.

Noyes, Alfred. *Mystery Ships: Trapping the U-boats.* London: Hodder and Stoughton, 1916.

Rössler, Eberhard. *Geschichte des deutschen Ubootsbaus.* München: J. F. Lehmanns Verlag, 1975.

Schmidt, Karl. *Panzer Vernichtung.* Berlin: Ulstein, 1935.

Weddigen, Dr. Otto. *Das erste Handels-Unterseeboot, Deutschland und sein Kapitän, Paul König.* Leipzig: Wiking Verlag, 1916.

ARTICLES

Abt, Clark C. "Submarine Tank Carrier." U.S. Naval Institute *Proceedings* (September 1984): 140–41.

Belote, James H. "The Lohmann Affair." *Studies in Intelligence* (Spring 1966): 31–38.

Brustat-Naval, Fritz. "Das *U-Deutschland* Unternehmen." *MOV-Nachrichten* (Jg. 15, 1966, Nr. 12): 236–37. Bibliothek für Zeitgeschichte, Stuttgart, BRD.

Duncan, Francis. "*Deutschland*—Merchant Submarine." U.S. Naval Institute *Proceedings* (April 1965): 113–25.

Ehlers, Wilhelm. "U-Deutschland." *Was wir vom Krieg nicht wissen.* Edited by F. Felger. (1929): 265–73. Bibliothek für Zeitgeschichte, Stuttgart, BRD.

Lundeberg, Philip K. "The German Naval Critique of the U-boat Campaign, 1915–1918." *Military Affairs*, vol. 27, Nr. 3 (Fall 1963): 105–18.

————. "Undersea Warfare and the Allied Strategy in World War I: Part I, To 1916." *The Smithsonian Journal of History*, vol. 1, Nr. 3 (Autumn 1966): 1–30.

————. "Undersea Warfare and the Allied Strategy in World War I: Part II, 1916–1918." *The Smithsonian Journal of History*, vol. 1, Nr. 4 (Winter 1966): 49–72.

Pease, Charles C. "Sink the Navy." U.S. Naval Institute *Proceedings* (September 1983): 30–36.

Rieschke, Hans-Georg. "Handels U-Boot U-Deutschland." *Marinekalender der DDR* (1981): 144–50. Bibliothek für Zeitgeschichte, Stuttgart, BRD.

Rohrbrecht, G. "Handels U-Boot Deutschland durchbrach zweimal die englische Blokade." *Seekiste* (1966, H8): 518–21. Bibliothek für Zeitgeschichte, Stuttgart, BRD.

Santoni, Alberto. "The First Ultra Secret: British Cryptanalysis in Naval Operations of the First World War." *Revue internationale d'histoire militaire* 63 (1985): 99–110.
United States Naval Institute *Proceedings*, Professional Notes Section:

"Admiral Jellicoe asks for More Small Craft." (May 1917): 1083–85.
"Anti-Submarine Bombs Tested." (May 1920): 769.
"Chain Net Submarine Defense." (Sept./Oct. 1915): 159.
"Depth Charges and Mines." (June 1920): 983–84.
"*Deutschland.*" (October 1917): 2297.
"*Deutschland* a Merchant Ship." (Sept./Oct. 1917): 1712–24.
"*Deutschland*—Merchant Submarine." (October 1965): 120.
"Five Lives Lost in Dismantling of *Deutschland.*" (November 1921): 1807.
"Hydrophones and Their Uses." (September 1919): 1637–38.
"Is There any Defense Against the Submarine?" (Mar./Apr. 1915): 575–76.
"Orders to British Merchantmen." (May 1917): 1083.
"Protection Against Submarines." (March 1917): 605.
"The Fate of the *Deutschland.*" (May 1919): 816–17.
"The German Commercial Submarines." (June 1917): 1240–42.
"The German Merchant Submarine *Deutschland.*" (Jul./Aug. 1916): 1307–11.
"The German Merchant Submarine *Deutschland.*" (Sep./Oct. 1916): 1675–76.
"The Gun as an Answer to the Submarine." (September 1917): 2144–45.
"The Problem with Anti-Submarine Defense." (Jan./Feb. 1916): 267–68.
"Walser's Hydrophone." (April 1919): 640–41.

NEWSPAPERS

New York Times, 1916 and 1917.
Oakland Tribune, 1943.

DOCUMENTS

Admiralty Historical Section. Packs and Miscellaneous Records, 1860–1924. ADM137; ADM137/1262; ADM137/3915; ADM137/4136; ADM137/4220; ADM137/4800. Public Records Office, Surrey, U.K.
Certified Copy of an Entry of Marriage: Paul L. König to Kathleen Marie Pennington, Nr. CAS886117/87. General Records Office, St. Catherine's House, Winchester, London, U.K.
Deutsche Dienststelle für die Benachrichtigung der nächsten Angehörigen von Gefallenen der ehemaligen deutschen Wehrmacht. Personalunterlagen für:
Eyring, Emil. 28 Aug. 1886
König, Paul L. 20 Mar. 1867
Krapohl, Franz. 12 Mar. 1878

Meusel, Karl. 4 Aug. 1881

Schwartzkopf, Karl. 30 Jul. 1875

Deutsche Dienststelle (WASt), Eichborndamm 167, Berlin 51, BRD

Office of Naval Intelligence:

"Cruise of the *Deutschland* in the Region of the Azores from 10 June to 16 August 1917." 4 April 1918.

"I. D. 1181, May 1917 to April 1918."

Johannes Spiess. "Six Years of Submarine Cruising." Undated, typed, 94 legal-size pages and; Marc W. Larimer. "Report of Inspection, German Naval Submarine *U-53*." 6 November 1916. Typed, 5 pages with scale drawing. All documents are in the author's possession.

Office of Naval Records and Library, "Reports on the visits of the *Deutschland* to Baltimore and New London during 1916." RG 45, Files JA-2 and JU, National Archives, Washington, D.C.

Records of Department of Commerce, Bureau of Navigation Correspondence, 1814–1934.

File 138092.

File 88535.

Steamboat Navigation Service Correspondence 1905–23.

File 73301.

National Archives, Washington, D.C.

Records of the Department of State Relating to World War I and its Termination, 1914–1929. Roll 179, file 763.72111B46–763.72111D81/5. National Archives, Washington, D.C.

Records of the German Navy, 1850–1945, Records Group 242, Microfilm Publication T1022. Roll 021, file PG 61710. Roll 022, file PG 61711 and PG 61712. Roll 095, file PG 62024. Roll 096, file PG 62024 (cont'd.) and PG 62025. Roll 558, file PG 75032. Roll 559, file PG 75032 (cont'd.) and PG 75033. Roll 560, file PG 75034. Roll 576, file PG 75056. Roll 596, file PG 75064. Roll 631, file PG 67344. Roll 647, file PG 75036. Roll 648, file PG 75036 (cont'd.). Roll 658, file PG 75195. Roll 659, file PG 75195 (cont'd.), PG 75196, and PG 75197. Roll 660, file PG 75197 (cont'd.). Roll 711, file PG 75019 and 75048. Roll 712, file PG 75048 (cont'd.). National Archives, Washington, D.C.

Telegramme der Deutschen Ozean Reederei, Bremen, an den Reichskanzler und umgekehrt, und Zeitungsartikeln über den Kapitän Paul König, Juni–Oktober 1916. File 00423. Zentrales Staatsarchiv, Potsdam, DDR.

APPENDIX

The *Deutschland* en route to Bremen. (Naval Historical Center)

DEUTSCHLAND SPECIFICATIONS

Length	outer hull:	65.0 meters	(213.25 feet)
	Pressure hull:	57.0 meters	(187.00 feet)
Beam	outer hull:	8.9 meters	(29.20 feet)
	Pressure hull:	5.8 meters	(19.00 feet)
Draft	surfaced:	5.3 meters	(17.40 feet)
	submerged:	9.3 meters	(30.50 feet)
Periscope depth:		13.0 meters	(42.00 feet)
Displacement	surface:		1,575 tons
	submerged:		1,860 tons
Speed	maximum surface:	11.0 knots	
	maximum submerged:	7.5 knots	
Range	surface:	approx. 8,000 nm @ 9.2 knots	
	submerged:	approx. 65 nm @ 3.0 knots	

INDEX